Frommer's®

P O R T A B L E

Dublin

2nd Edition

by Robert Emmet Meagher

with Mark Meagher and Elizabeth Neave

Macmillan • USA

ABOUT THE AUTHORS

Robert Emmet Meagher, a dual-citizen of Ireland and the United States, is Professor of Humanities at Hampshire College, Amherst, Massachusetts. The author of over a dozen books, plays, and translations, he has lived and worked in Ireland, twice holding visiting professorships at Trinity College Dublin.

Mark Meagher, an avid naturalist as well as a competitive cyclist and kayaker, has lived and studied in Ireland and is currently pursuing graduate studies in landscape architecture at the University of Pennsylvania.

Elizabeth Neave, after studying and teaching in Dublin, pursued her graduate studies in Education at Smith College and currently teaches elementary school in the Connecticut public schools.

MACMILLAN TRAVEL USA

A Pearson Education Macmillan Company
1633 Broadway
New York, NY 10019

Find us online at **www.mgr.com**

ISBN 0-02-862890-X
ISSN 1092-1265

Editor: Bob O'Sullivan
Production Editor: Carol Sheehan
Photo Editor: Richard Fox
Design by Michele Laseau
Digital Cartography by Ortelius Design
Page Creation by John Bitter, Natalie Evans and Sean Monkhouse

Cover photo: Ms. Muirne Harley

SPECIAL SALES

Bulk purchases (10+ copies) of Frommer's and selected Macmillan travel guides are available to corporations, organizations, mail-order catalogs, institutions, and charities at special discounts, and can be customized to suit individual needs. For more information write to Special Sales, Macmillan General Reference, 1633 Broadway, New York, NY 10019.

Manufactured in the United States of America

Contents

List of Maps

An Invitation to the Reader

There are so many more of you than there are of us that this book can only be informed and enhanced when you share your experiences with us. We welcome your letters. Let us know when we've led you straight and when astray—and let us in on your secret finds, provided that you're willing to have them shared with other readers in future editions. Anticipating your letters, thanks in advance for your contributions. You can address your letters to:

Frommer's Portable Dublin, 2nd Edition
Macmillan Travel
1633 Broadway
New York, NY 10019

An Additional Note

Please be advised that travel information is subject to change at any time—and this is especially true of prices. We therefore suggest that you write or call ahead for confirmation when making your travel plans. The authors, editors, and publisher cannot be held responsible for the experiences of readers while traveling. Your safety is important to us, however, so we encourage you to stay alert and be aware of your surroundings. Keep a close eye on cameras, purses, and wallets, all favorite targets of thieves and pickpockets.

What the Symbols Mean

✪ Frommer's Favorites

Our favorite places and experiences—outstanding for quality, value, or both.

The following abbreviations are used for credit cards:

AE	American Express	EURO	Eurocard
CB	Carte Blanche	JCB	Japan Credit Bank
DC	Diners Club	MC	MasterCard
DISC	Discover	V	Visa
ER	enRoute		

Find Frommer's Online

Arthur Frommer's Budget Travel Online (www.frommers.com) offers more than 6,000 pages of up-to-the-minute travel information—including the latest bargains and candid, personal articles updated daily by Arthur Frommer himself. No other Web site offers such comprehensive and timely coverage of the world of travel.

A Dublin Introduction

*I*f you haven't been to Dublin lately, then you haven't been to Dublin. Even native "Dubs," who leave and return after only several years, confess they don't believe their eyes. Greater Dublin—decreed long ago by Henry II to be "within the pale"—is now by popular consensus "out of sight." This is the lair of the Celtic Tiger, the O'Camelot of the fastest- growing economy in Europe.

The Celts are definitely back. Two millennia ago, Julius Caesar knew that they were the ones to beat, which he did, more or less. In 1998, however, Dublin evened the ancient score when it leapt past Rome to become the fifth most-visited city in Europe. Already, the year before, it had surpassed Rome, Milan, Amsterdam, and even London to be named by *Fortune* magazine the no. 1 city in Europe in which to do business. The word is out that, work or play, Dublin is the place to be.

The new Dublin, after decades of gestation, was born perhaps only 10 years ago as the city celebrated its first 1,000 years, most of which (700 years) it had spent as a British colony. Most but not all. To summon a thousand years was a stretch, even for the Irish imagination; and all that looking back begged the question of the future, the next 1,000 years. On this scale, even 700 years were a lot less than everything. The once-and-future Ireland was and would be Irish, and Dublin its epicenter. The 1988 Dublin Millennium was, in retrospect, more than a party. It was civic exercise. And exercise is addictive. For the first time in anyone's memory, Dublin had looked in the mirror and liked what it saw.

Under British rule, Dublin "peaked" in the 18th century, Dublin's Golden Age, when it was no. 2 in the empire. With a handful of notable exceptions, it's been slippage ever since. Until recently, that is. Dublin may have hit gold under George II, but it has gone platinum under the EU. Ireland entered the European Community in 1973 as its poorest member state, and has emerged 25 years later as its *wunderkind*. Nowhere is that transformation more evident than in Dublin, where the pace of change is staggering. It's like a construction site. If you don't walk past it every day, you miss something.

I suppose it all comes down to prosperity and pride; and Dublin currently has plenty of both. Twenty years ago most visitors to Ireland either bypassed Dublin altogether, or else made a mad dash from the ferry to the train station, determined to spend their first night beyond the pale. Now the opposite is the case. Dublin's centripetal force attracts millions of visitors a year and holds them there. In 1999, the Dublin Renaissance is in full swing. The time has passed when aspiring Irish artists owe it to themselves to emigrate. Today, they dig right in. If Joyce, Beckett, and Wilde could see Dublin today, they'd be back. Dublin is simply contagious; and it's not in the Guinness. (Fact is that the Irish now have one of the lowest alcohol consumption rates in Europe.) Neither is it in the water. (The Liffey only gets darker.) It's where it's always been, in the people. Dublin without the Dubliners would be like Elvis without his guitar, a sorry sight for all the glitter.

Of course, with every boom there's a bang. What's the downside, you ask? Spiralling property values, inflated price tags on everything from a pint to a Porsche, congestion, sprawl, extended work days, long commutes, crime, abuse, homelessness, teen suicide. It's all here, the legacy of success. To their credit, however, the Irish are still shocked by corruption and suffering, and possess a fairly strong national conscience with which to confront these problems. The dark spot of most immediate concern to tourists may be crime, and on this front Dublin has made dramatic progress in the past few years. After reaching an all-time high in 1995, crime in Dublin is down, way down, due in large part to fierce new anti-crime agencies and laws. If current trends continue, Dublin will enter 1999 with its lowest crime rate since 1980. At this rate, it's one of the safest cities in Europe. Furthermore, with the island poised to free itself from 30 years of sectarian troubles, security concerns (already minimal in Dublin) are likely to disappear altogether.

Finally, with cross-border and cross-channel collaboration at an all-time high, Dublin is emerging not only as the cultural and economic center of the Irish isle but as a peer of London in the North Atlantic. Over 2 million British visited Dublin last year and returned home with a touch of Celtic fever. If you liked *Riverdance*, you'll love Dublin.

1   The Lay of the Land

Dublin, like most ancient cities, lies sprawled along a river. In fact, three visible and three underground rivers converge and flow into the Irish Sea here, on the shore of Dublin Bay. The greatest of these, or perhaps just the least lazy, is the Liffey, which has divided Dublin into north and south for more than 1,000 years, much as tracks divide the core of a railroad town. Not as romantic as the Seine or as mighty as the Mississippi, the Liffey is just there, old and polluted, with walls to sit on or lean against when your legs give out. Still, it is and always has been at the center of things, and on a good day, it makes for a pretty picture.

The Liffey continues to divide the town as it once divided Viking from Celt and Norman from Norse. The "new Dublin" is mostly south of the Liffey. A walk from the top of Grafton Street down O'Connell and into north Dublin is a walk through time and, simultaneously, a glimpse of some of the pieces that must eventually be put together.

The tourist precinct of Dublin, as in most cities, is a small, well-defined compound comprising a large part of Dublin 2 and a smaller fraction of Dublin 1 (we'll talk about postal codes in a couple of pages): Grafton Street, St. Stephen's Green, and Temple Bar are the operative terms, and they are well worth the effort to see. That said, a visit to Dublin confined to these areas is not a visit to Dublin, the Dublin that kicked some of the greatest writers in the English language into song. Explore, get a haircut (in a barber shop, not a salon), get lost and ask directions, and you may uncover a time capsule from the Dublin of a century ago—or was it only a generation ago?

2 Frommer's Favorite Dublin Experiences

Whether you have a week or only a short while, here are a few of the best of what Dublin has to offer.

- **Bewley's in the Morning.** Most transatlantic flights arrive in Dublin in the early A.M., in time for morning coffee. Even though everyone says that Bewley's is the compulsory first stop for any visitor to Dublin, so do I (sometimes everyone is right.) Like the stout-dark waters of the Liffey, Bewley's coffee is a landmark, assuring you that you are in fact in Dublin. (And it won't imperil your health, like drinking from the Liffey would.) Sometimes the stampede of tourists gets pretty dense, but that never seems to crowd out the locals, who continue to claim the place as their own. So, right off, pick up the morning *Irish Times,* along with the latest issue of *In Dublin,* and stand in line at Bewley's for a mug of white coffee and a bun. (See chapter 5.)
- **Stroll, Consider, Feel Like a Scholar.** Dublin, at its center, is a noisy, hectic city, often thick with leaded car fumes. But there

are oases. Perhaps the most magical of these is Trinity College, across from the Bank of Ireland in College Green. Try this: Walk rapidly from Dame Street straight through the Trinity gates into Front Square and stop. Notice anything? If not, do it again. I'm talking about the instantaneous peace and quiet. Trinity is a walled university, a defensible position, sandbagged in 1916 and still fortified against the din of the surrounding city. Most visitors to Trinity march straight to the Old Library and its Book of Kells and then faithfully retrace their steps to the street. That's wrong. The point is to breathe the quiet, take a stroll through the campus, and sit and watch a student cricket or rugby match—because Trinity, too, is one of Ireland's treasures. (See chapter 6.)

- **Walk the Walk.** And let someone else talk the talk. The latest rage in Dublin is the escorted theme tour. It's good exercise, not only for the legs but also for the imagination. You'll learn to see Dublin from a new angle with each tour, depending on its slant: pubs, ghosts, rebels, writers, wackos . . . you name it. There are too many offerings to keep track of, especially as they tend to sprout up and die away from one season to the next. The historical walking tours leaving from Trinity College, as well as the new and notorious Zosimus Experience, are good places to start your habit. Soon a day without a walk will seem a day wasted. (See chapter 6.)

- **A Shopping Adventure for Cultured Gourmands.** Not all triathalons demand fine weather and aerobic effort. I would suggest starting a day at the National Museum on Kildare Street when the doors open at 10am, but not before making a 1pm reservation one block over at Fitzers on Dawson Street. The National Museum can be managed if not consumed in several hours, so you can get through just in time for lunch. Afterward, with pinions rested and appetite addressed, it's only a several-minute walk over to Nassau Street to the Kilkenny Shop, a one-stop introduction to some of Ireland's most tastefully designed woollens, ceramics, jewelry, and much more. There's even an on-site cafe for the inevitable mid-afternoon energy slide. (See chapters 5, 6, and 7.)

- **Where Tyrants & Martyrs Walked.** For anyone keenly interested in the modern history of Ireland and its struggles, Dublin Castle and Kilmainham Jail are must-sees. The castle was where the conquerors and colonizers of Ireland wove their webs. Here the Norse and Norman fortified themselves, and from here the British governed Ireland for centuries. Home to viceroys, G-men, and tortured patriots, its walls have many stories to tell—as do those of Kilmainham Jail, whose roster of former residents reads like a Who's Who of Irish history, from Robert Emmet to Eamon de Valera. It was here, in the prison courtyard, that a British firing squad made instant martyrs of the leaders of the 1916 Rising, and so helped turn a rampage into a war. The tours at both sites provide enough of the Irish story to bring these places alive for the visitor. (See chapter 6.)

- **A Day in the Sunny South.** Occasionally the sun does shine in Dublin, and brilliantly so. If you inherit such a day and don't want to waste it in the city, here's a plan: After breakfast, proceed to the nearest DART station and hop the next southbound train to Dalkey. After exploring the town, find your way to the small harbor facing Dalkey Island and, renting a boat from the Ferryman on Coliemore Road, row out and explore the uninhabited island and its ruins, making cautious acquaintance with the local goats and seals. By now, it'll be time for lunch at P.D.'s Woodhouse in Dalkey Center. Then, if the sun is still shining, take the DART farther south to Bray, walk the length of the strand, and find your way up to the stone cross atop Bray Head, taking in the views you've earned in the climb. Follow the cliff walk several miles to Greystones, where your reward is waiting: a pint and a meal not to be forgotten at Coopers. Gladly, a train from Greystones Station will take you back to Dublin center—just be sure to check a timetable. (See chapters 9 and 10.)

- **A Stroll Amid the Green.** Dublin center is surprisingly treeless; so, if you begin to crave foliage, know that relief is at hand. St. Stephen's Green, enclosed in 1664, is modest, charming, and readily available, but if you want more expanse, I have two suggestions, both a short bus ride from the center. First, there's the Phoenix Park (not Phoenix Park; "the" is part of its name), one of the world's largest city parks, more than double the size of New York's Central Park and home to Dublin's zoo, the Irish president, the U.S. ambassador, the All Ireland Polo Club, and a herd of wild deer. Another idea is to combine a trip to the National Botanical Gardens with a visit to Glasnevin Cemetery. They're next-door neighbors in the nearby suburb of Glasnevin, and both are free. The former boasts a series of remarkable glass houses designed by Richard Turner, while the latter offers rest to some of Ireland's most famous throwers of stones, like Jim Larkin, Eamon de Valera, and Michael Collins. (See chapters 6 and 9.)

2

Planning a Trip to Dublin

*I*t may be well to begin with a caution, offered in this case by John Steinbeck in *Travels With Charley:* "A journey is like a marriage. The certain way to be wrong is to think you control it." Fair enough. A trip too tightly packed and planned, with no room for the spontaneous and unexpected, is often not worth the effort. And yet, when we are so poorly prepared that surprise runs riot, we may wish we'd stayed home. In travel, as in Buddhism, the middle ground is to be recommended. Lay down your plans like pavement, and then romp on the grass at will. Our aim in this chapter is to help you prepare the way.

1 Visitor Information & Entry Requirements

SOURCES OF INFORMATION

To get your planning underway, contact the following offices of the Irish Tourist Board and/or the Northern Ireland Tourist Board. They're anxious to answer your questions, and they've got bags of genuinely helpful information, mostly free of charge. After you've perused the brochures, take a quick surf through the Net if you're online, to scoop up even more information.

IN THE UNITED STATES   Irish Tourist Board, 345 Park Ave., New York, NY 10154 (☎ **800/223-6470** from the U.S., or 212/418-0800; fax 212/371-9052).

IN CANADA   Irish Tourist Board, 160 Bloor St. E., Ste. 1150, Toronto, Ontario M4W 1B9 (☎ **416/929-2777;** fax 416/929-6783).

IN THE UNITED KINGDOM   Irish Tourist Board/Bord Failte, 150 New Bond St., London W1Y OAQ (☎ **0171/493-3201;** fax 0171/493-9065).

IN AUSTRALIA   Irish Tourist Board, 36 Carrington St., 5th Level, Sydney, NSW 2000 (☎ **02/9299-6177;** fax 02/9299-6323).

IN IRELAND   Irish Tourist Board/Bord Failte, Baggot Street Bridge, Dublin 2 (☎ **01/602-4000;** fax 01/602-4100) www.ireland.travel.ie.

INTERNET SITES

Ireland is far more Net-savvy than you might suspect. Most Irish towns, cities, sites of interest, hotels, government agencies, and more can be found on the Net; and, if you surf around long enough, you'll find them. Like the cells in our bodies or the hairstyles on supermodels, it is the nature of the Net to undergo constant change and proliferation, so don't curse us too loudly if the specific listings below have changed by the time they reach you. The point we're making here is that there is a mother lode of information about Ireland on the Net, and that these are some good places to position your shovel as you start digging:

> http://doras.tinet.ie
> www.indigo.ie
> www.internet-ireland.ie/
> www.iol.ie/discover
> www.niceone.com
> www.paddynet.com
> http://swift.kerna.com

In addition to these general listings, a number of cities, provinces, and regions have sites of their own on the Net, providing up-to-date local information. The URL or Internet address is the same for all of these, except for the last name of the city or area in question. For example, the city.net URL for Dublin is:

www.city.net/countries/ireland/dublin/

For Cork, replace /*dublin*/ with /*cork*/, and so on. At the time of writing, 18 cities and counties have sites posted. All of the major universities in Ireland also have their own sites. Three additional sites for Dublin are:

> www.dublins-fair-city.com
> www.shaw.iol.ie/smytho/dublin/
> www.visit.ie/dublin/

ENTRY REQUIREMENTS

DOCUMENTS   For citizens of the United States, Canada, Australia, and New Zealand entering the Republic of Ireland for a stay of up to 3 months, no visas are necessary, but a valid passport is required.

Citizens of the United Kingdom, when traveling on flights originating in Britain, do not need to show documentation to enter

Ireland. Nationals of the United Kingdom and Colonies not born in Great Britain or Northern Ireland must have a valid passport or national identity document.

CUSTOMS   Since the European Union's (EU) introduction of a single market on January 1, 1993, goods brought into Ireland and Northern Ireland fall into two categories: (1) goods bought duty-paid and value-added-tax (VAT)-paid in other EU countries; and (2) goods bought under duty-free and VAT-free allowances at duty-free shops.

Regarding the first category, provided that the goods are for personal use, there is no further duty or VAT to be paid. The limits for goods in this category are as follows: 800 cigarettes, 10 liters of spirits, 45 liters of wine, and 55 liters of beer. This category normally applies to Irish citizens, visitors from Britain, and travelers from other EU countries.

Regarding the second category, which pertains primarily to overseas visitors such as U.S. and Canadian citizens, the following duty-free and VAT-free items may be brought into the country for personal use: 200 cigarettes, 1 liter of liquor, 2 liters of wine, and other goods (including beer) not exceeding the value of £34 ($52.70) per adult. There are no restrictions on bringing currency into Ireland.

The Irish customs systems operate on a Green-, Red-, and Blue-Channel format. The first two choices are for passengers coming from the United States and non-EU countries. The Green Channel is for anyone not exceeding the duty-free allowances, while the Red Channel is for anyone with extra goods to declare. If you are like most visitors, bringing in only your own clothes and personal effects, choose the Green Channel. The Blue Channel, the latest addition to the system, is exclusively for use by passengers entering Ireland from another EU country.

In addition to your luggage, you may bring in sports equipment for your own recreational use or electronic equipment for your own business or professional use while in Ireland. Prohibited goods include firearms, ammunition, and explosives; narcotics; meat, poultry, plants, and their by-products; and domestic animals from outside the United Kingdom.

2 Money

CASH/CURRENCY   Until the adoption of a single EU currency (the Euro), the 26 counties of the Republic of Ireland continue to have an independent currency system, the basic unit of which is the Irish pound £ or punt. Inside Ireland, it is mostly referred to as "the pound," as distinct from the British pound, known as "the pound sterling." The Irish and British pounds trade independently on the currency market and fluctuate more or less freely with respect to each other and to the dollar.

Euros are scheduled to enter Irish pockets in 2002 and will likely exist side by side with pounds for up to 6 months. As early as New Year's 1999, however, the value of the Euro will be fixed against those currencies, including the punt, committed to joining a single European monetary system. This event is sure to put some pressure on the value of the punt during 1998; and its conversion value on "Euro day" is a matter of intense speculation. Irish exporters (and tourists) want a weak punt, while importers want the opposite.

Both the Irish and the British pounds are generically symbolized by a £ sign. The Irish pound is, however, officially designated by the £ sign preceded by IR: IR£. Each unit of paper currency is called a note. The pound notes, which are printed in denominations of £5, £10, £20, £50, and £100, come in different sizes and colors (the larger the size, the greater the value). There are still some £1 notes in circulation, although these are being phased out in favor of the £1 coin. (The old £1 note is a work of art, so try to find one before they disappear.) Since 1971, the Irish monetary system has been on the decimal system; so, for instance, every pound is divided into 100 pence ("p"); coins come in denominations of £1, 50p, 20p, 10p, 5p, and 1p.

Note: The value of the Irish pound fluctuates daily, so it is best to begin checking the exchange rates well in advance of your visit so as to gain a sense of their recent range. It's always a gamble when and where to convert and how much. Shop around and avoid exchanging in airports and train stations. Banks are best, and on any given day one bank will be offering a better rate than another. Since any purchase on a U.S. credit card offers an exchange rate far more favorable than anything an individual is likely to negotiate, I make a point of converting as little currency as possible and using my credit card to the max. Whatever you do, don't convert small amounts daily, as if you were shopping for bread. The fees alone will impoverish you. Rates of exchange are, of course, available daily in most newspapers, and on the Net you can consult **www.xe.net/currency/** or, if you want your math done for you, check out the GNN/Klobas Currency Converter at **www.macgrawnet.com/currenc.htm**.

TRAVELER'S CHECKS   Traveler's checks are readily accepted in the Republic of Ireland, and they bring a better exchange rate than does cash. In general, banks provide the best exchange rates, followed

Irish Punt & U.S. Dollar Equivalents

At the time of writing the pound sterling stands at $1.65, and our best guess for the future value of the punt is $1.55, which are the figures used to calculate all dollar costs in this book.

IR£	U.S.$	U.S.$	IR£
0.50	0.80	0.50	0.30
1.00	1.55	1.00	0.65
5.00	7.75	5.00	3.20
10.00	15.50	10.00	6.45
50.00	77.50	50.00	32.25
100.00	155.00	100.00	64.50

by bureaux de change. Most banks and exchange bureaus post their daily exchange rates up front, so you can window-shop for the best rate.

Hotels, restaurants, and stores also accept traveler's checks, though often at a less than favorable rate. *Note:* Personal checks, even when presented with your passport, are not usually accepted by banks or places of business, unless you are a member of the Eurocheque scheme or have made prior arrangements in advance.

CREDIT CARDS Leading international credit cards such as American Express, Carte Blanche, Diners Club, MasterCard (also known as Access or Eurocard), and Visa (also known as Visa/ Barclay) are readily acceptable throughout all 32 counties. Most establishments display on their windows or shop fronts the symbols or logos of the specific credit cards they accept. MasterCard and Visa are the most widely accepted, with American Express a close third.

3 When to Go

CLIMATE

You have to be part psychic to even begin making bets on Irish weather, but don't bet too heavily. The only thing consistent about Irish weather is its changeability; often, the best of times and the worst of times may be only hours, or minutes, apart.

With that disclaimer solidly in place, it's safe to offer a few useful observations. If you think east equals dry and west equals wet, you'll be right except when you're wrong, which will be less than half the time. More specifically, the driest and sunniest parts of

Ireland are the northeast and the southeast, which is not to say that they are reliably either dry or sunny.

Irish thermometers, gratefully, are a lot less busy than their barometers. That's to say that the temperatures in Ireland are mild and fluctuate within what any New Englander would call "spring." The generally coldest months, January and February, bring frosts but seldom snow, and the warmest months, July and August, rarely become hot. Remember, in Ireland anything over 70° is "hot" and 32° is considered freezing. Both are unusual. For a complete guide to Irish weather on the Net, including year-round averages and daily updates, consult www.iol.ie/~discover/meteo1.htm.

When packing, "layers" is the word to remember, any time of year. And don't forget wool—the Irish attraction to it is no accident. *One further tip:* The Irish are becoming more and more casual in their dress, so you can think Oregon rather than Manhattan.

In sum, the weather is neither the reason for coming to Ireland nor a reason for staying away, unless you're looking for the beaches of Mexico or Greece, which remain in Mexico and Greece.

Average Monthly Temperatures in Dublin

	Jan	Feb	Mar	Apr	May	June	July	Aug	Sept	Oct	Nov	Dec
Temp (°F)	36–46	37–48	37–49	38–52	42–57	46–62	51–66	50–65	48–62	44–56	39–49	38–47
Temp (°C)	2–8	3–9	3–9	3–11	6–14	8–17	11–19	10–18	9–17	7–13	4–9	3–8

HOLIDAYS

The Republic observes the following national holidays: New Year's Day (January 1); St. Patrick's Day (March 17); Good Friday (mostly observed, though not statutory); Easter Monday; May Day (first Monday in May); first Monday in June and August (Summer Bank Holidays); last Monday in October (Autumn Bank Holiday); Christmas (December 25); and St. Stephen's Day (December 26).

The only Irish holiday that's likely to attract tourists to Dublin is St. Patrick's Day, which in Ireland is traditionally a religious and family day. The massive parade and adjunct delirium associated with March 17 in Boston, New York, and Chicago is a recent import to Ireland—an accommodation on Ireland's part to an idea hatched abroad. The tail wags the dog: Dublin's St. Patrick's Day parade is an imitation of those in the United States, not the original thing. Although the Irish participation in and taste for the event are growing, many of the bands and marchers, and a great many of the crowd, are visitors, creating what they came over to watch. For some, this is the day of all days to be in Dublin; and who's to say it's not? I'd recommend another day, though. Any other day.

What Things Cost in Dublin	U.S. $
Taxi from the airport to the city center (£12)	18.60
Express bus from airport to city center (£2.50)	3.90
Bus minimum fare (55p)	.85
Local telephone call (30p)	.50
Double room at the Shelbourne Hotel (expensive) (£225)	348.75
Double room at Stauntons on the Green (moderate) (£99)	153.45
Double room at Jurys Christchurch (inexpensive) (£58)	89.90
Breakfast for one at Bewley's (budget) (£3.25)	5.05
Lunch for one at Patrick Guilbaud (expensive) (£22)	34.10
Lunch for one at La Mere Zou (moderate) (£9.50)	14.75
Dinner for one, without wine, at The Commons (expensive) (£35)	54.25
Dinner for one at Roly's Bistro (moderate) (£21)	32.55
Dinner for one at Chez Jules (inexpensive) (£8.90)	13.80
Pint of Guinness (£2.20)	3.40
Shot of Irish whiskey (£1.85)	2.90
Glass of wine (£3.50)	5.45
Coca-Cola in a cafe (90p)	1.40
Cup of coffee (£1)	1.55
Admission to see the Book of Kells at Trinity College (£3.50)	5.45
Admission to the National Museum	Free
Movie ticket (£4.75)	7.35
Ticket to the Abbey Theatre (£12)	18.60

DUBLIN CALENDAR OF EVENTS

January

- **2nd Dublin International Theatre Symposium.** Samuel Beckett Centre, Trinity College, Dublin 2. Contact Mary O'Donovan (☎ **01/280-0544;** fax 01/239-0918; E-mail: panpan@iol.ie.) January 3 to 8.

February

- **Rugby International, Ireland v. Scotland.** Landsdowne Road, Ballsbridge. Contact **Irish Rugby Football Union,** 62 Lansdowne Rd., Dublin 4 (☎ **01/668-4601;** fax 01/660-5640). February 7.

March

- **Dublin Film Festival.** The best in Irish and international cinema. More than 100 films are featured, with screenings of the best of Irish and world cinema, plus seminars and lectures on filmmaking. At cinemas throughout Dublin. Contact Aine O'Halloran (☎ **01/679-2937;** fax 01/679-2929; www.iol.ie/dff/). March 3 to 12.

- **The 1999 National St. Patrick's Day Festival.** Street theater, sports, music, and other festivities culminating in Ireland's grandest parade, with marching bands, drill teams, floats, and delegations from around the world. Contact Grainne Walker, Festival Office, St. Stephen's Green House, Earlsfort Terrace, Dublin 2 (☎ **01/676-3208;** fax 01/676-3208; E-mail: info@paddyfest.ie). March 13 to 17.

April

- **Feis Ceoil.** In spite of its Gaelic name, this 11-day springtime event is not a traditional music gathering. It is a mostly classical competitive music festival that covers all instruments, including voice. There are more than 150 categories featuring orchestral and choral events, with duets, trios, and ensembles of all sizes. Located at RDS, Ballsbridge. For full information, contact **Feis Ceoil Office,** 37 Molesworth St., Dublin 2 (☎ **01/676-7365;** fax 01/676-7429). March 13 to 17.

June

- **AIB Music Festival in Great Irish Houses.** This is a continuous 10-day festival of classical music performed by leading Irish and international artists in some of the Dublin area's great Georgian buildings and mansions. There are various venues throughout Dublin and neighboring Counties Wicklow and Kildare. Contact Crawford Tipping, Blackrock Post Office, County Dublin (☎ **01/278-1528;** fax 01/278-1529). June 3 to 13.

- ✪ **Bloomsday.** Dublin's unique day of festivity commemorates 24 hours in the life of Leopold Bloom, the central character of James Joyce's *Ulysses.* Every aspect of the city, including the menus at restaurants and pubs, seeks to duplicate the aromas, sights, sounds, and tastes of Dublin on June 16, 1904. Special ceremonies are held at the James Joyce Tower and Museum, and there are guided walks of Joycean sights. Located along the streets of Dublin and at various venues. Contact the **James Joyce Centre,** 35 N. Great George's St., Dublin 1 (☎ **01/878-8547;** fax 01/878-8488; www.jamesjoyce.ie). June 16.

July

- **Dun Laoghaire Festival.** A weeklong celebration in the seafront suburb of Dun Laoghaire, 7 miles south of Dublin, with arts and crafts, concerts, band recitals, sports events, and talent competitions. Mid-July.

- ✪ **Guinness Blues Festival.** Dublin's "West Bank" plays host to bands from England, Ireland, and the United States, offering more than 200 hours of blues performances, films, and workshops, including a free open-air concert at College Green and a "blues trail" of free live blues in 18 different pubs. Along streets and in pubs in the Temple Bar area. Contact Una Lisa Tinley (☎ **01/497-0381;** fax 01/491-0631; E-mail: production@ carpediem.iol.ie). July 24 to 26.

- **Summer Schools.** Study sessions meeting in Dublin include the Irish Theatre Summer School in conjunction with the Gaiety School of Acting at Trinity College, the Synge Summer School in County Wicklow, the James Joyce Summer School at Newman House, and the International Summer Schools in Irish Studies at Trinity College and the National University of Ireland. Contact the **Irish Tourist Board.** July and August.

August

- ✪ **Kerrygold Dublin Horse Show.** This is the principal sporting and social event on the Irish national calendar, attracting visitors from all parts of the world. More than 2,000 horses, the cream of Irish bloodstock, are entered for this show, with dressage, jumping competitions each day, and more. Highlights include a fashionable ladies' day (don't forget your hat!), formal hunt balls each evening, and the awarding of the Aga Khan Trophy and the Nation's Cup by the president of Ireland. Located at the RDS Showgrounds, Ballsbridge. Contact Niamh Kelly, RDS, Merrion Road, Ballsbridge, Dublin 4 (☎ **01/668-0866;** fax 01/660-4014). August 5 to 9.

- **Summer Music Festival.** St. Stephen's Green is the setting for this series of free lunchtime band concerts of popular and Irish traditional music, as well as afternoon open-air performances of Shakespearean plays, sponsored by the Office of Public Works. Last 2 weeks of August.

- **Cutty Sark Tall Ships Race.** The finish of this colorful race will be celebrated in Dublin Port with 4 days of festivity. Last 2 weeks of August.

September

✪ **All-Ireland Hurling and Football Final.** Tickets must be obtained months in advance for these two national amateur sporting events, the equivalent of Super Bowls for Irish national sports. Located at Croke Park, Dublin 3. Contact the **Gaelic Athletic Association** (☎ **01/836-3222;** fax 01/836-6420). Two weekends in September; dates vary from year to year.

- **Irish Antique Dealers' Fair.** Annual show sponsored jointly by the RDS and the Irish Antique Dealers' Association. This is Ireland's premier annual antique fair. It's located at the RDS Showgrounds, Ballsbridge. Contact George Stacpoole, Irish Antique Dealers' Association, Adare, County Limerick (☎ **061/ 396409;** fax 061/396733). September 23 to 27.

October

✪ **Dublin Theatre Festival.** A world-class theater festival showcasing new plays by Irish authors and presenting a range of productions from abroad. At theaters throughout Dublin. Contact Tony O Dálaigh, director, 47 Nassau St., Dublin 2 (☎ **01/677-8439;** fax 01/679-7709). October 5 to 17.

✪ **Dublin City Marathon.** More than 3,000 runners from both sides of the Atlantic and the Irish Sea participate in this popular run through the streets of Dublin City. For entry forms and information, contact the **Dublin Marathon Office,** 2 Clare St., Dublin 2 (☎ **01/676-4647;** fax 01/676-1383). Last Monday in October.

December

- **Dublin Grand Opera.** This is the second half of Dublin's twice-yearly operatic fling, with great works presented by the Dublin Grand Opera Society at the Gaiety Theatre. Early December.

- **National Crafts Fair of Ireland.** Retail crafts fair, displaying the work of Ireland's finest craftsworkers. Located at the RDS Showgrounds, Ballsbridge. Contact Patrick O'Sullivan (☎ **01/ 867-1517;** fax 01/878-6276). December 16 to 20.

- **Christmas Horse Racing Festival.** Three days of winter racing for thoroughbreds at Leopardstown Racetrack. December 26 to 29.

4 Health & Insurance

HEALTH   As a general rule, no health documents are required to enter Ireland or Northern Ireland from the United States, Canada, the United Kingdom, Australia, New Zealand, or most other countries. If in the last 14 days a traveler has visited areas where a contagious disease is prevalent, however, proof of immunization for such disease may be required.

If you have a condition that may require emergency care but may not be readily recognizable, you would do well to consider joining **Medic Alert,** P.O. Box 819009, Turlock, CA 95381 (☎ **800/ 825-3785**), which provides ID tags, cards, and a 24-hour emergency information hotline. If you are diabetic, you can call the **American Diabetes Association,** 1660 Duke St., Alexandria, VA 22314 (☎ **800/232-6733**), for a copy of *Travel and Diabetes.*

If you require the services of a physician, dentist, or other health professional during your stay in Ireland, your accommodations host may be in the best position to recommend someone local. Otherwise, you can call the **Irish Medical Organization,** 10 Fitzwilliam Place, Dublin (☎ **01/676-7273**), for a referral.

INSURANCE   When planning a trip, it is wise to consider insurance coverage for the various risk aspects of travel: health and accident, cancellation or disruption of services, and lost or stolen luggage. Travel insurance makes especially good sense when purchasing non-refundable airline tickets.

Before buying any new coverage, check your own insurance policies (automobile, medical, and homeowner) to ascertain if they cover the elements of travel abroad. Also check the membership contracts of automobile and travel clubs, and the benefits extended by credit card companies.

If you decide you need further coverage, consult your travel agent or tour planner. In many cases, tour operators provide insurance as part of a package or offer optional coverage for a small additional fee. Alternatively, you may wish to contact one of the following companies, specializing in short-term policies for travelers:

- **M. H. Ross Insurance Brokers,** P.O. Box 9159, Van Nuys, CA 91409-9159 (☎ **800/423-3632;** fax 818/892-6576; E-mail: rosswiteby@aol.com).
- **Travel Guard International,** 1145 Clark St., Stevens Point, WI 54481-2980 (☎ **800/826-1300;** fax 800/955-8785; www.noelgroup.com).

- **Travel Insurance International,** Travelers Insurance Co., P.O. Box 280568, Hartford, CT 06128-0568 (☎ **800/243-3174;** fax 860/528-8005). Travelers' policies regarding trip cancellation and pre-existing conditions make them particularly attractive for senior citizens or anyone with a pre-existing medical condition.

5 Tips for Travelers with Special Needs

FOR TRAVELERS WITH DISABILITIES

For the last 30 years, the **National Rehabilitation Board of Ireland,** the Square Shopping Center, Dublin 24 (☎ **01/462-0444**), has encouraged facilities to accommodate the disabled. Consequently, more and more hotels and public buildings now have ramps or graded entrances, and rooms specially fitted for wheelchair access.

Unfortunately, many of the older hotels, guest houses, and landmark buildings still have steep steps both outside and within. For a list of the properties that cater to the needs of the disabled, contact the National Rehabilitation Board in advance.

The **Irish Wheelchair Association,** 24 Blackheath Dr., Clontarf, Dublin 3 (☎ **01/833-8241**), loans free wheelchairs for travelers in Ireland. A donation is appreciated. Branch offices are located at Parnell Street, Kilkenny (☎ **056/62775**); White Street, Cork (☎ **021/966544**); Henry Street, Limerick (☎ **061/313691**); and Dominick Street, Galway (☎ **091/565598**).

If you plan to travel by rail in Ireland, be sure to check out Iarnrod Eireann's Web site at **www.clubi.ie/RailNet/**, which includes services for travelers with disabilities.

For advice on travel to Northern Ireland, contact **Disability Action,** 2 Anandale Ave., Belfast (☎ **01232/491011**).

FOR SENIOR CITIZENS

Seniors, known in Ireland and Northern Ireland as OAPs (old age pensioners), enjoy a variety of discounts and privileges. Native OAPs ride the public transport system free of charge, but this privilege does not extend to tourists. Visiting seniors can avail themselves of other discounts, particularly on admission to attractions and theaters. Always ask about a senior discount if special rates are not posted; the discount is usually 10%.

The Irish Tourist Board publishes a list of reduced rate hotel packages for seniors, **Golden Holidays/For the Over 55s.** These packages are usually available in the months of March to June, and September to November.

Some tour operators in the United States, such as **CIE Tours** (☎ **800/CIE-TOUR** or 201/292-3438), which operates in Ireland and Northern Ireland, give senior citizens over age 55 cash discounts on selected departures of regular tour programs throughout the year. In addition, **SAGA Tours** operates tours to Ireland specifically geared to seniors or anyone over 50. Contact: **SAGA Tours,** 222 Berkeley St., Boston, MA 02116 (☎ **800/343-0273** or 617/262-2262; fax 617/ 375-5950). **Elder Hostel**, meanwhile, offers a range of educational travel programs for seniors. Contact **Elder Hostel,** P.O. Box 1959, Wakefield, MA 01880-5959 (☎ **617/426-8056;** www.elderhostel. org.) for a free Elder Hostel international catalogue.

FOR STUDENTS, TEACHERS & YOUTH

With almost half of its population under age 25, Ireland is well geared to students, whether you're planning to study there or are just passing through.

The country has a distinguished and vital academic tradition. Dublin alone is home to three universities—Trinity College Dublin, University College Dublin, and Dublin University—and to many other fine schools and institutes of higher learning. Campuses of the National University of Ireland are located in Cork, Limerick, Galway, and Maynooth. In Northern Ireland, the leading universities are Queen's University in Belfast and Ulster University, with branches in Belfast, Coleraine, and Derry.

Two excellent sourcebooks will help you to explore the opportunities for study in Ireland: *The Transitions Abroad Alternative Travel Directory,* an annual guide to living, learning, and working overseas; and *Work, Study, Travel Abroad: The Whole World Handbook,* compiled by CIEE, the Council on International Educational Exchange. Both are available in bookstores.

Ireland in general is extremely student-friendly. Most attractions have a reduced student-rate admission charge, obtainable on the presentation of a valid student ID card, and a range of travel discounts are available to students, teachers (at any grade level, kindergarten through university), and youth (anyone under 25). For further information on international student/teacher/youth identity cards and fares, call the national office of **Council Travel** at ☎ **888/COUNCIL,** where they can make your reservations or refer you to the Council Travel office nearest you. Council Travel operates over 40 offices in the United States and works through a network of world affiliates. (Even if you're not eligible for any of Council's student/teacher/youth discounts, they offer full travel services, with the advantage of a growing network of local offices and overseas affiliates.)

In Canada, CIEE's counterpart is **Travel CUTS,** 187 College St., Toronto, Ontario M5T1P7 (☎ **416/979-2406;** fax 416/979-8167).

In Ireland, Council Travel's affiliate is **USIT,** the **Irish Student Travel Service,** 19 Aston Quay, Dublin 2 (☎ **01/679-8833**). In Northern Ireland, contact USIT in the Sountain Centre, College Street, Belfast BT1-6ET (☎ **1232/324073**); or at Queens University Travel, Student Union Bldg., University Road, Belfast BT7-1PE (☎ **1232/241-830**). In the United States, USIT is located at 895 Amsterdam Ave., New York, NY 10025 (☎ **212/663-5435**). (For the hopelessly curious among you, USIT is the acronym for the organization's original name, "Union of Students of Ireland Travel," but as the gentleman told me when I asked, "It doesn't stand for anything anymore. It's just USIT.")

U.S. firms offering educational programs to Ireland include: **Academic Travel Abroad,** 3210 Grace St. NW, Washington, DC 20007 (☎ **800/556-7896** or 202/785-9000); **Cultural Heritage Alliance,** 107–115 S. Second St., Philadelphia, PA 19106 (☎ **800/323-4466** or 215/923-7060); and **Irish American Cultural Institute,** 1 Lackawanna Place, Morristown, NJ 07960 (☎ **800/232-3746** or 612/962-6040).

FOR FAMILIES

Roughly a quarter of the Irish population is under 15 years of age, so it's no wonder that Ireland is so youth and family oriented. A love of children (*lots* of them) is one of the hallmarks of the Irish-Catholic tradition, and of the country in general, so you'll always find people quick to be helpful and to suggest places to go and things to do with children.

Instead of hotels or B&Bs, families might well consider a farm stay or a vacation rental home, where children are likely to have the opportunity to meet and to make friends with local children. The information provided above regarding farmhouse accommodations and self-catering will be helpful in pursuing such options.

En route, if given 24-hour advance notice, airlines will arrange for a special child menu, and will warm any baby food you bring with you. On arrival, car-rental companies will have children's car seats on hand, provided a request has been made ahead of time. Throughout the island, entrance fees and tickets on public transportation are often reduced by at least half for children, and inclusive family rates for parents with children may be available. In this guide, a "family" rate, unless otherwise stated, is for two adults with two children. Additional increments are most often charged for larger families. Aside from all too familiar fast-food fare, many hotels and restaurants offer children's menus. Baby-sitting is provided in some hotels, guest houses, and B&Bs, and can be arranged in others.

OTHER HELPFUL RESOURCES

Travel With Your Children (TWYCH), 45 W. 18th St., 7th Floor, New York, NY 10011 (☎ **212/206-0688**), can send you an information packet of its publications, such as *Family Travel Times,* and a sample issue for $2.

Wilderness Press, 2440 Bancroft Way, Berkeley, CA 94704 (☎ **800/443-7227**) offers *Sharing Nature with Children* and *Backpacking with Babies and Small Children.*

Mason-Grant Publications, P.O. Box 6547, Portsmouth, NH 03802 (☎ **603/436-1608**) offers *Take Your Kids to Europe* by Cynthia W. Harriman, a guide to budget family travel.

FOR GAY & LESBIAN TRAVELERS

Gay Ireland has rapidly come out of the closet since homosexuality became legal in the North in 1982 and in the Republic in July 1993. Though the gay and lesbian community has received increasing support over the last several years, much of Ireland on the whole continues to discourage its gay population. In cities such as Dublin, Cork, and Galway, gay and lesbian visitors will find more formal support and an open, if small, gay community.

Two essential publications for the gay or lesbian visitor to Ireland are the *Gay Community News* and *In Dublin* magazine.

Gay Community News is a free newspaper of comprehensive Irish gay-related information published the last Friday of each month and widely available in the city center. You can find a copy for sure at the **National Lesbian and Gay Federation (NLGF),** 6 S. William St., Dublin 2 (☎ **01/671-0939**), where it is published and where you can obtain advice on gay-related legal issues. The *Gay Community News* is also distributed by Books Upstairs at 36 College Green across from Trinity College; Waterstone's on Dawson Street, also near Trinity; the Well Fed Cafe on Crow Street in Temple Bar; the George on South Greater St. George's Street off Dame Street; and other progressive haunts.

In Dublin, which comes out twice a month and is for sale at news agents and bookstores throughout the city, has a page of gay events, current club information, AIDS and health information resources, accommodation options, and helpful organizations.

The following organizations and help lines are staffed by knowledgeable and friendly people:

National Lesbian and Gay Federation (NLGF), 6 S. William St., Dublin 2 (☎ **01/671-0939;** fax 01/671-3549; http://homepage.tinet.ie/~nlgf). Monday to Friday noon to 5pm.

Gay Switchboard Dublin at Carmichael House, North Brunswick Street, Dublin 7 (☎ **01/872-1055;** fax 01/873-5737), Sunday to Friday 8 to 10pm and Saturday 3:30 to 6pm.

Lesbian Line Dublin (☎ **01/872-9911**), Thursday 7 to 9pm.

LOT (Lesbians Organizing Together), the central umbrella group of the lesbian community, 5 Capel St. (☎/fax **01/ 872-7770**). Drop-in Fridays 10am to 4pm. (LOT also sponsors LEA/Lesbian Education Awareness, ☎/fax 01/ 872-0460, E-mail: leanow@indigo.ie.) Further information and newsletter on the World Wide Web: http://qrd.tcp.com/ qrd/www/world/europe/ireland/leanow.html.

outhouse, a new gay and lesbian resource center, 6 S. William St. (☎/fax **01/670-6377**).

AIDS Helpline Dublin (☎ **01/872-4277**), Monday to Friday, 7 to 9pm and Saturday 3 to 5pm, offering assistance with HIV/AIDS prevention, testing, and treatment.

Gay and Lesbian travelers seeking information and assistance on travel abroad may wish to consult the **International Gay and Lesbian Travel Association (IGLTA),** 4331 North Federal Hwy., Suite 304, Fort Lauderdale, FL 33308 (☎ **800/448-8550** or 954/ 776-2626; fax 954/776-3303; www.iglta.org). Additional helpful resources include the following publications: *Ferrari's Places for Men, Ferrari's Places for Women,* and *Inn Places: US and Worldwide Gay Accommodations,* all three published by Ferrari Publications, P.O. Box 37887, Phoenix, AZ 85069, www.q-net.com; and *Women Going Places,* Inland Book Company, P.O. Box 12061, East Haven, CT 06512. Also, Council Travel (☎ **888/COUNCIL** for an office near you) can provide a free pamphlet—*AIDS and International Travel*—that includes information on hotlines, HIV testing, blood transfusions, and traveling with AIDS overseas.

6 Getting to Ireland

BY PLANE

About half of all visitors from North America arrive in Ireland via direct transatlantic flights to Dublin Airport, Shannon Airport, or Belfast International Airport. (Since March 27, 1994, transatlantic flights to the Republic are no longer required to stop in Shannon.) The other half fly first into Britain or Continental Europe and then "backtrack" into Ireland by air or sea. In the Republic, there are seven smaller regional airports, all of which have service to Dublin and several of which receive some EC international traffic: Cork, Donegal, Galway, Kerry, Knock, Sligo, and Waterford. As services and schedules are always subject to change, be sure to consult your preferred airline or travel agent as soon as you begin to sketch your itinerary. The routes and carriers listed below are provided to suggest the range of possibilities for air travel to Ireland.

Dublin International Airport (☎ 01/704-4222) is located 7 miles north of the city center. **Dublin Bus** (☎ 01/873-4222) provides express coach service from the airport into the city's central bus station, Busarus, Store Street. Service runs daily, 7:30am until 7:45pm (8:30pm Sun), with departures every 20 to 30 minutes. One-way fare is £2.50 ($4) for adults and £1.25 ($2) for children under age 12. These services are expanded during high season, and a local city bus (no. 41) is also available to the city center for £1.10 ($1.80).

For speed and ease, a taxi is the best way to get directly to your hotel or guest house. Depending on your destination, fares average between £10 and £13 ($16 and $20.80). Taxis are lined up at a first-come, first-served taxi stand outside of the arrivals terminal.

Major international and local car-rental companies operate desks at Dublin Airport (for a list of companies, see "By Car" under "Getting Around Dublin" in chapter 3).

FROM THE UNITED STATES

The Irish national "air fleet" or **Aer Lingus** (☎ 800/223-6537) is the traditional leader in providing transatlantic flights to Ireland. Aer Lingus offers scheduled flights from Boston, Chicago, Newark, and New York to Dublin, Shannon, and Belfast International Airports, with connecting flights to Ireland's regional airports. A new fleet of wide-body Airbus 330 aircraft was introduced in summer 1994, and on March 14, 1996, Aer Lingus announced a new corporate identity and "a major period of customer-led product and service changes." Connections are available from more than 100 U.S. cities via American, Delta, TWA, or US Airways.

Note: Aer Lingus offers educational discounts to full-time students, which can be booked through CIEE/Council Travel, listed above, and an attractively priced Eurosaver Green Pass for those who wish to combine an Aer Lingus round-trip transatlantic flight to Ireland with a side trip to Britain or the Continent, or a domestic flight within Ireland, including the North.

Excellent transatlantic service is also provided by **Delta Airlines** (☎ **800/241-4141**), offering scheduled daily flights from Atlanta to both Dublin and Shannon, with feed-in connections from Delta's network of gateways throughout the United States. Delta also has a co-share arrangement with Aer Lingus, which allows Delta to offer daily service to Ireland from New York/JFK, at very competitive prices. Delta proves that it takes an expert to tell the difference between Southern and Irish hospitality.

The newest carrier to offer (as of June 1998) transatlantic service to Ireland is **Continental Airlines** (☎ **800/231-0856**) with one flight a day from Newark to Shannon and Dublin. In addition, limited (Mon and Fri) scheduled service from Miami to Shannon is offered by **Aeroflot** (☎ **888/340-6400**). Finally, **American Trans Air** (☎ **800/382-5892**) offers scheduled service from New York to Belfast.

There is no disputing that Aer Lingus offers a taste of Ireland prior to arrival, but no matter who carries you there, Ireland is only hours off, and so it makes sense to shop around for a flight that best suits your schedule and budget.

BACKTRACKING TO IRELAND

Many travelers opt to fly to Britain and backtrack into Dublin (see "From Britain to Ireland," below). Carriers serving Britain from the United States include **American Airlines** (☎ 800/433-7300); **British Airways** (☎ 800/247-9297); **Continental Airlines** (☎ 800/231-0856); **Delta Airlines** (☎ 800/241-4141); **Northwest Airlines** (☎ 800/447-4747); **TWA** (☎ 800/892-4141); **United** (☎ 800/241-6522); **US Airways** (☎ 800/428-4322); and **Virgin Atlantic Airways** (☎ 800/862-8621).

FROM BRITAIN TO IRELAND

Air service from Britain into Dublin is operated by **Aer Lingus** (☎ **800/223-6537** from the U.S., or 081/899-4747 in Britain) from Birmingham, Bristol, Edinburgh, Glasgow, Leeds/Bradford, London/Heathrow, Manchester, and Newcastle; **British Midland** (☎ **800/788-0555** from the U.S., or 01345/554554 in Britain) from London/Heathrow; **Jersey European** (☎ **01232/676676** in Belfast) from Belfast, Derry, Exeter, Jersey; **British Airways Express** (☎ **0345/222111** in Britain) from Cardiff, Isle of Man, and Jersey; **Ryanair** (☎ **800/365-5563** from the U.S., or 0171/435-7101 in Britain) from Birmingham, Bristol, Glasgow, Liverpool, London/Gatwick, London/Heathrow, London/Stansted, Luton, and Manchester; **Cityjet** (☎ **01/844-5566** in Ireland) from London city airport. There is also regular though quite limited service from Britain into Ireland's regional airports.

FROM THE CONTINENT

Major air connections into Dublin from the continent include service from Brussels via **Aer Lingus** and **Sabena** (☎ 800/952-2000); Copenhagen via Aer Lingus and **SAS;** Paris via Aer Lingus and **Air France;** Munich via **Lufthansa** (☎ 800/645-3880); Rome via Aer Lingus and **Alitalia;** Amsterdam via Aer Lingus; Lisbon via **TAP Air Portugal** (☎ 800/221-7370); and Zurich via Aer Lingus and **Crossair.**

BEST-VALUE AIRFARES

The expression "You get what you pay for, and you pay for what you get" has dubious relevance to airfares. We all know that the fellow in the seat next to us, the silent fellow with the grin, may be paying a lot less than we are. Budget fares are not always loudly hawked. Like newts, they sometimes hide under rocks, but a little looking around can uncover them. One place to look is on the Net, by consulting lowest-fare search sites such as:

> http://expedia.msn.com
> www.bestfares.com
> www.Travelocity.com

Avoiding high season, the defining dates of which vary somewhat, is the first and most effective step anyone can take in reducing the cost of travel, lodging, car rental, and so on. The next step is to plan far enough ahead to be able to meet advance-purchase restrictions, which mostly vary from a week to a month. That brings you to a fork in the road: between scheduled service and charters. On any given day, charters are likely to be less costly. They also offer fewer frills, and their tickets are ordinarily nonrefundable. Among airlines offering scheduled service, there is no predicting who will be making the best offer on any given day.

BY FERRY

If you're traveling to Ireland from Britain or the Continent, especially if you're behind the wheel of a car, ferries can get you there. The Irish Sea has a reputation, however, so it's always a good idea to consider an over-the-counter pill or patch to guard against seasickness.

Note: Prices fluctuate seasonally and further depend on your route, time of travel, and whether you are on foot or in a car. It's best to check with your travel agent for up-to-date details.

Irish Ferries (☎ **201/768-1187** from the U.S.) operates from Holyhead, Wales, to Dublin. **StenaLine** (☎ **800/677-8585** from the U.S.) sails from Holyhead to Dun Laoghaire, 8 miles south of Dublin.

From elsewhere in Europe, **Irish Ferries** also sails from Roscoff and Cherbourg, France, to Rosslare. **Brittany Ferries** (☎ **021/277801** in Cork) connects Roscoff and St. Malo, France, to Cork. (*Note:* Because the Irish Ferries company is a member of the Eurail system, you can travel free on the ferries between Rosslare and Roscoff or Cherbourg if you hold a valid Eurailpass.)

7 Getting to Dublin from Other Parts of Ireland

BY TRAIN   Irish Rail (☎ **01/836-6222**) operates daily train service into Dublin from Belfast in Northern Ireland and all major cities in the Irish Republic, including Cork, Galway, Limerick, Killarney, Sligo, Wexford, and Waterford. Trains from the south, west, and southwest arrive at Heuston Station, Kingsbridge, off St. John's Road; from the north and northwest at Connolly Station, Amiens Street; and from the southeast at Pearse Station, Westland Row, Tara Street.

BY BUS   Bus Eireann (☎ **01/836-6111**) operates daily express coach and local bus services from all major cities and towns in Ireland into Dublin's central bus station, Busaras, Store Street.

BY CAR   If you are arriving by car from other parts of Ireland or via car ferry from Britain, all main roads lead into the heart of Dublin and are well signposted to An Lar (City Centre). To bypass the city center, the East Link (toll bridge 55p/50¢) and West Link are signposted, and M50 circuits the city on three sides.

3

Getting to Know Dublin

*W*hen I was living in Dublin in the mid-'80s, I got to know the city by commuting every morning with a gentleman who navigated his tiny Ford through back alleys and major byways like a fighter pilot in the battle of Midway—city map spread across the steering wheel, radio tuned to a perpetual traffic report, eagle eyes scanning for any opening, horn honking madly as he sped through blind intersections. This was the adventurer's way of learning one's way around Dublin. This was the brave way. This is how Hemingway would have done it.

Barring that opportunity, here's a short course in Dublin navigation to get you going.

1 Dublin Orientation

Dublin is 138 miles NE of Shannon Airport, 160 miles NE of Cork, 104 miles S of Belfast, 192 miles NE of Killarney, 136 miles E of Galway, 147 miles SE of Derry, 88 miles N of Wexford.

VISITOR INFORMATION **Dublin Tourism** operates five visitor centers in greater Dublin that are open year-round. The principal center is at **St. Andrew's Church,** Suffolk Street, Dublin 2, open from June through August Monday to Saturday from 9am to 8:30pm and Sunday 11am to 5:30pm, and the rest of the year Monday through Saturday 9am to 5:30pm. For accommodation and ticket reservations throughout Ireland by credit card, call ☎ 01/605-7777. The other four centers are at the **Arrivals Hall of Dublin Airport** (☎ 01/844-5387), open daily in the summer from 8am to 10:30pm and the rest of the year from 8am until 10pm; the **Dun Laoghaire Ferry Terminal** (☎ 01/284-6361), open daily 10am to 9pm (subject to ferry arrivals); **Baggot Street Bridge,** Dublin 2 (☎ 01/284-4768), open Monday to Friday 9:15am to 5:15pm; and **The Square,** Tallaght, Dublin 24 (☎ 01/462-0671), open Monday to Saturday 9:30am to 5pm (closed noon to 12:30pm). Dublin Tourism also operates a 24-hour tourist information line (☎ 1550/112-233) for 58p (90¢) per minute. In addition, the **Temple Bar Audio-visual Centre** operates an automated mation line at (☎ **01/671-5717**).

CITY LAYOUT

Compared with other European capitals, Dublin is a relatively small metropolis and easily traversed. The city center, identified in Irish on bus destination signs as "An Lar," is bisected by the River Liffey flowing west to east into Dublin Bay and is ringed by canals, the north half by the Royal Canal and the south half by the Grand Canal.

To the north of the Royal Canal are the northside suburbs such as Drumcondra, Glasnevin, Howth, Clontarf, and Malahide; to the south of the Grand Canal are the southside suburbs of Ballsbridge, Blackrock, Dun Laoghaire, Dalkey, Killiney, Rathgar, Rathmines, and other residential areas.

MAIN ARTERIES, STREETS & SQUARES   The focal point of Dublin is the River Liffey, with no fewer than 14 bridges connecting its north and south banks. On the north side of the river, the main thoroughfare is O'Connell Street, a wide, two-way avenue that starts at the riverside quays and runs northward to Parnell Square. Enhanced by statues, trees, and a modern fountain, O'Connell Street of earlier days was the mainstream of the city, and it is still important today although neither as fashionable nor as safe as it used to be.

On the south side of the Liffey, Grafton Street is Dublin's main upscale shopping street and has clearly bent over backward in recent years to attract and please tourists. Narrow and restricted to pedestrians, Grafton Street sits at the center of Dublin's commercial district, surrounded by smaller and larger streets where a variety of shops, restaurants, and hotels are situated. At the south end of Grafton Street is St. Stephen's Green, a lovely park and urban oasis ringed by rows of historic Georgian townhouses, fine hotels, and restaurants.

Nassau Street, which starts at the north end of Grafton Street and rims the south side of Trinity College, is noted not only for its fine shops but because it leads to Merrion Square, another fashionable Georgian park noted for the historic brick-front townhouses that surround it. Merrion Square is also adjacent to Leinster House, the Irish House of Parliament, the National Gallery, and the National Museum.

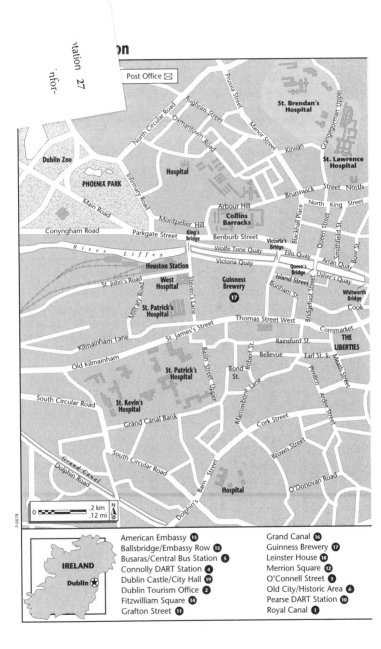

Post Office ⊠

St. Brendan's Hospital

Prussia Street

Aughrim Street

North Circular Road

Oxmantown Road

Manor Street

Kirwan

Grangegorman Upper

St. Lawrence Hospital

Dublin Zoo

PHOENIX PARK

Infirmary Road

Hospital

Brunswick   Street   North

North   King   Street

Blackhall Place

Queen Street

Smithfield St.

Main Road

Montpelier Hill

Arbour Hill

Collins Barracks

Bow St.

Conyngham Road

Parkgate Street

King's Bridge

Benburb Street

Victoria's Bridge

Ellis Quay

Arran Quay

River   Liffey

Wolfe Tone Quay

Victoria Quay

Queen's Bridge

Island Street

Usher's Quay

Heuston Station

St. John's Road

West Hospital

Steven's Lane

Guinness Brewery 17

Bonham St.

Bridgefoot Street

Whitworth Bridge

Cook

Military Road

St. Patrick's Hospital

Thomas Street West

Cornmarket

THE LIBERTIES

Kilmainham Lane

St. James's Street

Rainsford St.

Old Kilmainham

St. Patrick's Hospital

Basin Street Upper

Bond St.

Bellevue

Earl St. S.

Meath St.

Robert St.

South Circular Road

St. Kevin's Hospital

Marrowbone Lane

Pimlico

Ardee Street

Grand Canal Bank

Cork Street

Brown Street

Grand Canal

South Circular Road

Dolphin Road

Dolphin's Barn Street

Hospital

O'Donovan Road

0   .2 km
     .12 mi

N

P-0078

IRELAND

Dublin ★

American Embassy 15
Ballsbridge/Embassy Row 15
Busaras/Central Bus Station 5
Connolly DART Station 4
Dublin Castle/City Hall 19
Dublin Tourism Office 2
Fitzwilliam Square 14
Grafton Street 11

Grand Canal 16
Guinness Brewery 17
Leinster House 18
Merrion Square 12
O'Connell Street 3
Old City/Historic Area 6
Pearse DART Station 10
Royal Canal 1

28

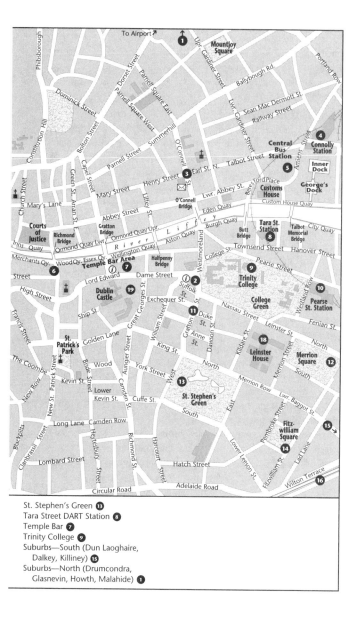

In the older section of the city, High Street is the gateway to medieval and Viking Dublin, from the city's two medieval cathedrals to the old city walls and nearby Dublin Castle. The other noteworthy street in the older part of the city is Francis Street, the antiques row of Dublin.

FINDING AN ADDRESS   Like London, the streets of Dublin are a maze of names, without a numerical grid system and seemingly assembled with no logical pattern in mind. Some are wide, some narrow, many are one-way, and a few run two ways. They form rectangles, triangles, and perpendicular angles, and run parallel to each other. For the most part, however, the larger thoroughfares are identified as streets or roads and the smaller ones are called lanes, alleys, rows, closes, and places.

Most names are posted not on street signs but high on the corners of buildings at the end of each street. The names are usually given in English and Irish, but a few of the older ones have Irish signs only. On each street, most buildings are numbered, but numbers are often not displayed and are seldom used by the locals. "At the top of Grafton Street" may be as specific an address as you will get. I recommend you buy a detailed city map and ask freely for directions.

For starters, always ask if an address is on the north or south side of the Liffey. That'll put you in the ballpark, narrowing the possibilities by 50% in one swipe. Another helpful strategy for finding your way is to acclimate yourself to the various postal zones within the city. Although there are more than 24 different zones, most of the attractions—hotels, restaurants, pubs, shops, and other activities of greatest interest to visitors—lie within six zones: Dublin 1 and 9 on the north side of the city, and Dublin 2, 4, 6, and 8 on the south side of the city. There is a map of Dublin's postal zones in the front section of all local telephone books. Keep in mind that odd-numbered zones are north of the Liffey, and even-numbered zones are south.

A complication to finding your way is that there is nothing to prevent one zone from having a street with the same name as one found in another zone. For instance, you'll find a Pembroke Lane in Dublin 2, off Baggot Street, and you'll find another Pembroke Lane off Raglan Road near the American Embassy in Dublin 4. This only underscores the fact that attention to the postal zones can be crucial.

One rule that you can depend on for further direction is the designation of streets as Upper or Lower. Streets that are Lower are always closer to the River Liffey. Finally, remember that Dubliners usually give directions that are defined by local landmarks or major sights, such as "beside Trinity College" or "just off St. Stephen's Green."

NEIGHBORHOODS IN BRIEF

O'Connell Street (North of the Liffey) Once a fashionable and historic focal point in Dublin, this area has lost much of its charm and importance in recent years. A wide and sweeping thoroughfare, O'Connell Street is rimmed by shops, fast-food restaurants, and movie theaters, as well as a few great landmarks like the General Post Office and the Gresham Hotel. Within walking distance of O'Connell Street are four theaters plus the Catholic Pro-Cathedral, the Moore Street open markets, the all-pedestrian shopping area of Henry Street, the new Financial Services Centre, the ILAC Centre, the Jervis Shopping Centre, and the Central Bus Station. Regrettably, it is wise to be cautious after hours, especially after dark, in this section of the city. Most of this area lies in the Dublin 1 postal code.

Trinity College Area On the south side of the River Liffey, the Trinity College complex is a 42-acre center of academia in the heart of the city, surrounded by fine bookstores and shops. This area lies in the Dublin 2 postal code.

Temple Bar Wedged between Trinity College and the Old City, this section has recently been spruced up and made the scene of massive development as the cultural and entertainment hub of Dublin. As Dublin's self-proclaimed Left Bank, Temple Bar is the place to see and to be seen. It offers a vibrant array of unique shops, art galleries, recording studios, theaters, trendy restaurants, and atmospheric pubs. Largely the stomping ground of the young, it's easy to feel over the hill here if you're past 25. This area lies in the Dublin 2 and Dublin 8 postal code.

Old City/Historic Area Dating from Viking and medieval times, this cobble-stoned enclave includes Dublin Castle, the remnants of the city's original walls, and the city's two main cathedrals, Christ Church and St. Patrick's. The adjacent Liberties section, just west of High Street, takes its name from the fact that the people who lived here long ago were exempt from the local jurisdiction within the city walls. Although it prospered in its early days, the Liberties fell on hard times in the 17th and 18th centuries and is only now feeling a touch of urban renewal. Highlights here range from the Guinness Brewery and Royal Hospital to the original Cornmarket area. Most of this area lies in the Dublin 8 zone.

St. Stephen's Green/Grafton Street Area   A focal point for visitors to Dublin, this district is home to some of the city's finest hotels, restaurants, and shops. There are some residential townhouses near the Green, but this area is primarily a business neighborhood. It is part of the Dublin 2 zone.

Fitzwilliam & Merrion Square   These two little square parks are surrounded by fashionable brick-faced Georgian townhouses, each with its own distinctive and colorful doorway. Some of Dublin's most famous citizens once resided here, although today many of the houses have been turned into offices for doctors, lawyers, and other professionals. This area is part of the Dublin 2 zone.

Ballsbridge/Embassy Row   Situated south of the Grand Canal, this is Dublin's most prestigious suburb, yet it is within walking distance of downtown. Although primarily a residential area, it is also the home of some of the city's leading hotels, restaurants, and embassies, including that of the United States. This area is part of the Dublin 4 zone.

2 Getting Around Dublin

BY BUS

Dublin Bus operates a fleet of green double-decker buses, high-frequency single-deck buses, and minibuses (called 'imps') throughout the city and its suburbs. Most buses originate on or near O'Connell Street, Abbey Street, and Eden Quay on the north side; and from Aston Quay, College Street, or Fleet Street on the south side. Bus stops are located every 2 or 3 blocks. Destinations and bus numbers are posted above the front windows; buses destined for the city center are marked with the Irish Gaelic words "An Lar."

Bus service runs daily throughout the city, starting at 6am (10am on Sunday), with the last bus at 11:30pm, excluding Thursday, Friday, and Saturday nights, when there is a Nitelink service from city center to the suburbs running from midnight to 3am. Frequency ranges from every 10 to 15 minutes for most runs; schedules are posted on revolving notice boards at each bus stop.

Inner city fares are calculated on distances traveled; minimum fare is 55p (85¢); maximum fare is £1.25 ($1.95). Nitelink fare is a flat £2.50 ($3.90). Buy your tickets from the driver as you enter the bus; exact change is welcomed but not required. Notes of £5 or higher, however, may not be accepted. One-day and 4-day passes are available at reduced rates: 1-day bus-only for £3.30 ($5.10) and 4-day bus and city rail for £10 ($15.50). With 4-day passes, bus travel is restricted to after 9:45am.

For more information, contact **Dublin Bus,** 59 Upper O'Connell St., Dublin 1 (☎ **01/873-4222**).

BY DART

Dublin's electric rapid transit system, known as **DART (Dublin Area Rapid Transit),** links several city-center stations at Tara Street, Pearse Street, and Amiens Street (Connolly Station) with suburbs and seaside communities as far as Howth to the north and Bray to the south.

The DART operates from 7am to 11:30pm Monday through Saturday, and from 9:30am to 11:30pm on Sunday, and is admirably punctual. Schedules are available at all stations during operating hours, but, depending on the time of day and the particular station, you can generally expect that the time between trains will be 10 to 20 minutes. Minimum single-journey fare is 80p ($1.25). An individual 1-day RAMBLER ticket for unlimited DART travel is available for £3.50 ($5.45), and a family ticket (any two adults with up to two children) for £6 ($9.30). A 4-day bus and rail **Dublin Explorer** pass for one costs £10 ($15.50). Longer weekly and monthly commuter passes require ID cards and are not geared for tourists. For further information, contact **DART,** Pearse Station Street, Dublin 2 (☎ **01/703-3504**).

BY TAXI

Dublin taxis do not cruise the streets looking for fares; instead, they line up at ranks. Ranks are located outside all of the leading hotels, at bus and train stations, and on prime thoroughfares such as Upper O'Connell Street, College Green, and the north side of St. Stephen's Green. You can also phone for a taxi. Some of the companies that operate a 24-hour radio-call service are **Co-Op** (☎ **01/677-7777**); **National** (☎ **01/677-2222**); and **VIP Taxis** (☎ **01/478-3333**). If you need a wake-up call, VIP offers that service, along with especially courteous dependability.

Taxi rates are fixed by law and posted in each taxi. The minimum fare for one passenger within a 10-mile radius of O'Connell Street is now £1.90 ($2.95) for any distance not exceeding ⁵/₉ mile or 3 minutes and 20 seconds; after that, it's 10p (15¢) for each additional ninth of a mile or 40 seconds. At peak times in Dublin's often backed-up traffic, it's the minutes and not the miles that add up. The per-journey additional charge for each extra passenger and for each suitcase is 40p (60¢). The most costly add-ons are £1.20 ($1.85) for dispatched pick-up and £1.30 ($2) for service from Dublin airport. *Be warned:* Some hotel or guest house staff, when asked to arrange for a taxi, will tack on as much as £3 ($4.65) for their services, although this practice violates city taxi regulations.

BY CAR

Unless you're going to be doing a lot of driving from Dublin to neighboring counties, it is not logistically or economically advisable to rent a car. In fact, getting around the city and its environs is much easier without a car.

If you must drive in Dublin, remember to keep to the *left-hand side of the road* and not drive in bus lanes. The speed limit within the city is 30 miles per hour and seat belts must be worn at all times by driver and passengers.

RENTALS   Most major international **car-rental firms** are represented in Dublin, as are many Irish-based companies, with desks at the airport and/or full-service offices downtown. The rates vary greatly according to company, season, type of car, and duration of rental. In high season, the average weekly cost of a car, from subcompact standard to full-size automatic, ranges from £245 all the way up to £1,100 ($379.75 to $1,705), which makes this a prime moment to remind you of the advantage of making car-rental arrangements well in advance from home.

International firms represented in Dublin include: **Avis/Johnson and Perrott,** 1 Hanover St. E., Dublin 1 (☎ 01/605-7500) and Dublin Airport (☎ 01/605-7500); **Budget,** at Dublin Airport (☎ 01/844-5919); **Dan Dooley Rent-a-Car,** 42/43 Westland Row, Dublin 2 (☎ 01/677-2723) and at Dublin Airport (☎ 01/844-5156); **Hertz,** 149 Upper Leeson St., Dublin 4 (☎ 01/660-2255) and at Dublin Airport (☎ 01/844-5466); **Murray's Europcar,** Baggot Street Bridge, Dublin 4 (☎ 01/668-1777) and at Dublin Airport (☎ 01/844-4179); and **Thrifty,** 14 Duke St., Dublin 2 (☎ 01/679-9420).

Dublin Area Rapid Transit (DART) Routes

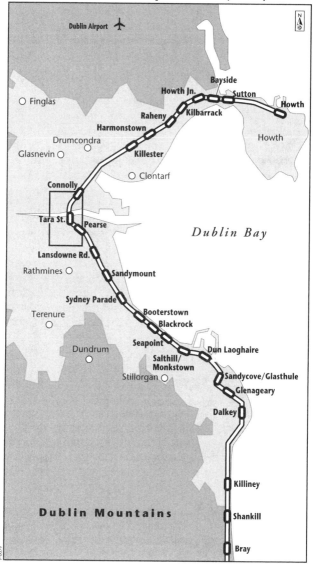

PARKING   During normal business hours, **free parking** on Dublin streets is an endangered option soon to be extinct. Never park in bus lanes or along a curb with double yellow lines. Fines for parking illegally are £15 ($23.25); if a car is towed away, it costs £100 ($155) to retrieve it. What's more, as of May 1998, a new peril faces parked vehicles. The infamous "Texas boot" or wheel clamp has come to Ireland, and the cost of removing it starts at £65 ($100.75).

Individual **parking meters** in the city center are currently being phased out in favor of multi-bay meters and "pay-and-display" **disc parking.** In Dublin, five discs can be purchased for £4 ($6.20), and each ticket is good for either 1 or 2 hours, depending on the location of the parking site. The most reliable and safest places to park are at surface parking lots or in multistory car parks in central locations such as Kildare Street, Lower Abbey Street, Marlborough Street, and St. Stephen's Green West. Parking lots charge on average £1.40 ($2.15) per hour and £13 ($20.15) for 24 hours. Night rates vary from £3.50 ($4.45) to £6 ($9.30).

The bottom line here is that you're better off without a car in Dublin, as the city is aggressively discouraging the car as the vehicle of choice for commuters, much less for tourists.

BY BICYCLE

The steady flow of Dublin traffic rushing down one-way streets may be a little intimidating for most cyclists, but there are many opportunities for more relaxed pedaling in residential areas and suburbs, along the seafront, and around Phoenix Park. The Dublin Tourism office can supply you with bicycle touring information and suggested routes.

Bicycle-rental averages £8 ($12.40) per day or £30 ($46.50) per week, with a £40 ($60) deposit. In the downtown area, bicycles can be rented from **Rent-a-Bike International,** 58 Lower Gardiner St., Dublin 1 (☎ **01/872-5399;** fax 01/836-4763); and **C. Harding for Bicycles,** 30 Bachelor's Walk, Dublin 1 (☎ **01/873-2455**).

ON FOOT

Small and compact, Dublin is ideal for walking, so long as you remember to look left and right (in the direction opposite your inclinations) for oncoming traffic and obey traffic signals. Each traffic light has timed "walk/don't walk" signals for pedestrians. Pedestrians have the right of way at specially marked, zebra-striped crossings; as a warning, there are usually two flashing lights at these intersections.

FAST FACTS: Dublin

Airport   See "Dublin Orientation" earlier in this chapter.

American Express   The American Express office is opposite Trinity College, just off College Green, at 116 Grafton St., Dublin 2 (☎ 01/677-2874). It's open Monday to Friday 9am to 5pm and Saturday 9am to noon; the foreign exchange operates Monday to Saturday 9am to 5pm and Sunday 11am to 4pm. In an emergency, traveler's checks can be reported lost or stolen by dialing collect ☎ 1-44-1-273-571-600.

Area Code   The area code for telephone numbers within Dublin city and county is **01.**

Baby-sitters   With advance notice, most hotels and guest houses will arrange for baby-sitting.

Business Hours   Banks are open Monday through Wednesday and on Friday from 10am to 12:30pm and from 1:30 to 3pm, on Thursday from 10am to 12:30pm and from 1:30 to 5pm. Some banks are beginning to stay open through the lunch hour. Most business offices are open from 9am to 5pm, Monday through Friday. Stores and shops are open from 9am to 5:30pm Monday through Wednesday and Friday to Saturday, and from 9am to 8pm on Thursday. Some bookshops and tourist-oriented stores also open on Sunday from 11am or noon until 4 or 5pm. During the peak season (May through Sept), many gift and souvenir shops post Sunday hours.

Car Rentals   See "Getting Around Dublin," above.

Currency Exchange   A currency exchange service in Ireland is signposted as a bureau de change. There are bureaux de change at all banks and at many branches of the Irish Post Office system, known as An Post. A bureau de change operates daily during flight arrival and departure times at Dublin Airport; a foreign currency note-exchanger machine is also available on a 24-hour basis in the main Arrivals Hall. In addition, many hotels and travel agencies offer exchange bureau services, although the best rate of exchange is usually given at banks.

Dentist   For dental emergencies, contact the **Eastern Health Board Headquarters,** Dr. Steevens Hospital, Dublin 8 (☎ **01/679-0700**). See also "Dental Surgeons" in the Golden Pages (yellow pages) of the telephone book.

Doctor   In an emergency, most hotels and guest houses will contact a house doctor for you. You can also call either the **Eastern Health Board Headquarters,** Dr. Steevens Hospital, Dublin 8 (☎ **01/679-0700**); or the **Irish Medical Organization,** 10 Fitzwilliam Place, Dublin 2 (☎ **01/676-7273**), 9:15am to 5:15pm. See also "Doctors—Medical" in the Golden Pages of the telephone book.

Drugstores   Centrally located drugstores, known locally as pharmacies or chemist shops, include **Hamilton Long and Co.,** 5 Lower O'Connell St. (☎ **01/874-8456**); and **Dame Street Pharmacy,** 16 Dame St., Dublin 2 (☎ **01/670-4523**). A late-night chemist shop is **Byrnes Late Night Pharmacy,** 4 Merrion Rd., Dublin 4 (☎ **01/838-6750**).

Embassies/Consulates   The **United States** Embassy is located at 42 Elgin Rd., Ballsbridge, Dublin 4 (☎ 01/668-8777); **Canadian** Embassy, 65/68 St. Stephen's Green, Dublin 2 (☎ 01/478-1988); **British** Embassy, 29 Merrion Rd., Dublin 4 (☎ 01/205-3700); **Australian** Embassy, Fitzwilton House, Wilton Terrace, Dublin 2 (☎ 01/676-1517).

Emergencies   For police, fire, or other emergencies, dial ☎ **999.**

Eyeglasses   For 1-hour service on glasses or contact lenses, try **Specsavers,** Unit 9, GPO Arcade, Henry Street (☎ **01/872-8155**), also at 112 Grafton St., Dublin 2 (☎ 01/677-6980); or look in the Golden Pages of the telephone book under "Opticians—Ophthalmic."

Gay & Lesbian Resources   Gay Switchboard Dublin, Carmichael House, North Brunswick Street, Dublin 7 (☎ **01/872-1055;** fax 01/873-5737; E-mail: gsd@iol.ie); **Lesbian and Gay Federation National,** 10 Fownes St. Upper, Dublin 2 (☎ **01/671-0939**); **LOT/Lesbians Organizing Together,** 5 Capel St., Dublin 1 (☎ **01/872-7770**).

Hairdressers/Barbers   The leading hairstyling names for women and men are **Peter Mark and John Adam.** Peter Mark has more than two dozen locations throughout Dublin and its suburbs, including 74 Grafton St., Dublin 2 (☎ **01/671-4399**), and 11A Upper O'Connell St., Dublin 1 (☎ **01/874-5589**). John Adam has shops at 13A Merrion Row, Dublin 2 (☎ **01/661-0354**) and 112A Baggot St., Dublin 2 (☎ **01/661-1952**). Also consult the Golden Pages under "Hairdressers."

Hospitals   For emergency care, two of the most modern health-care facilities are **St. Vincent's Hospital,** Elm Park (☎ **01/ 269-4533**), on the south side of the city; and **Beaumont Hospital,** Beaumont (☎ **01/837-7755**), on the north side.

Hotlines   In Ireland, hotlines are called helplines. For emergencies, police, or fire, dial ☎ **999; Aids Helpline** (☎ **01/872-4277**), Monday to Friday 7 to 9pm and Saturday 3 to 5pm; **Alcoholics Anonymous** (☎ **01/453-8998** and after hours 01/679-5967); **Narcotics Anonymous** (☎ **01/830-0944**); **Rape Crisis Centre** (☎ **01/661-4911**) and **FreeFone** (☎ **1800/778-888,** after 5:30pm and weekends **01/661-4564);** and **Samaritans** (☎ **01/ 872-7700** and 1850/609-090).

Information   For information on finding a telephone number, dial ☎ **1190.** For visitor information, see "Visitor Information" under "Dublin Orientation," above.

Laundry/Dry Cleaning   Most hotels provide same-day or next-day laundry and/or dry-cleaning services. If you wish to make your own arrangements, two centrally located choices are **Craft Cleaners,** 12 Upper Baggot St., Dublin 2 (☎ **01/668-8198**); and **Grafton Cleaners,** 32 S. William St., Dublin 2 (☎ **01/679-4309**). More are listed under "Dry Cleaners" in the Golden Pages of the telephone book.

Libraries   For research materials and periodicals, try the **National Library of Ireland,** Kildare Street, Dublin 2 (☎ **01/603-0200**); or **Dublin's Central Library,** ILAC Centre, Henry Street, Dublin 1 (☎ **01/873-4333**).

Lost Property   Most hotels have a lost-property service, usually under the aegis of the housekeeping department. For items lost in public places, contact the **Dublin Garda Siochana (Police) Headquarters,** Harcourt Square, Dublin 2 (☎ **01/475-5555**).

Newspapers/Magazines   The three morning Irish dailies are the *Irish Times* (except Sun), *Irish Independent,* and *The Examiner.* In the afternoon, one tabloid, *The Herald,* hits the stands. There are also two weeklies, *The Sunday World* and *The Sunday Tribune.* Papers from other European cities can be purchased at **Eason and Son,** 40 Lower O'Connell St., Dublin 1 (☎ **01/873-3811**). The leading magazines for upcoming events and happenings are: *In Dublin,* published every 2 weeks (£1.50 at newsagents; $2.35); and *The Event Guide,* www.dkm.ie/events, also published biweekly, containing a useful and up-to-date listing of events throughout Ireland, with a focus on Dublin (available free of cost practically wherever you look for it). *Where: Dublin,* published bi-monthly, is aimed specifically at tourists and visitors and is a useful one-stop source for shopping, dining, and entertainment (free at most hotels). Note that the *Irish Times* has an award-winning Web site at www.irish-times.com, where you can keep your finger on the Irish pulse 6 days a week.

Photographic Needs   For photographic equipment, supplies, and repairs, visit **Dublin Camera Exchange,** 9B Trinity St., Dublin 2 (☎ **01/679-3410**), also at 63 S. Great George's St., Dublin 2 (☎ **01/478-4125**); or **City Cameras,** 23A Dawson St., Dublin 2 (☎ **01/676-2891**). For fast developing, try the **Camera Centre,** 56 Grafton St., Dublin 2 (☎ **01/677-5594**); or **One Hour Photo,** 5 St. Stephen's Green, Dublin 2 (☎ **01/671-8578**), 110 Grafton St., Dublin 2 (☎ **01/677-4472**), and at the ILAC Centre, Henry Street, Dublin 1 (☎ **01/872-8824**).

Police   Dial ☎ **999** in an emergency. The metropolitan headquarters for the **Dublin Garda Siochana (Police)** is in the Phoenix Park, Dublin 8 (☎ **01/677-1156**).

Post Office   **The General Post Office (GPO)** is located on O'Connell Street, Dublin 1 (☎ **01/705-7000**), www.anpost.ie. Hours are Monday through Saturday 8am to 8pm, Sunday and holidays 10:30am to 6pm. Branch offices, identified by the sign "Oifig An Post/Post Office," are open Monday through Saturday only, 9am to 6pm.

Radio/TV   **RTÉ (Radio Telefís Éireann)** is the national broadcasting authority and controls two TV channels—RTÉ 1 and Network 2—and three radio stations—RTÉ 1, 2FM, and Radió na Gaeltachta (all Irish-language programming). Besides RTÉ programming, there are other privately owned local stations, including Anna Livia Radio on 103.8 FM and Classic Hits Radio and Ireland Radio News on 98 FM. In addition, programs from Britain's BBC-TV (British Broadcasting Corporation) and ITN-TV (Independent) can be picked up by most receivers in the Dublin area. BBC Radio 1, 2, and 3 can also be heard. Satellite programs, via CNN, SKY News, and other international operators are also fed into the Dublin area.

Shoe Repairs   Two reliable shops in mid-city are **O'Connell's Shoe Repair,** 3 Upper Baggot St. (☎ **01/667-2020**); and **Mister Minit,** Parnell Mall, ILAC Centre, Henry Street (☎ **01/872-3037**).

Weather   Phone ☎ **1-850/241-222.**

Yellow Pages   The classified section of the Dublin telephone book is called the Golden Pages.

4

Dublin Accommodations

*F*rom legendary old-world landmarks to sleek glass-and-concrete high-rises, Dublin offers a great diversity of places to stay. It may not be the cheapest city to visit, but even travelers on a budget should be able to find comfortable and attractive accommodations.

Dublin's hotels and guest houses are now inspected, registered, and graded by Tourism Quality Services. In 1994, the Irish Tourist Board introduced a grading system that ranks them with one to five stars, consistent with other European countries and international standards. Five hotels in Dublin currently merit the five-star rating: Berkeley Court, Conrad, Jurys, Shelbourne, and Westbury.

In general, rates for Dublin hotels do not vary as greatly with the seasons as they do in the Irish countryside. Some hotels charge slightly higher prices during special events, such as the Dublin Horse Show. For the best deals, try to reserve a room in Dublin over a weekend, and ask if there is a reduction or a weekend package in effect. Some Dublin hotels cut their rates by as much as 50% on Friday and Saturday nights, when business traffic is low.

In Dublin and throughout Ireland, **bed-and-breakfast homes** are open to lodgers by the night or longer. A warm bed and a solid, hot breakfast can be expected, and other meals are negotiable. Although B&Bs are regulated and inspected by the Department of Tourism (look for the Shamrock seal of approval), they are all different, as are your hosts. The Irish Tourist Board, for a small fee, will send a 400-page detailed listing of the approved B&Bs, complete with color photos of each (see "Visitor Information & Entry Requirements" in chapter 2 for their address). Or, better yet, you can follow our recommendations. Needless to say, you receive the personal touch when you stay in someone's home, and more often than not this is a real bonus. For those on a budget, this choice is hard to beat. Make your reservation at least 24 hours in advance (48 in high season); your room will ordinarily be held until 6pm. The cost for a room with private bath is roughly $22 to $32 per person, per night. *Note:* Most B&Bs do not accept credit cards.

Ireland's **hotels and guest houses** are the hospitality professionals. A full guide titled *Be Our Guest* is distributed by the Irish Hotel Federation and is available from the Irish Tourist Board. Hotels and guest houses, depending on their size and scope, offer a good deal more than a bed for the night and a breakfast to get you under way—everything from restaurants, night clubs, and on-premises pubs to health spas with saunas and tennis courts. All hotels and guest houses are inspected and rated by the Board of Tourism; hotels may aspire to five stars, while guest houses can reach no higher than four. The least expensive options may cost no more than a homestyle bed and breakfast, and the most expensive can be 10 times that.

TIPS ON ACCOMMODATIONS   Many older hotels and guest houses throughout Ireland consider the lobby level as the ground floor (not the first floor); the first floor is the next floor up, or what Americans would call the second floor. So, if your room is on the first floor, that means it is one flight up, not on ground level.

Elevators, readily available in hotels but not so plentiful in guest houses, are called lifts. Remember to press "G" for the main floor or lobby, not "1."

Concierges or hall porters, as they are sometimes called, arrange all types of services, from taking luggage or delivering packages to your room to obtaining theater tickets, booking a rental or chauffeur-driven car, selling postage stamps and mailing letters/ cards, dispensing tourist literature, or reserving taxis (for which they sometimes levy a hidden surcharge). Many of Dublin's concierges consider their craft a real art form and are members of the prestigious international organization known as Les Clefs d'Or, so you may have to prepare yourself to be pampered!

The vast majority of Irish hotels, as well as many B&B's, provide baby-sitting services, especially with appropriate notice. Ireland has long been a deeply family-centered culture, where at the same time adults traditionally socialize in pubs rather than at one another's homes; so baby-sitting is an art long since mastered.

Note: Many hotels and guest houses close for a few days or more on and around Christmas, even when they announce that they are open year-round. Consequently, if you plan to visit Ireland during the Christmas holidays, double-check that the hotels, restaurants, and attractions you are counting on will in fact be open. Furthermore, in this quide, what is true of Sundays is nearly always true for Bank Holidays.

1 Rates

All room charges quoted include 12.5% government tax (VAT) in the Republic of Ireland and 17.5% VAT in Northern Ireland, but do not (unless otherwise noted) include service charges, which are usually between 10% and 15%, with the majority adding 12.5%. Most hotels and guest houses will automatically add the service charge onto your final bill, although in recent years many family-run or limited-service places have begun the practice of not charging for service, leaving it as an option for the guest. Home-style B&Bs do not ordinarily charge for service.

We have classified "places to stay" into categories of price. The price levels as specified below and followed throughout this guide indicate the cost of a double room for two per night, including tax but not service charges.

Very Expensive	£150 and up ($233 and up)
Expensive	£120–£150 ($186–$233)
Moderate	£60–£120 ($93–$186)
Inexpensive	£30–£60 ($47–$93)

Ordinarily, the Irish cite the per-person price of a double room, a policy not followed in this guide, which for the sake of uniform comparison assumes double occupancy. Most accommodations will make adjustments for children. Children accompanying their parents are very often assessed on an ad hoc sliding scale. In other words, a smallish, angelic child may well incur only a nominal if any fee, while a hellion may pay full price. So it pays to have your children put their best, most silent feet forward when making their entry into a hotel or guest house.

If you have a talent for it, room prices in hotels—especially privately owned hotels in the off-season—can be negotiated downward. I have it on the best of authorities (the experienced manager of a revered old hotel) that a polite entry into such negotiations would be to ask, "Is that your best rate?" or "Can you do a little bit better?" The same hotelier described to me an occasion when a big-booted Texan slammed a fistful of bills down on the reception desk and bellowed "Fifty bucks, take it or leave it." This approach to negotiation is not recommended.

A note on terminology: The Irish use the phrase "en suite" to indicate a room with private bath. A "double" has a double bed, while a "twin" has two single beds. Queen and king size beds are not common except in large, deluxe hotels.

2   Reservations

Many hotels can be booked through toll-free 800 numbers in the United States; and, better yet, the prices offered through these booking services can be appreciably (as much as 40%) lower than those offered at the door. For those properties that do not have a U.S. reservation number, the fastest way to reserve is by telephone, fax or E-mail. Fax or E-mail are advisable since they provide you with a written confirmation. You can then follow up by sending a deposit check (usually the equivalent of one night's room rate) or by giving out your credit card number, which I for one still hesitate to do over the Net.

If you arrive in Ireland without a reservation, the staff members at the various tourist offices throughout the Republic and Northern Ireland will gladly find you a room via a computerized reservation service known as **Gulliver.** You can also call the Gulliver line directly yourself by dialing ☎ **00-800/668-668-66.** This is a nationwide and cross-border "freephone" facility for credit-card bookings, operated daily 8am to 11pm. Gulliver is now accessible as well from the US by dialing ☎ 011-800/668-668-66.

3   Quality & Value

Despite the various systems of approval, regulation, and rating, guest accommodations in Ireland are quite uneven in quality and cost. A budget hostel may be cleaner and more accommodating than a guest house or hotel and may be only a third as costly. Tourism in Ireland is a boom industry and there is a general rush to be a part of it. Understandably and regrettably, the gatekeepers are not as rigorous as their reputation; so it is always well to consult a fellow traveler or a reliable guide book in booking your lodgings. Which, of course, is what you're doing.

If possible, it is always advisable to ask to see your room before committing yourself to a stay. In any given lodging, the size and quality of the rooms can vary considerably, often without any corresponding variation in cost. This is particularly true of single rooms, which even in a semiluxurious hotel can approach boarding-house standards. Don't be discouraged by this, but be alert so you're not disappointed. Be sure, if you have complaints, to state them at once and unambiguously, which will likely bring an immediate resolution. Saving up your disappointments so as to file them all at once like your taxes seldom gets you anywhere.

4　Putting a Roof Over Your Head—Dublin Accommodations

HISTORIC OLD CITY & TEMPLE BAR/TRINITY COLLEGE AREA

VERY EXPENSIVE

Clarence. 6/8 Wellington Quay, Dublin 2. ☎ **01/670-9000.** Fax 01/677-7800. www.theclarence.ie. 50 units. MINIBAR TV TEL. £175–£190 ($271.25–$294.50) double; £400 ($620) 1-bedroom suite; £535 ($829.25) 2-bedroom suite; £1,450 ($2,247.50) penthouse suite. No service charge. AE, DC, MC, V. Bus: 51B, 51C, 68, 69, 79.

Situated between the south bank of the Liffey and Temple Bar, this Regency-style hotel belongs to an investment group that includes the rock band U2. Built in 1852, the Clarence was totally refurbished in 1996 to offer larger rooms and suites upgraded to deluxe standards. The rooms (some nonsmoking) are elegant and contemporary, with king-size orthopedic beds, PC/fax connection, satellite TV, VCR, and private safe. Services include valet service and cellular phone hire. The hotel offers a bar and noted restaurant.

EXPENSIVE

Central. 1–5 Exchequer St., Dublin 2. ☎ **01/679-7302.** Fax 01/679-7303. 72 units. MINIBAR TV TEL. £98–£135 ($151.90–$209.25) double. Includes full Irish breakfast and service charge. AE, DC, MC, V. Bus: 22A.

Midway between Trinity College and Dublin Castle at the corner of Great George's Street, this century-old five-story hotel was renovated in 1991 and totally refurbished in 1997. The public areas retain a Victorian atmosphere, enhanced by an impressive collection of contemporary Irish art. Guest rooms, cheerfully decorated with colorful Irish-made furnishings, offer such extras as a garment press, hair dryer, and tea/coffeemaker. There's a Victorian-style dining room, two bars, concierge, and room service. No on-premises parking, but a public lot is nearby.

Temple Bar Hotel. Fleet St., Temple Bar, Dublin 2. ☎ **800/44-UTELL** from the U.S., or 01/677-3333. Fax 01/677-3088. 108 units. TV TEL. £125 ($193.75) double. No service charge. MC, V. DART to Tara St. Station. Bus: 78A or 78B.

If you want to be in the heart of the action in the Temple Bar district, then this is a prime place to stay. Opened in summer 1993, this five-story hotel was developed from a row of town houses and great care was taken to preserve the Georgian brick-front facade with a Victorian mansard roof. Guest rooms are modern with traditional furnishings, including amenities such as a garment press, towel warmer, hair dryer, and tea/coffeemaker. Facilities include a skylit garden-style restaurant, the Terrace Cafe, and an Old Dublin–theme pub, Buskers, as well as access to a nearby health club. Fee-parking on street.

MODERATE

Blooms. Anglesea St., Dublin 2. ☎ **800/44-UTELL** from the U.S., or 01/671-5622. Fax 01/671-5997. www.blooms.ie. 86 units. TV TEL. £110 ($170.50) double. Service charge 12.5%. AE, DC, MC, V. DART to Tara St. Station. Bus: 21A, 46A, 46B, 51B, 51C, 68, 69, 86.

Lovers of Irish literature will feel at home at Blooms. Named after Leopold Bloom, a character in James Joyce's *Ulysses,* this hotel is in the heart of Dublin, near Trinity College and on the edge of the Temple Bar district. The bedrooms are modern and functional, with useful extras like garment presses and hair dryers. Concierge, 24-hour room service, and valet/laundry service are available, and the hotel has an enclosed private parking lot.

For formal dining, reserve a table at the Bia restaurant, or for more informal fare, try the Anglesea Bar. Late-night entertainment is available in the basement-level nightclub known simply as M.

INEXPENSIVE

Harding Hotel. Copper Alley, Christchurch, Dublin 2. ☎ **01/679-6500.** Fax 01/679-6504. www.iol.ie/usitaccm/. 53 units, with shower only. TV TEL. £50 ($77.50) double, £60 ($93) triple. No service charge. MC, V. Bus: 21A, 50, 50A, 78, 78A, 78B.

The Harding is conveniently tucked away along Dublin's oldest medieval street, with striking views of neighboring Christchurch to the west. The rooms are surprisingly large, and are furnished simply in a contemporary style, with lots of pine and with bright blue and yellow print fabrics. Each room is equipped with shower, hair dryer, phone, and coffee/tea-making facilities. Single and family rooms are available; and the hotel is fully wheelchair accessible.

Jurys Christchurch Inn. Christ Church Place, Dublin 8. ☎ **800/44-UTELL** from the U.S., or 01/475-0111. Fax 01/475-0488. www.jurys.com. 183 units. A/C TV TEL. £58 ($89.90) single, double, or family room. No service charge. AE, CB, DC, MC, V. Bus: 21A, 50, 50A, 78, 78A, 78B.

An ideal location and a winning concept—to offer quality hotel lodging at budget cost—have combined to make this one of Dublin's most sought-after accommodations. In the summer of 1997, Jurys Christchurch set a new Dublin record with 5 straight months of 100% occupancy. Totally refurbished in 1998, the rooms are ample, bright, and inviting. Facilities include a moderately priced

Dublin Accommodations

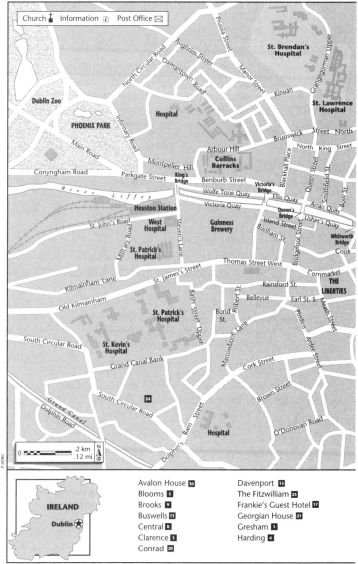

Church ✝ Information ⓘ Post Office ⊠

Prussia Street
Aughrim Street
North Circular Road
Oxmantown Road
Manor Street
Kirwan
Grangegorman Upper
St. Brendan's Hospital
St. Lawrence Hospital
Dublin Zoo
Infirman Road
PHOENIX PARK
Hospital
Brunswick Street North
North King Street
Blackhall Place
Queen Street
Smithfield St.
Bow St.
Main Road
Montpelier Hill
Arbour Hill
Collins Barracks
Conyngham Road
Parkgate Street
King's Bridge
Benburb Street
Victoria's Bridge
Wolfe Tone Quay
Ellis Quay
Arran Quay
River Liffey
Victoria Quay
Queen's Bridge
Island Street
Usher's Quay
Heuston Station
West Hospital
Guinness Brewery
Bonham St.
Bridgefoot Street
Whitworth Bridge
St. John's Road
Steven's Lane
Cook
Military Road
St. Patrick's Hospital
Thomas Street West
Cornmarket
Kilmainham Lane
St. James's Street
Basin Street Upper
Rainsford St.
THE LIBERTIES
Old Kilmainham
Robert St.
Bellevue
Earl St. S.
Meath Street
Pimlico
St. Patrick's Hospital
Bond St.
Marrowbone Lane
Ardee Street
South Circular Road
St. Kevin's Hospital
Grand Canal Bank
Cork Street
Brown Street
South Circular Road
24
Dolphin's Barn Street
O'Donovan Road
Grand Canal
Dolphin Road
Hospital

0   .2 km
     .12 mi
N

P-0080

IRELAND
Dublin ★

Avalon House 16
Blooms 5
Brooks 9
Buswells 11
Central 8
Clarence 3
Conrad 20

Davenport 13
The Fitzwilliam 23
Frankie's Guest Hotel 17
Georgian House 21
Gresham 1
Harding 6

48

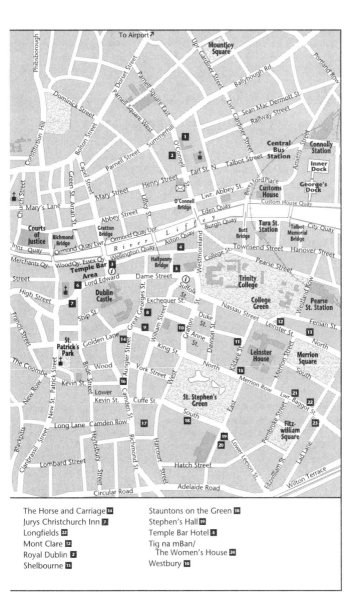

The Horse and Carriage 🄴
Jurys Christchurch Inn 🄶
Longfields 🄳
Mont Clare 🄵
Royal Dublin 🄴
Shelbourne 🄴

Stauntons on the Green 🄴
Stephen's Hall 🄴
Temple Bar Hotel 🄴
Tig na mBan/
   The Women's House 🄴
Westbury 🄴

49

restaurant, pub lounge, and discounted parking at an adjacent parking lot. Nonsmoking rooms are available, and baby-sitting may be arranged on request. Make your reservations early and request a fifth-floor room facing west for a memorable view of Christchurch. *Tip:* Rooms 501, 507, and 419 are especially spacious.

ST. STEPHEN'S GREEN/GRAFTON STREET AREA
VERY EXPENSIVE

Brooks Hotel. 59–62 Drury St., Dublin 2. ☎ **01/670-4000.** Fax 01/670-4455. www.iol.ie/bizpark/s/sinnott. 75 units. A/C MINIBAR TV TEL. £150–£200 ($232.50–$310) double. No service charge. AE, CB, DC, MC, V. DART to Tara St. or Pearse Station. Bus: 10, 11A, 11B, 13, 20B.

The Brooks Hotel opened its doors in June 1997 and has since welcomed many corporate and holiday visitors to its comfortable quarters. Quality furnishings include orthopedic beds, handmade oak furniture from Galway, and a tasteful decor varying in color scheme from room to room. Individually controlled heating/cooling units, three phones, powerful showers with bath, hair dryers, trouser presses, and ironing boards are standard issue, as are fax, E-mail, and current adapters. Three of the six floors are designated for nonsmokers. Superior and executive rooms provide such extras as VCRs, antique radios, and high king-size beds.

The visitors lounge, paneled in French oak, provides a restful oasis for tea or sherry and the newspaper, while the lobby-side bar provides a lively setting for more spirited social gatherings. An adjacent car park is available to guests at discounted overnight and weekend rates.

Conrad International. Earlsfort Terrace, Dublin 2. ☎**800/HILTONS** from the U.S., or 01/676-5555. Fax 01/676-5424. www.conrad-international.ie. 197 units. A/C MINIBAR TV TEL. £200 ($310) double; £410–£700 ($635.50–$1,085) suite. Service charge 15%. AE, DC, MC, V. DART to Pearse Station. Bus: 11A, 11B, 13, 14A.

A member of the international subsidiary of Hilton Hotels and one of the city's newest deluxe hotels, this seven-story red-brick high-rise is situated opposite the National Concert Hall and across from the southeast corner of St. Stephen's Green. The spacious public areas are rich in marble, brass, contemporary art, and lots of leafy plants. Each guest room is outfitted with contemporary furnishings, blond woods, and pastel tones, with extras such as electronic safety lock, minibar, writing desk, bathrobes, and three telephone lines. All beds have orthopedic mattresses.

Dining/Diversions: Choices include The Alexandra, a clubby room known for a range of gourmet Continental and Irish fare;

Plurabelle, a brasserie-style restaurant; The Lobby Lounge, for traditional afternoon tea or drinks with piano background music; and Alfie Byrne's, a pub named for a former lord mayor of Dublin and serving light lunches.

Amenities: 24-hour room service, concierge, valet, shoe-shine, express checkout, foreign currency exchange, car parking garage, hairdressing salon.

✪ **The Shelbourne.** 27 St. Stephen's Green, Dublin 2. ☎ **800/225-5843** from the U.S., or 01/676-6471. Fax 01/661-6006. www.shelbourne.ie. 164 units. MINIBAR TV TEL. £175–£225 ($271.25–$348.75) double; £325–£775 ($503.75–$1,201.25) suite. Service charge 15%. AE, CB, DC, MC. DART to Pearse Station. Bus: 10, 11A, 11B, 13, 20B.

With a fanciful red-brick and white-trimmed facade enhanced by wrought-iron railings and window boxes brimming with flowers, this grand six-story hostelry stands out on the north side of St. Stephen's Green. Built in 1824, it has played a significant role in Irish history (the new nation's constitution was signed in Room 112 in 1921) and it has often been host to international leaders, stars of stage and screen, and literary giants. The public areas, replete with glowing fireplaces, Waterford chandeliers, and original art, are popular rendezvous spots for Dubliners. The guest rooms vary in size, but all offer up-to-date comforts and are furnished with antique and period pieces. The front units overlook the bucolic setting of St. Stephen's Green. In 1996, nearly $2.5 million was spent refurbishing the Shelbourne's bedrooms and meeting rooms.

Needless to say, you don't stay here just for the beds, which represent the Irish preference for a mattress somewhere beyond soft and short of firm.

Dining/Diversions: The Dining Room offers Irish/Continental cuisine, while the Horseshoe Bar or Shelbourne Bar are both ideal for a convivial drink. The Lord Mayor's Lounge is favored by the locals for a proper afternoon tea.

Amenities: 24-hour room service, concierge, baby-sitting, safe deposit boxes, foreign currency exchange, private enclosed parking lot, beauty salon, boutiques, access to nearby health club.

Westbury Hotel. Grafton St., Dublin 2. ☎ **800/44-UTELL** from the U.S., or 01/679-1122. Fax 01/679-7078. 206 units. A/C TV TEL. £205–£265 ($317.75–$410.75) double; £305–£450 ($472.75–$697.50) suite; £595 ($922.25) presidential suite. Service charge 15%. Breakfast £9.95 ($15.40). AE, DC, DISC, MC, V. DART to Tara St. or Pearse Station. Bus: 10, 11A, 11B, 13, 20B.

A tasteful hybrid of modern and traditional design, this relatively new midtown hotel blends a sleekly styled contemporary facade with a serene interior of soft pastel tones and antique furnishings. It sits in the heart of the city's fashionable shopping district and near all the major sights. The guest rooms, many with half-canopy or four-poster beds, are furnished with dark woods, brass trim, and floral designer fabrics. Many of the suites have Jacuzzis.

Dining/Diversions: Choices include The Russell Room, a French/Irish restaurant; The Sandbank, a nautical-style pub serving fresh seafood; Charlie's Coffee Shop for a quick meal; and the Terrace Bar and Lounge, a favorite venue for afternoon tea or a drink, with live piano music.

Amenities: 24-hour room service, concierge, express checkout, hairdressing salon, 20-shop arcade, underground parking, fitness room, access to Riverview Health and Fitness Club.

EXPENSIVE

Buswells. 25 Molesworth St., Dublin 2. ☎ **800/473-9527** from the U.S., or 01/676-4013. Fax 01/676-2090. 72 units. TV TEL. £146 ($226.30) double. Includes full breakfast. No service charge. AE, CB, DC, MC, V. DART to Pearse Station. Bus: 10, 11A, 11B, 13, 20B.

Situated on a street that's oddly quiet (considering it's only 2 blocks from Trinity College and opposite the National Museum), this vintage four-story hotel has long been a meeting point for artists, poets, scholars, and politicians. Originally two Georgian town houses dating from 1736, it was launched as a hotel in 1928. After having been managed by three generations of the Duff family, Buswells was purchased by the Sean Quinn Hotel group in 1996. The public rooms contain period furniture, intricate plasterwork, Wedgwood flourishes, old prints, and memorabilia. Extensive refurbishment throughout the hotel is underway and should be completed by the time this guide reaches print. The Georgian decor and character will be preserved. Facilities include an à la carte restaurant, carvery, two bars, concierge, and room service.

Georgian House. 18 Lower Baggot St., Dublin 2. ☎ **01/661-8832.** Fax 01/661-8834. E-mail: hotel@georgianhouse.ie. 30 units. TV TEL. £72–£140 ($111.60–$217) double. Service charge 10%. Rates include full breakfast. AE, DC, MC, V. DART to Pearse Station. Bus: 10.

Located less than 2 blocks from St. Stephen's Green, this four-story, 200-year-old brick town house sits in the heart of Georgian Dublin, within walking distance of most major attractions. Bedrooms are smallish, but offer all the essentials and a colorful decor with pine furniture. As at most small hotels in landmark buildings, there is no elevator, but there is an enclosed parking lot at the rear; a restaurant specializing in seafood, The Ante Room, in the basement; and a lively in-house pub, Maguire's. A major expansion is planned for April 1999.

Stephens Hall. 14–17 Lower Leeson St., Earlsfort Terrace, Dublin 2. ☎ **800/ 223-6510** from the U.S., or 01/661-0585. Fax 01/661-0606. 37 suites. TV TEL. £150–£230 ($232.50–$356.50) double. No service charge. AE, CB, DC, MC, V. DART to Pearse Station. Bus: 11A, 11B, 13, 14A, 46A, 46B, 86.

With a gracious Georgian exterior and entranceway, this is Dublin's first all-suite hotel, situated on the southeast corner of St. Stephen's Green. It's ideal for visitors who plan an extended stay or who want to entertain and/or do their own cooking. All of the suites were re-decorated in March/April 1996. Each contains a hallway, sitting room, dining area, kitchen, bathroom, and either one or two bed-rooms. The luxury penthouse suites, on the upper floors, offer views of the city, while the ground-level town house suites have private entrances. Free underground parking.

Amenities: Concierge, twice-daily maid service, baby-sitting, safe deposit boxes, valet parking, bistro and bar, underground parking, access to nearby health club.

MODERATE

Stauntons on the Green. 83 St. Stephen's Green, Dublin 2. ☎ **01/ 478-2300.** Fax 01/478-2263. http://indigo.ie/~hotel. 32 units. TV TEL. £89– £99 ($137.95–$153.45) double. 10% discount for seniors; 50% for children sharing room with parents. Rates include full breakfast. No service charge. AE, DC, MC, V. DART to Pearse Station. Bus: 14A or 62.

Opened in 1993, this beautifully restored guest house occupies a four-story Georgian town house on the south side of St. Stephen's Green, next door to the Irish Department of Foreign Affairs. There is no elevator, but there are rooms on the ground level. The guest rooms are decorated in traditional style, enhanced by tall windows and high ceilings; front rooms overlook the Green, and rooms at the back have views of the adjacent Iveagh Gardens. Beds are firm. Pub-lic areas include a breakfast room and a parlor with open fireplace. Valet parking £5 ($7.75) per day.

INEXPENSIVE

Frankie's Guest Hotel. 8 Camden Place (off Harcourt St.), Dublin 2. ☎ **01/ 478-3087.** 12 units (9 with shower). TV. £58 ($89.90) double. Rates include breakfast. AE, EURO, MC, V. Safe backstreet parking. Bus: 62.

Frankie has been running this very pleasant guest hotel for 8 years, adding to the lovely walkway and roof garden and maintaining the small but fresh, simple white rooms to a high standard. Set on a quiet back street, the house has a Mediterranean feel, welcoming mature gay, lesbian, and straight visitors alike. There is a double bedroom downstairs that can accommodate a traveler with disabilities. It is an easy walk to St. Stephen's Green and Grafton Street and you can make coffee or tea in your room to renew yourself. I recommend that you book this place well in advance, especially for a weekend stay.

The Horse and Carriage Guest Hotel. 15 Aungier St., Dublin 2 (Aungier continues S. Great George's St.). ☎ **01/478-3537.** Fax 01/478-4010. E-mail: liamtony@indigo.ie. 9 units with shared bathrooms. TV. £45–£70 ($69.75–$108.50). All rates include breakfast and unlimited use of the attached Incognito Sauna Club facilities. AE, MC, V. Pay parking lot nearby. Bus: 14, 14A, 47, 47A.

Set in the heart of busy Dublin center, this three-year-old hotel, warmly welcoming people of all ages and orientations, has predominantly gay male visitors. The Incognito Sauna Club is part of the hotel complex and the atmosphere is very casual and bustling. Most rooms have soft king-size beds, and the shared bathrooms are very clean and private. The three highest priced rooms, the "carriage rooms," are more spacious and quieter than the others, which face a busy street. Heavily flowered wallpaper makes the rooms feel small and a bit dark, but all the accommodations are comfortable. The hotel has won awards for its remodeled turn-of-the-century facade. Hosts Liam Ledwidge and Tony Keogan are very helpful and well informed on Dublin life.

Tig na mBan/The Women's House. 24 Church Ave. South, Rialto, Dublin 8 (in Dolphin's Barn area off Reuben Ave., between St. Anthony's Rd. and Haroldville Ave.). ☎ **01/473-1781.** 4 units with shared bathrooms. £28 ($43.40) double. No credit cards. On-street parking. Bus: 19 or 19A.

A 10-minute bus ride south of Dublin center will bring you to the welcoming and cozy Women's House, which offers women travelers a wide range of options: single, up to four women sharing, standard B&B, and self-catering, all with optional evening meal. Every room has tea/coffee-making facilities. The knowledgeable owners will help you plan your stay in Dublin and give you the latest on women's and gay events. This is a very popular spot, so be sure to book well in advance.

FITZWILLIAM SQUARE/MERRION SQUARE AREA
VERY EXPENSIVE

Davenport Hotel. Merrion Sq., Dublin 2. ☎ **800/327-0200** from the U.S., or 01/661-6800. Fax 01/661-5663. 116 units. A/C TV TEL. £200–£230 ($310–$356.50) double. Service charge 12.5%. AE, DC, MC, V. DART to Pearse Station. Bus: 5, 7A, 8, 62.

Opened as a hotel in 1993, this building incorporates the neoclassical facade of Merrion Hall, an 1863 church. Inside there is an impressive domed entranceway with a six-story atrium lobby of marble flooring and plaster moldings, encircled by classic Georgian windows and pillars. The guest rooms, in a newly built section, have traditional furnishings, orthopedic beds, textured wall coverings, quilted floral bedspreads and matching drapes, and brass accoutrements. The hotel shares valet parking arrangements with its sister hotel, the Mont Clare, which is across the street.

Dining/Diversions: The Georgian-theme restaurant, Lanyon's, is named after a leading Irish architect of the 19th century. The clubby President's Bar, decorated with framed pictures of world leaders, past and present, serves drinks as well as morning coffee and afternoon tea.

Amenities: Room service, concierge, valet laundry, three telephone lines in each room plus a computer data line, work desk, personal safe, garment press, tea/coffee welcome tray, mirrored closet, and hair dryer.

EXPENSIVE

✪ **Longfield's.** 10 Lower Fitzwilliam St., Dublin 2. ☎ **01/676-1367.** Fax 01/676-1542. 26 units. MINIBAR TV TEL. £104–£149 ($161.20–$230.95) double. No service charge. Rates include full breakfast. AE, DC, MC, V. DART to Pearse Station. Bus: 10.

Created from two 18th-century Georgian town houses, this small, classy hotel is named after Richard Longfield, also known as Viscount Longueville, who originally owned this site and was a member of the Irish Parliament 2 centuries ago. Totally restored and recently refurbished, it combines Georgian decor and reproduction period furnishings of dark woods and brass trim. Bedrooms offer extras such as clock radios and hair dryers. Like the eye of a storm, Longfield's is in the midst yet remarkably quiet, an elegant yet unpretentious getaway 5 minutes' walk from Stephen's Green. Facilities include a restaurant with bar, room service, and foreign currency exchange, but no parking lot.

Mont Clare Hotel. Merrion Sq., Clare St., Dublin 2. ☎ **800/44-UTELL** from the U.S., or 01/661-6799. Fax 01/661-5663. 74 units. AC MINIBAR TV TEL. £140 ($217) double. Service charge 12.5%. AE, DC, MC, V. DART to Pearse Station. Bus: 5, 7A, 8, 62.

Overlooking the northwest corner of Merrion Square, this vintage six-story brick-faced hotel was thoroughly restored and refurbished in recent years. It has a typically Georgian facade, matched tastefully inside by period furnishings of dark woods and polished brass. All of the guest rooms were completely refurbished in August 1997 and given a brighter, more contemporary feel.

Dining/Diversions: The main restaurant, Goldsmith's (named for Oliver Goldsmith, one of Ireland's great writers), has a literary theme. There is also a traditional lounge bar.

Amenities: 24-hour room service, concierge, foreign currency exchange, private valet parking lot, hair dryer, tea/coffeemaker, and garment press.

MODERATE

The Fitzwilliam. 41 Upper Fitzwilliam St., Dublin 2. ☎ **01/662-5155.** Fax 01/676-7488. 12 units. TV TEL. £60–£80 ($93–$124) double. Service charge 10%. Rates include full breakfast. AE, DC, MC, V. DART to Pearse Station. Bus: 10.

Named for the wide thoroughfare it overlooks, this cozy guest house is a restored and refurbished 18th-century Georgian home. The entrance parlor has a homey atmosphere, with a marble fireplace and antique furnishings, while the bedrooms are outfitted with contemporary amenities including hair dryers and clock radios. Facilities include a French restaurant. Free overnight parking.

BALLSBRIDGE/EMBASSY ROW AREA
VERY EXPENSIVE

Berkeley Court. Lansdowne Rd., Ballsbridge, Dublin 4. ☎ **800/42-DOYLE** from the U.S., or 01/660-1711. Fax 01/661-7238. 217 units. TV TEL. £165–£185 ($255.75–$286.75) double; £250–£450 ($387.50–$697.50) suite; £1,600 ($2,480) penthouse suite. Service charge 15%. Breakfast £10.75 ($16.65). AE, DC, MC, V. DART to Lansdowne Rd. Bus: 7, 8, 45.

The flagship of the Irish-owned Doyle Hotel group and the first Irish member of Leading Hotels of the World, the Berkeley Court (pronounced *bar*-kley) is nestled in a residential area near the American Embassy on well-tended grounds that were once part of the Botanic Gardens of University College. A favorite haunt of diplomats and international business leaders, the hotel is known for its posh lobby decorated with fine antiques, original paintings, mirrored columns, and Irish-made carpets and furnishings. The guest rooms, which aim to convey an air of elegance, have designer fabrics, semicanopy firm beds, dark woods, and bathrooms fitted with marble accouterments. There are only 20 nonsmoking rooms available, so be specific when making reservations.

Dining/Diversions: Choices include the formal Berkeley Room for gourmet dining; the skylit Conservatory for casual meals; the Royal Court, a Gothic-style bar for drinks; and the Court Lounge, a proper setting for afternoon tea or a relaxing drink.

Ballsbridge / Embassy Row Area Accommodations

Anglesea Town House **12**
Ariel House **7**
Berkeley Court **5**
Burlington **1**
Butlers Town House **4**
Donnybrook Manor **13**
Doyle Montrose **14**
Doyle Tara **15**

Glenveagh Town House **3**
Hibernian Hotel **2**
Jurys Hotel and Towers **8**
Lansdowne Lodge **6**
Lansdowne Village **9**
Morehampton House **11**
Mount Herbert **10**

Amenities: 24-hour room service, concierge, laundry service, express checkout, foreign currency exchange, shopping boutiques, health club, Jacuzzis in suites, free valet parking.

Burlington. Upper Leeson St., Dublin 4. ☎ **800/42-DOYLE** from the U.S., or 01/660-5222. Fax 01/660-3172. www.doyle-hotels.ie. 504 units. TV TEL. £158–£173 ($244.90–$268.15) double, £350 ($542.50) suite. Service charge 15%. AE, CB, DC, MC, V. Bus: 10 or 18.

A favorite headquarters for conventions, meetings, conferences, and group tours, this is the largest hotel in Ireland, situated a block south of the Grand Canal in a fashionable residential section within walking distance of St. Stephen's Green. It's a modern, crisply furnished seven-story property that is constantly being refurbished. The bedrooms are outfitted with brass-bound oak furniture and designer fabrics. The interconnecting units are ideal for families.

Dining/Diversions: Choices include the Sussex, a large formal dining room; a buffet restaurant; and a coffee shop for light meals. For a real Old Dublin pub atmosphere, try Buck Mulligans, which serves a carvery-style lunch (read: lots of meat) and light evening meals as well as drinks. Annabel's is the basement-level nightclub. From May to early October, the main ballroom offers Doyle's Irish Cabaret, a three-hour cabaret dinner show.

Amenities: 24-hour room service, concierge, valet/laundry service, foreign currency exchange, underground and outdoor parking, gift shops, newsstand, hairdressing salons.

Hibernian Hotel. Eastmoreland Place, Ballsbridge, Dublin 4. ☎ **800/525-4800** from the U.S., or 01/668-7666. Fax 01/660-2655. www.slh.com/slh/pages/i/ianirea.html. 40 units. TV TEL. £145–£160 ($240–$248) double; £180 ($288) junior suite. No service charge. Rates include full Irish breakfast. AE, DC, MC, V. Bus: 10.

Although it bears a similar name, this is not a reincarnation of the legendary Royal Hibernian Hotel that was ensconced on Dawson Street until the early 1980s. Instead, this handsome four-story Victorian building was originally part of Baggot Street Hospital. After a complete restoration, it was modeled into a hotel in 1993, and offers its guests up-to-date comforts with the charm of a country inn. In 1995, it became a member of the "Small Luxury Hotels of the World," and in 1997 was named their Hotel of the Year. The public areas are filled with antiques, graceful pillars, and floral arrangements. The top floor sports a beautifully restored dome-shaped skylight. The bedrooms, of varying size and layout, are outfitted with orthopedic beds and are individually decorated with dark woods, floral fabrics, and specially commissioned paintings of Dublin and wildlife scenes. Some nonsmoking rooms are available. In-room conveniences include a full-length mirror, garment press, hair dryer, and tea/coffeemaker. Unlike some converted 19th-century buildings, it has an elevator. Guests can use the private parking lot for no extra charge.

Dining: On the lobby level, a cozy, parlorlike guests' bar and a conservatory-style restaurant with a Georgian decor.

Amenities: Room service, concierge, 24-hour butler, turn-down service, valet laundry.

Jurys Hotel and Towers. Pembroke Rd., Ballsbridge, Dublin 4. ☎ **800/843-3311** from the U.S., or 01/660-5000. Fax 01/660-5540. www.jurys.com. 390 units. TV TEL. Main hotel £180 ($279) double; Towers wing (with continental breakfast) £210 ($325.50) double. Service charge 12.5%. AE, DC, MC, V. DART to Lansdowne Rd. Station. Bus: 5, 7, 7A, 8.

Setting a progressive tone in a city steeped in tradition, this unique hotel welcomes guests to a skylit, three-story atrium lobby with a marble and teak decor. Situated on its own grounds opposite the American Embassy, this sprawling property is actually two interconnected hotels in one: a modern, eight-story high-rise and a new 100-unit tower with its own check-in desk, separate elevators, and private entrance, as well as full access to all of the main hotel's amenities. The guest rooms in the main wing, recently refurbished, have dark wood furnishings, brass trim, and designer fabrics. The Towers section, a first for the Irish capital, is an exclusive wing of oversize concierge-style rooms with bay windows. Each unit has computer-card key access, stocked minibar, three telephone lines, well-lit work area with desk, reclining chair, tile and marble bathroom, walk-in closet, and either a king- or queen-size bed. Decor varies, from contemporary light woods with floral fabrics to dark tones with Far Eastern motifs. Towers guests also enjoy exclusive use of a private hospitality lounge with library, board room, and access to complimentary continental breakfast, daily newspapers, and coffee/tea service throughout the day.

Dining/Diversions: Choices include the Embassy Garden for Irish/Continental cuisine; The Kish for seafood; and The Coffee Dock, an around-the-clock coffee shop. This is also the home of Jurys Irish Cabaret Show, Ireland's longest-running evening entertainment; The Dubliner Bar, a pub with a turn-of-the century theme; and the skylit Pavilion Lounge, overlooking the indoor/outdoor pool.

Amenities: 24-hour room service, concierge, foreign currency exchange, valet/laundry service, safe deposit boxes, express checkout, heated indoor/outdoor pool, therapeutic hot whirlpool, hairdressing salons, craft/clothes shop, Aer Lingus ticket office, outdoor parking.

EXPENSIVE

Butlers Town House. 44 Lansdowne Rd., Ballsbridge, Dublin 4. ☎ **800/44-UTELL** from the U.S., 01/667-4022. Fax 01/667-3960. 20 units. A/C TV TEL. £129 ($199.95) double. AE, DC, MC, V. DART to Lansdowne Rd. Station. Bus: 7, 7A, 8, 45.

This beautifully restored and expanded Victorian town house opened its doors to guests for the first time in 1997. The aim here has been a formal yet welcoming elegance, class without the starched collar. The rooms are richly furnished with either four-poster or half-tester beds, and equipped with their own climate control, activated from a hand-held remote. It's hard to elude comfort here, and the staff are especially solicitous. The hotel offers free tea and coffee all day. Breakfast, afternoon tea, and high tea are served in the atrium dining room. A limited-menu room service dinner is available daily. Baby-sitting may be arranged. One handicapped-equipped room is offered. The gem here, in our opinion, is the Glendalough Room, which can be requested if you book early. In addition to laundry and dry cleaning, secretarial services are available; and every room has a computer modem. You'll find that there isn't much Helen Finnegan, the manager, has overlooked here.

Doyle Montrose. Stillorgan Rd., Dublin 4. ☎ **800/42-DOYLE** or 800/44-UTELL from the U.S., or 01/269-3311. Fax 01/269-1164. 179 units. TV TEL. £117 ($181.35) double. Service charge 15%. AE, CB, DC, MC, V. Bus: 10, 46, 46A, 46B, 63.

Nestled on its own palm tree–lined grounds in a residential neighborhood, across from the Belfield campus of Dublin's University College, this modern four-story hotel sits beside the main road (N11) to the southeast of Ireland. The largest hotel on the southern outskirts of the city, it is a 10-minute drive from downtown, and offers ample outdoor car parking. Guest rooms are modern and functional, with colorful Irish-made furnishings.

Dining/Diversions: Facilities include a restaurant, The Belfield Room, plus a grill room and skylit lounge bar.

Amenities: Concierge, room service, laundry service, health center, souvenir shop, full-service bank.

MODERATE

Anglesea Town House. 63 Anglesea Rd., Ballsbridge, Dublin 4. ☎ **01/668-3877.** Fax 01/668-3461. 7 units. TV TEL. £90 ($139.50) double. No service charge. Rates include full breakfast. AE, MC, V. DART to Lansdowne Rd. Station. Bus: 10, 46A, 46B, 63, 84.

A true bed-and-breakfast experience is the best way to describe this 1903 Edwardian-style guest house. Located in the Ballsbridge section of the city, close to the Royal Dublin Showgrounds and the American Embassy, it is furnished with comfort in mind—rocking chairs, settees, a sundeck, and lots of flowering plants, as well as all modern conveniences in every guest room. You can count on a warm welcome from hostess Helen Kirrane, and the homemade breakfast is worth getting up for.

✪ **Ariel House.** 50/52 Lansdowne Rd., Ballsbridge, Dublin 4. ☎ **01/668-5512.** Fax 01/668-5845. 28 units. TV TEL. £50–£150 ($77.50–$232.50) double. Full Irish breakfast £7.50 ($11.65), continental breakfast £4.50 ($7). MC, V. DART to Lansdowne Rd. Station. Bus: 7, 7A, 8, 45.

Ariel House, a bastion of distinction and quality, sets the standard for Dublin guest houses. Michael and Maurice O'Brien are warm and consummate hosts. Opened over 25 years ago by Dublin-born and San Francisco–trained hotelier Michael O'Brien, Ariel House—with an historic mid-19th-century mansion as its core—has been expanded and enhanced over the years to its present scale. Guests are welcome to relax in the Victorian-style drawing room with its Waterford glass chandeliers, open fireplace, and delicately carved cornices. The bedrooms are individually decorated with period furniture, fine paintings and watercolors, and crisp Irish linens, as well as modern extras such as a hair dryer, garment press, tea/coffeemaker, and iron/ironing board. Facilities include a conservatory-style dining room that serves breakfast, morning coffee, and afternoon tea; a wine bar; and a private car park. It is conveniently located 1 block from the DART station.

Doyle Tara. Merrion Rd., Dublin 4. ☎ **800/42-DOYLE** from the U.S., or 01/269-4666. Fax 01/269-1027. www.doyle-hotels.ie. 100 units. TV TEL. £89 ($137.95) double. Service charge 15%. AE, DC, MC, V. DART to Booterstown Station. Bus: 5, 7, 7A, 8.

Positioned along the coast road between downtown Dublin and the ferryport of Dun Laoghaire, just 10 minutes from the city center, this modern seven-story hotel offers wide-windowed views of Dublin Bay. There is ample parking on the premises, which is nice if you have a car. For those who prefer to use public transport, it's within easy walking distance of major bus routes and a DART station. Guest rooms, with every modern convenience, contain attractive Irish-made furnishings. Concierge, room service, and laundry service are available, and there are a foreign currency exchange and a souvenir shop on the premises. For dining, there's a conservatory-style restaurant and a Joycean lounge bar.

Glenveagh Town House. 31 Northumberland Rd., Ballsbridge, Dublin 4. ☎ **01/668-4612.** Fax 01/668-4559. 13 units (9 with shower only). TV TEL. £60–£80 ($93–$124) double. No service charge. Rates include full breakfast. MC, V. DART to Lansdowne Rd. Station. Bus: 5, 6, 6A, 7A, 8, 18, 45.

Fashioned into a guest house by the Cunningham family, this converted three-story Georgian residence is situated south of the Grand Canal on a tree-lined residential street, heavily trafficked during the day yet rather quiet at night. It offers a homey atmosphere with a glowing fireplace in the sitting room, high ceilings, and tall windows bedecked with floral drapery. Guest rooms are decorated with light woods, lots of frilly pastel fabrics, and all the modern conveniences. There is a free parking lot.

Lansdowne Lodge. 6 Lansdowne Terrace, Shelbourne Rd., Ballsbridge, Dublin 4. ☎ **01/660-5755.** Fax 01/660-5662. 12 units. TV TEL. £50–£80 ($77.50–$124) double. £5 ($7.75) children over 5. Service charge 10%. Rates include full breakfast. MC, V. DART to Lansdowne Rd. Station. Bus: 5, 7, 8.

With a lovely two-story brick facade, this guest house enjoys a very convenient location, between Lansdowne and Haddington Roads, and within a block of the DART station and major bus routes. Owner Finbarr Smyth offers a variety of individually styled bedrooms with armchairs and homey furnishings, including decorative bed coverings and framed paintings. All the bedrooms have been newly renovated and have firm beds, and nonsmoking rooms available on request. The grounds include a garden and private parking lot.

Mount Herbert. 7 Herbert Rd., Ballsbridge, Dublin 4. ☎ **01/668-4321.** Fax 01/660-7077. 200 units. TV TEL. £79–£89 ($122.45–$137.95) double. No service charge. AE, DC, MC, V. DART to Lansdowne Rd. Station. Bus: 2, 3, 5, 7, 7A, 8, 18, 45.

Over 40 years ago the Loughran family welcomed their first guests to what had once been the family home of Lord Robinson. This gracious residence, with its own mature floodlit gardens, forms the core of a now somewhat sprawling complex. Over the past 4 decades, the Mount Herbert has expanded from four guest rooms to 200, and the result is a curious mix of family hospitality and large-scale uniformity. The guest rooms are bright, comfortable, and convenient to the city center, though without remarkable charm. Tea/coffeemaking facilities and garment presses are standard. Guest facilities include a restaurant, wine bar, sauna, indoor solarium, gift shop, and guest parking for up to 100 cars.

INEXPENSIVE

Morehampton House Guest Hostel. 78 Morehampton Rd., Donnybrook, Dublin 4. ☎ **01/668-8866.** Fax 01/668-8794. www.kilkennycats.ie/1stchoice/. 85 beds (some rooms with private bathroom). £27–£34 ($41.85–$52.70) double in twin-bed rooms. MC, V. Bus: 10, 46A, 46B.

In a residential area south of the city center and within a 15-minute walk from St. Stephen's Green, this four-story Victorian house has been recently converted into a hostel. Designed for the budget-minded traveler, it offers a range of twin rooms, multi-bed rooms, and dorm-style accommodations. Facilities include a 24-hour reception desk, TV room, common room, self-catering kitchen, car and bike parking, and lovely gardens.

SELF-CATERING

Donnybrook Manor. Donnybrook Manor, Donnybrook, Dublin 4. ☎ **01/676-6784.** Fax 01/676-6868. www.dubchamber.ie/brookman. 20 units (2/3/4 bedroom). TV TEL. £450–£800 ($697.50–$1,240) per week, depending on size of apartment and season. 4-day minimum stay. AE, DC, MC, V. Bus: 10, 46A, 46B.

Donnybrook Manor, a community of tasteful red-brick townhouses with stained glass doors, is strategically situated in Donnybrook, only a 25-minute walk from Grafton Street and College Green. Set well back from Donnybrook Road (N11) in its own parklands, the town houses are all but oblivious of the surrounding city. Newly refurbished and equipped with virtually every appliance and convenience you could want in a home-away-from-home, these present a very attractive and cost-efficient alternative to hotel or guest house living for couples, families, or groups wishing to base themselves in Dublin for 4 or more days. The immediate environs are thick with exceptional gourmet shops such as the Butler's Pantry, the Gallic Kitchen, Roy Fox, and Terroirs, guaranteeing the finest of provisions for home-cooked feasts. Otherwise, you can order out via "Restaurant Express" or walk to a range of fine restaurants. Each town house has its own enclosed garden, complete with table and chairs for sitting outdoors. Cots, cribs, and high chairs are available for the asking. Naomi Kidney, your host at Donnybrook Manor, goes the extra mile to respond to your needs and help make your stay memorable.

Lansdowne Village. Newbridge Ave. off Lansdowne Rd., Ballsbridge, Dublin 4. ☎ **01/668-3534.** Fax 01/660-6465. 19 units (2/3 bedroom). TV TEL. £380–£550 ($589–$852.50) per week, depending on size of apartment and season. Shorter periods available at reduced rates Oct–Mar. MC, V. DART to Lansdowne Rd. Station. Bus: 2, 3, 5, 7, 7A, 8, 18, 45.

Lansdowne Village is itself a modest and appealing residential development on the banks of the River Dodder and directly across from Lansdowne stadium. Within this community, Trident Holiday Homes offers fully-equipped 2 and 3 bedroom rental units, each with an additional pull-out double-bed sofa in the living room. They are bright and comfortable, trim and well maintained so that everything really works. The location is ideal—not only are you a 5-minute walk from the DART and less than a half hour's walk from Stephen's Green, but the Sandymount Strand, a favorite walking spot for Dubliners and perfect for an after-dinner stroll, is only 10 minutes away on foot. There are a number of shops and supermarkets nearby, so you can manage here quite well without a car. The smaller units are perfect for couples, perhaps with one child, while the considerably more spacious 3-bedroom units are recommended for larger families or for more than one couple.

O'CONNELL STREET AREA
VERY EXPENSIVE

Gresham. 23 Upper O'Connell St., Dublin 1. ☎ **01/874-6881.** Fax 01/878-7175. 206 units. TV TEL. £160–£200 ($248–$310)) double, £250–£700 ($387.50–$1,085) suite. Service charge 12.5%. AE, CB, DC, MC, V. DART to Connolly Station. Bus: 40A, 40B, 40C, 51A.

Centrally located on the city's main business thoroughfare, this Regency-style hotel is one of Ireland's oldest (est. 1817) and best-known lodging establishments. Although much of the tourist trade in Dublin has shifted south of the River Liffey in recent years, the Gresham is still synonymous with stylish Irish hospitality and provides easy access to the Abbey and Gate Theatres and other northside attractions. The lobby and public areas are a panorama of marble floors, molded plasterwork, and crystal chandeliers. With high ceilings and individual decor, guest rooms vary in size and style, with heavy emphasis on deep blue and pink tones, soft lighting, tiled bathrooms, and period furniture, including padded headboards and armoires. Nonsmoking rooms are available. One-of-a-kind luxury terrace suites grace the upper front floors.

Dining/Diversions: Choices include the bi-level Aberdeen Restaurant for formal meals; and Toddy's, a trendy pub/lounge offering light meals all day. Another bar, Magnums, attracts a late-night crowd.

Amenities: Concierge, 24-hour room service, valet laundry service, private parking garage, ice machines, foreign currency exchange.

MODERATE

Royal Dublin. 40 Upper O'Connell St., Dublin 1. ☎ **800/528-1234** from the U.S., or 01/873-3666. Fax 01/873-3120. 120 units. TV TEL. £98–£123 ($151.90–$190.65) double. Includes full Irish breakfast and service charge. AE, DC, MC, V. DART to Connolly Station. Bus: 36A, 40A, 40B, 40C, 51A.

Romantically floodlit at night, this modern five-story hotel is positioned near Parnell Square at the north end of Dublin's main thoroughfare, within walking distance of all the main theaters and northside attractions. It combines a contemporary skylit lobby full of art deco overtones with adjacent lounge areas that were part of the original building dating from 1752. These Georgian-themed rooms are rich in high molded ceilings, ornate cornices, crystal chandeliers, gilt-edged mirrors, and open fireplaces. The bedrooms are strictly modern with light woods, pastel fabrics, and three-sided full-length windows that extend over the busy street below. Corridors are extremely well lit, with individual lights at each doorway. Concierge, 24-hour room service, and laundry service are available, and there's a currency exchange bureau, underground car park, and car-rental desk in the hotel. Dining choices include the Cafe Royale Brasserie for full meals; Raffles Bar, a clubby, skylit room with portraits of Irish literary greats, for snacks or drinks; and the Georgian Lounge for morning coffee or afternoon tea beside the open fireplace.

5

Dining in Dublin

*Y*ou're here. You're famished. Where do you go? A formal, old-world hotel dining room? Or perhaps a casual bistro or wine bar? Ethnic cuisine, maybe? Dublin has the goods, across a wide range of price categories. Expect, however, generally higher prices than you'd pay for comparable fare in a comparable U.S. city. (Hey, Dublin's hip—you always have to pay for hip.) As befits a European capital, there's plenty of continental cuisine, with a particular leaning toward French and Italian influences, plus a fine selection of international eateries, with menus from Scandinavia, Russia, the Mediterranean, China, and even exotic fare from someplace called California.

1 Not Just Boiled Potatoes Anymore

In the last 25 years, Irish cuisine has undergone a major makeover. Previously—before, in the words of Julia Child, "nutrition reared its ugly head"—Ireland enjoyed a singular reputation for overcooked meats, waterlogged vegetables, piles of potatoes, and cream-on-cream desserts. Recently, however, healthful preparation and appealing presentation of fresh natural ingredients have become the norm, or at least the measure of success.

The transformation of Irish cuisine did not have to start from scratch. The raw materials had always been there—beef and lamb nurtured on Irish pastures, an abundance of freshwater fish and ocean seafood, a bounty of agrarian produce, and dairy goods straight from the local creamery. It seems that travel inspired Irish chefs to take the next step. Abroad, they learned the arts of French nouvelle cuisine and California au courant. At the same time, visitors came to Ireland in greater numbers and requested crisper, more recognizable vegetables and a wider selection of seafood. In kitchens from Dublin to Donegal, the "new Irish cuisine" now reigns. To prove it, Irish chefs regularly bring home dozens of gold medals from the International Food Olympics.

A word of caution: Although a new standard has been set for Irish cooking, it is still quite common to find vegetables boiled into oblivion, and the once rampant white sauce is far from endangered or extinct.

MEALS & DINING CUSTOMS

Mealtimes in Ireland are similar to those in the United States, with most hotels and restaurants offering breakfast from 6 or 7am to around 10am, lunch from noon to 2 or 3pm, and dinner from 6 or 7pm to 10 or 11pm.

Breakfast in Ireland can be continental (juice, rolls or toast, coffee or tea) or "full Irish" (juice, fruits, yogurt, cereal, eggs, bacon, sausage, brown bread, toast or scones, coffee or tea, and sometimes fish). If you choose the full breakfast, you'll probably be content with a snack for lunch. In the cities, lunch can be a light or full meal, and the evening dinner is usually the main family meal of the day. The upper-priced restaurants prefer to sell set lunches, usually three or four courses, but most others offer snacks, sandwiches, salads, or a variety of hot and cold entrees.

To all of this, add morning coffee, usually around 11am, and afternoon tea around 3 or 4pm. The latter can be as simple as a cup of tea on the run or as formal as a sit-down gathering at a fine hotel with a brewed pot of tea, finger sandwiches, pastries, and other sweets arrayed on a silver tray and accompanied by piano or harp music. After a proper afternoon tea, some visitors have been known to skip dinner.

THE CUISINE

The star of most menus is seafood, formerly considered penitential fare. In particular, it's hard to equal wild Irish salmon, caught daily and rushed direct to your plate. Served steamed or broiled with a wedge of lemon, it's pink, delicate, and sweet. It's ideal as an appetizer (or starter, as the Irish say), slowly oak-smoked and thinly sliced with capers and lemon. Most visitors become so addicted to it that they take home at least a side of the stuff, vacuum-packaged for travel.

Another good prospect is the Dublin Bay prawn, one of Ireland's most popular seafoods. It's a more tender version of a shrimp but a cousin to the Norway lobster in flavor. Plump and succulent, prawns are equally tempting served either hot with melted butter or cold with a light cocktail sauce. Want more? There's Galway Bay oysters, Kinsale and Wexford mussels, Kerry scallops, Dingle Bay lobster, and Donegal crab. Dig in.

And lest you think the Irish have gone Inuit, there's the traditional land-based fare. Irish beef, for instance, has always been a favorite with the natives as well as with visitors, and it's exported all over the world. These days you'll not only get your choice of steaks, but you can also order filet of beef en croute, stir-fry beef, beef stuffed with oysters, beef flambéed in Irish whiskey, or beef sautéed in Guinness. And then there's lamb, lean racks and legs of which are the pride of Irish chefs. Ever wonder about all those sheep roaming the countryside? Not all of them are there to be made into sweaters.

As part of the standard, traditional Irish breakfast, you'll almost certainly be served a hefty portion of pork, whether it's the famous Limerick ham, zesty homemade sausages, or thick country bacon, which is one of the great pleasures of life (assuming you're not a vegetarian).

Traditional roast chicken will usually be the tasty free-range variety, accompanied by lean Irish bacon or ham and an herby bread stuffing. Breast of chicken wrapped around local mushrooms or smoked salmon mousse are also popular choices.

One of Ireland's most humble foods is also one of its greatest culinary treasures—brown bread. Made of stone-ground whole meal flour, buttermilk, and other "secret" ingredients, Irish brown bread is served on the tables of every restaurant in the country. Brown bread, be it light or dark, firm or crumbly, sweet or nutty, is always delicious—especially when the crust is crispy. Shedding all restraint, add a little rich creamery butter or homemade raspberry jam.

Some traditional dishes adapted to the new lighter cuisine might include boxty (a potato pancake filled with meats, vegetables, or fish), crubeens (pigs' feet), colcannon (potatoes mashed with scallions and cabbage), coddle (boiled bacon, sausages, onions, and potatoes), boiled bacon and cabbage (a precursor to the Irish-American St. Patrick's Day favorite, corned beef and cabbage), and, above all, the classic Irish lamb stew.

Irish desserts (sometimes called sweets) range from cakes (often called gateaux), pies, and American-style cheesecakes to a seasonal array of fruit salads or simple dishes of fresh strawberries. With a little effort, you can still find some of the rich traditional dishes such as trifle, a fruit salad combined with custard and sherry-soaked cake and topped with a roof of rich double cream, and plum pudding, a whiskey-based soft fruitcake usually reserved for Christmas and special occasions. Other native desserts include barm brack, a light and yeasty fruitcake, and raisin-filled soda cake.

Irish farmhouse cheeses offer a piquant alternative to rich and sweet confections. More than 60 cheeses are now produced throughout the land, and many restaurants pride themselves on the quantity and quality of their all-domestic cheeseboards.

2 Reservations

Except for self-service eateries, informal cafes, and some popular seafood spots, most all restaurants encourage reservations. The more expensive restaurants absolutely require reservations, since there is little turnover—once a table is booked, it is yours for the whole lunch period or for the evening until closing. Friday and Saturday nights (and Sunday lunch) seatings are often booked out a week or more in advance at some places, so have a few choices in mind if you are booking at the last minute.

Here's a tip for Americans who don't mind dining early: If you stop into or phone a restaurant and find that it is booked up from 8 or 8:30pm onward, ask if you can dine early (at 6:30 or 7pm), with a promise to leave by 8pm, and you will sometimes get a table. A few restaurants are even experimenting with early-bird menus at reduced prices to attract people for early evening seating. Irish restaurateurs are just beginning to learn that it is doubly profitable to have more than one seating a night.

In most restaurants, two menus are offered: table d'hôte, a set three- or four-course lunch or dinner, with a variety of choices, for a fixed price; and à la carte, a menu offering a wide choice of appetizers (starters), soups, main courses, salads or vegetables, and desserts (sweets), each individually priced. With the former, you pay the set price whether you take each course or not, but if you do take each course, the total price offers very good value. With the latter, you choose what you want and pay accordingly. If you are just a salad-and-entree person, à la carte will probably work out to be less expensive; but if you want all the courses and the trimmings, then stick with the table d'hôte.

In the better restaurants, the table d'hôte menu is pushed at lunchtime, particularly for the business clientele. In the evening, both menus are readily available. In the less-expensive restaurants, coffee shops, and cafes, you can usually order à la carte at any time, whether it be a soup and sandwich for lunch or steak and salad at night.

Here's a tip for those on a budget: If you want to try a top-rated restaurant but can't afford or accept the dinner prices, then have your main meal there in the middle of the day by trying the table d'hôte set lunch menu. You'll experience the same great cuisine at half the price of a nighttime meal.

3   Prices

Meal prices at restaurants include 12^1/$_2$% VAT, but service charge is extra. In more than half of all restaurants, a set service charge is added automatically to your bill—this can range from 10% to 15%. In the remaining restaurants, it is now the custom not to add any service charge, leaving the amount of the tip up to you. Needless to say, this diversity of policy can be confusing for a visitor, but each restaurant normally prints its policy on the menu. If it's not clear, ask.

When no service charge is added, then you should tip as you normally would in the United States—up to 15% depending on the quality of the service. If 10% to 12^1/$_2$% has already been added to your bill, then you should leave an appropriate amount that will total 15% if service has been satisfactory.

We have classified the restaurants described in this book into categories of price. The price levels are based on what it costs for a complete dinner (or lunch, if dinner is not served) for one person including tax and tip, but not wine or alcoholic beverages.

Very Expensive	£35 and up ($56 and up)
Expensive	£25–£35 ($40–$56)
Moderate	£10–£25 ($16–$40)
Inexpensive	£5–£10 ($8–$16)
Budget	under £5 (under $8)

MONEY-SAVING TIP   Some restaurants, in all categories of price, offer a fixed-price three-course tourist menu during certain hours and days. These menus offer limited choices, but are usually lower in price than the restaurant's regular table d'hôte menu. Look for a tourist menu with a green Irish chef symbol in the window, listing the choices and the hours when the prices are in effect.

SOME DINING TIPS   If you are fond of a cocktail or beer before or during your meal, be sure to check in advance if a restaurant has a full license—some restaurants are only licensed to sell wine.

Don't be surprised if you are not ushered to your table as soon as you arrive at a restaurant. This is not a delaying tactic—many of the better dining rooms carry on the old custom of seating you in a lounge or bar area while you sip an aperitif and peruse the menu.

Your waiter then comes to discuss the choices and to take your order. You are not called to the table until the first course is about to be served.

4 Keeping Body & Soul Together—Restaurants in Dublin

HISTORIC OLD CITY/LIBERTIES AREA

EXPENSIVE/MODERATE

Lord Edward. 23 Christchurch Place, Dublin 8. ☎ **01/454-2420.** Reservations required. Main courses £9.95–£15.95 ($15.40–$24.70). Fixed-price dinner £20 ($31). AE, DC, MC, V. Mon–Fri noon–10:45pm, Sat 6–10:45pm. Bus: 50, 54A, 56A, 65, 65A, 77, 77A, 123, 150. SEAFOOD.

Established in 1890 and situated in the heart of the Old City opposite Christ Church Cathedral, this cozy upstairs dining room claims to be Dublin's oldest seafood restaurant. A dozen different preparations of sole, including au gratin and Veronique, are served; there are seven variations of prawns, from thermidor to Provençal; fresh lobster is prepared au naturel or in sauces; and there's fresh fish from salmon and sea trout to plaice and turbot—grilled, fried, meunière, or poached. Vegetarian dishes are also available. At lunchtime, light snacks and simpler fare are served in the bar.

Old Dublin. 90/91 Francis St., Dublin 8. ☎ **01/454-2028.** Reservations recommended. Fixed-price lunch £13.50 ($20.90) and 10% service; fixed-price dinner £21 ($32.55) and 21% service. Main courses £11.50–£15.50 ($17.80–$24). AE, DC, MC, V. Mon–Fri 12:30–2:15pm and 6–11pm, Sat 6–11pm. Bus: 21A, 78A, 78B. SCANDINAVIAN/RUSSIAN.

Located in the heart of Dublin's antique row, this restaurant is also on the edge of the city's medieval quarter, once settled by Vikings. It's not surprising, therefore, that many recipes featured here reflect this background, with a long list of imaginative Scandinavian and Russian dishes. Among the best entrees are *novgorod*, a rare beef thinly sliced and served on sauerkraut with fried barley, mushrooms, garlic butter, sour cream, and caviar; salmon kulebjaka, a pastry filled with salmon, dill herbs, rice, egg, mushrooms, and onion; black sole Metsa, filled with mussels and served with prawn butter and white wine; and a varied selection of vegetarian dishes.

INEXPENSIVE

Leo Burdock's. 2 Werburgh St., Dublin 8. Bus: 21A, 50, 50A, 78, 78A, 78B. FISH AND CHIPS/FAST FOOD.

Established in 1913, this quintessential fish-and-chips take-out shop was a cherished Dublin institution until it was devastated in a recent

Dublin Dining

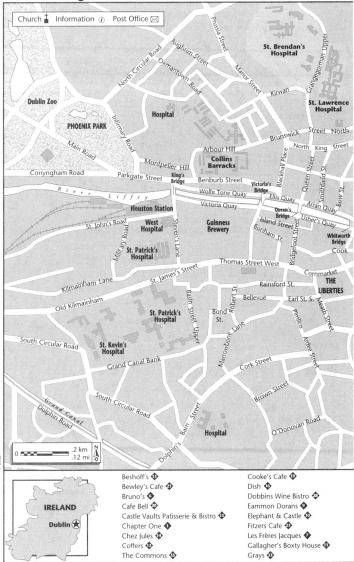

Church ✝ Information ⓘ Post Office ✉

Prussia Street
St. Brendan's Hospital
Grangegorman Upper
Aughrim Street
North Circular Road
Oxmantown Road
Manor Street
Kirwan
St. Lawrence Hospital
Dublin Zoo
Infirmary Road
PHOENIX PARK
Hospital
Brunswick Street North
Arbour Hill
North King Street
Main Road
Montpelier Hill
Collins Barracks
Blackhall Place
Queen Street
Smithfield St.
Bow St.
Conyngham Road
Parkgate Street
King's Bridge
Benburb Street
Victoria's Bridge
River Liffey
Wolfe Tone Quay
Ellis Quay
Arran Quay
Heuston Station
Victoria Quay
Queen's Bridge
Usher's Quay
St. John's Road
West Hospital
Steven's Lane
Guinness Brewery
Island Street
Bonham St.
Bridgefoot Street
Whitworth Bridge
Cook
Military Road
St. Patrick's Hospital
Thomas Street West
Cornmarket
THE LIBERTIES
Kilmainham Lane
St. James's Street
Rainsford St.
Bailm Street Upper
Robert St.
Bellevue
Earl St. S.
Meath Street
Pimlico
Old Kilmainham
St. Patrick's Hospital
Bond St.
Marrowbone Lane
Ardee Street
South Circular Road
St. Kevin's Hospital
Grand Canal Bank
Cork Street
Grand Canal
Dolphin Road
South Circular Road
Bailm Street
Brown Street
O'Donovan Road
Dolphin's
Hospital

0 .2 km / .12 mi
N

P-0062

IRELAND
Dublin ★

Beshoff's ⑰	Cooke's Cafe ⑯
Bewley's Cafe ㉑	Dish ⑮
Bruno's ❻	Dobbins Wine Bistro ㉓
Cafe Bell ㉒	Eammon Dorans ❾
Castle Vaults Patisserie & Bistro ⑬	Elephant & Castle ⑱
Chapter One ❶	Fitzers Cafe ㉔
Chez Jules ⑭	Les Frères Jacques ❼
Coffers ⑫	Gallagher's Boxty House ⑪
The Commons ㉕	Grays ⑲

72

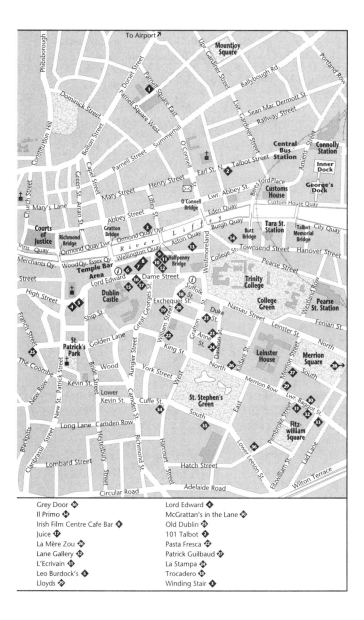

Grey Door 🔵	Lord Edward 🔵
Il Primo 🔵	McGrattan's in the Lane 🔵
Irish Film Centre Cafe Bar 🔵	Old Dublin 🔵
Juice 🔵	101 Talbot 🔵
La Mère Zou 🔵	Pasta Fresca 🔵
Lane Gallery 🔵	Patrick Guilbaud 🔵
L'Ecrivain 🔵	La Stampa 🔵
Leo Burdock's 🔵	Trocadero 🔵
Lloyds 🔵	Winding Stair 🔵

fire. Currently rebuilding, Burdock's should be back in operation and better than ever by the time this guide reaches the stands.

TEMPLE BAR/TRINITY COLLEGE AREA
EXPENSIVE

Les Frères Jacques. 74 Dame St., Dublin 2. ☎ **01/679-4555.** Reservations recommended. Fixed-price lunch £13 ($20.25); fixed-price dinner £20 ($31). À la carte also available. AE, DC, MC, V. Mon–Fri 12:30–2:30pm and 7–11pm, Sat 7–11pm. Bus: 50, 50A, 54, 56, 77. FRENCH.

Well-situated between Crampton Court and Sycamore Street opposite Dublin Castle, this restaurant brings a touch of haute cuisine to the lower edge of the trendy Temple Bar district. The menu offers such creative entrees as filet of beef in red wine and bone marrow sauce; duck supreme on a sweet corn pancake in tangy ginger sauce; rosette of spring lamb in meat juice sabayon and tomato coulis with crispy potato straws; veal on rainbow pasta with garlic and basil sauce; and grilled lobster from the tank flamed in whiskey.

MODERATE

bruno's. 30 E. Essex St., Dublin 2. ☎ **01/670-6767.** Reservations recommended. Main courses £8.75–£12.50 ($13.55–$19.40). Fixed-price dinners £9.95 ($15.40) and £11.95 ($18.50). Service charge 10% on tables over 4. DC, MC, V. Daily noon–midnight. DART to Tara St. Station. Bus: 21A, 46A, 46B, 51B, 51C, 68, 69, 86. MODERN CONTINENTAL.

Born in 1998, bruno's is one of the new kids on the block in Temple Bar. The atmosphere is light and modern, and the food is consistently excellent without flourish or pretence. The spinach and goat cheese tart; salad of prawns with honey, lime, sesame seeds, and jalapeño peppers; and the bruschetta of chicken are all worthy of mention. This is a sure-fire spot for a flawlessly prepared, interesting lunch or dinner without serious damage to the budget.

Dish. 2 Crow St., Dublin 2. ☎ **01/671-1248.** Reservations recommended. Main courses £10.50–£13.95 ($16.30–$21.60). Service charge 10% on tables of 6 or more. AE, DC, MC, V. Daily noon–11:30pm. DART to Tara St. Station. Bus: 21A, 46A, 46B, 51B, 51C, 68, 69, 86. NOUVEAU INTERNATIONAL.

With floor to ceiling windows, wide-beamed pine floors, light walls and dark blue linens, Dish presents a relaxed, tasteful atmosphere. One of Dublin's newest restaurants, of 1998 vintage, Dish already makes a strong case for itself. The menu is eclectic and enticing, with an emphasis on fresh grilled seafood and Mediterranean flavors, complex without being confusing. The grilled salmon with avocado, papaya and tequila-lime dressing; the baked hake; and the chargrilled tiger prawns were outstanding. The desserts we tried—caramelized

lemon tart with cassis sauce and the amaretti chocolate cheesecake—
were superior. Dish promises to be one of Temple Bar's finest venues, and at a modest price.

INEXPENSIVE

Chez Jules. 16a D'Olier St., Dublin 2 (across from the north wall of Trinity College). ☎ **01/677-0499.** Reservations recommended. Main courses £5.95–
£10.90 ($9.20–$16.90); fixed-price menus available before 7/8pm, £6.50–£8.90
($10.10–$13.80). No service charge. MC, V. Mon–Sat noon–3pm and 6–11pm,
Sun 6–11pm. DART to Tara St. Station. Bus: 5, 7A, 8, 15A, 15B, 15C, 46, 55,
62, 63, 83, 84. FRENCH COUNTRY.

One of Dublin's newer ventures, Chez Jules fills a niche: relaxed
French dining at pub-grub prices. Except for the checkered tablecloths, this is a dining hall, with long tables, benches, bright lights,
and bustle. The staff is especially warm and friendly. Some of the
dishes, like the au gratin potatoes, are delivered in their skillet. The
menu is modest, augmented by daily specials on the chalkboard.
This is solid, tasty French country fare, most affordable and satisfying. The vin de pays house wines are very drinkable and a real
bargain.

Elephant & Castle. 18 Temple Bar, Dublin 2. ☎ **01/679-3121.** Reservations
not necessary. Lunch main courses £5.50–£8.95 ($8.55–$13.90); dinner main
courses £6.50–£14.95 ($10.10–$23.20). AE, DC, MC, V. Mon–Thurs 8am–
11:30pm, Fri–Sat 8am–midnight. DART to Tara St. Station. Bus: 21A, 46A, 46B,
51B, 51C, 68, 69, 86. CALIFORNIAN/INTERNATIONAL.

Located in the heart of the Temple Bar district, this is an informal
and fun restaurant, a favorite with kids, with simple pinewood tables
and benches and a decor blending modern art with statues of
elephants and cartoon figures. The menu is eclectic, and includes
everything from exotic salads and multi-ingredient omelets to sesame
chicken with spinach and cucumber; fettuccine with shrimp, sun-
dried tomatoes, and saffron; linguine with goat cheese, tomato, broccoli, and thyme; and a house-special Elephant Burger with curried
sour cream, bacon, scallions, cheddar, and tomato.

Gallagher's Boxty House. 20–21 Temple Bar, Dublin 2. ☎ **01/677-2762.**
Reservations recommended. Fixed-price 3-course meal £4.95 ($7.70) until 5pm;
dinner main courses £5–£11.95 ($7.75–$18.50). MC, V. Daily noon–11:30pm.
DART to Tara St. Station. Bus: 21A, 46A, 46B, 51B, 51C, 68, 69, 86. TRADI-
TIONAL IRISH.

Old-style Irish cooking is hard to find in Dublin restaurants; but
here is one spot that keeps traditions alive. Gallagher's puts a
particular emphasis on Irish stew, bacon and cabbage, and a dish
called "boxty" (an Irish potato pancake grilled and rolled with various

fillings such as beef, lamb, chicken, fish, or combinations like bacon and cabbage). It's primarily a tourist venue, a culinary souvenir shop, as it were; and it's also almost always brimming full.

Juice. Castle House, S. Great George's St., Dublin 2. ☎ **01/473-7856.** Reservations recommended Fri–Sat. Main courses £6.95–£9.95 ($10.80–$15.40); early bird fixed-price dinner Mon–Thurs 5:30–7pm £7.95 ($12.30). Service charge 10%. EURO, MC, V. Sun–Thurs 11am–10pm, Fri–Sat 11am–midnight, Fri–Sat late-night light menu midnight–4am. Bus: 50, 50A, 54, 56, 77. VEGETARIAN.

Juice tempts carnivorous, vegan, macrobiotic, celiac, and yeast-free diners alike, using organic produce to create delicious dressings and entrees among its largely conventional but very well-prepared offerings. The avocado fillet of blue cheese and broccoli wrapped in filo was superb, and I highly recommend the spinach and ricotta cheese cannelloni. The latter is included in the early bird dinner—a great deal. Coffees, fresh-squeezed juices, organic wines, and late weekend hours add to the lure of this modern, casual eatery frequented by mature diners who know their food. The one anomaly here is that a restaurant so focused on health should often be rather clouded in smoke.

BUDGET

Beshoffs. 14 Westmoreland St., Dublin 2. ☎ **01/677-8026.** Reservations not necessary. All items £1.90–£4.50 ($2.95–$7). No credit cards. Sun–Thurs 11:30am–11pm, Fri–Sat 11:30am–3am. DART to Tara St. Station. Bus: 7A, 8, 15A, 15B, 15C, 46, 55, 62, 63, 83, 84. SEAFOOD/FISH AND CHIPS.

It's no wonder that the Beshoff name is synonymous with fresh fish in Dublin—Ivan Beshoff settled here in 1913 from Odessa, Russia, and started a fish business that developed into this top-notch fish-and-chips eatery, reminiscent of an Edwardian oyster bar. The atmosphere is informal and the self-service menu is simple: crisp chips (french fries) are served with a choice of fresh fish, from the original recipe of cod to classier variations using salmon, shark, prawns, and other local sea fare—some days as many as 20 different varieties. The potatoes are grown on a 300-acre farm in Tipperary and freshly cut each day. A second shop is located at 6 Upper O'Connell St. in the International Food Court (☎ **01/872-4400**).

Castle Vaults Patisserie and Bistro. Dublin Castle, Palace St. (off Dame St.), Dublin 2. ☎ **01/677-0678** or 01/679-3713. Reservations not necessary. Full breakfast £3.50 ($5.40). Fixed-price lunch £5.50 ($8.50). No credit cards. Mon–Fri 8:30am–4:45pm, Sat–Sun 12:30–4:45pm. Bus: 50, 50A, 54, 56A, or 77. INTERNATIONAL/SELF-SERVICE.

With stone walls, paned windows, and colorful medieval banners, the old vaults of Dublin Castle serve as the setting for this bustling indoor-outdoor cafe. The menu focuses on a lovely range of pastries prepared on the premises, snacks, and light lunch items such as homemade soups, pâtés, quiche, lasagna, sausage rolls, stuffed baked potatoes, salads, and sandwiches.

Irish Film Centre Cafe Bar. 6 Eustace St., Temple Bar, Dublin 2. ☎ **01/677-8079.** Reservations not necessary. Lunch and dinner prices range from £3.50–£8 ($5.45–$12.40). MC, V. Daily 12:30–3pm and 5:30–9pm. Bus: 21A, 78A, 78B. IRISH/INTERNATIONAL.

One of the most popular drinking spots in Temple Bar, the Cafe Bar features an excellent menu that changes daily. A vegetarian/Middle Eastern menu is available for both lunch and dinner. The weekend entertainment usually includes music or comedy.

ST. STEPHEN'S GREEN/GRAFTON STREET AREA
VERY EXPENSIVE
The Commons. 86 St. Stephen's Green, Dublin 2. ☎ **01/475-2597** or 01/478-0530. Reservations required. Fixed-price lunch £20 ($31); fixed-price dinner £35 ($54.25). AE, DC, MC, V. Mon–Fri 12:30–2:15pm and 7–10pm, Sat 7–10pm. DART to Pearse Station. Bus: 11, 13, 10 or 46A. MODERN EUROPEAN.

Nestled on the south side of St. Stephen's Green, this Michelin-starred restaurant occupies the basement level of Newman House, the historic seat of Ireland's major university, comprised of two elegant town houses dating back to 1740. The interior of the dining rooms is a blend of Georgian architecture, cloister-style arches, and original contemporary artworks with Joycean influences. For an aperitif in fine weather, there is a lovely stone courtyard terrace surrounded by a "secret garden" of lush plants and trees. The inventive menu changes daily, but you'll often see dishes such as confit of duck leg on a beetroot boxty, grilled shark with peppered carrot, and loin of rabbit with a stuffing of marinated prune.

MODERATE
Cookes Café. 14 S. William St., Dublin 2. ☎ **01/679-0536.** Reservations required. Fixed-price lunch menu £14.95 ($23.17). Early-bird menu 6–7:30pm £14.95 ($23.20). Dinner main courses £10–£17 ($15.50–$26.35). Service charge 12 ⅓%. AE, DC, MC, V. Mon–Sat 12:30–3pm, 6–11pm; Sun 12:30–3pm, 6–8pm. DART to Tara St. Station. Bus: 16A, 19A, 22A, 55, 83. CALIFORNIAN/MEDITERRANEAN.

Named for owner/chef Johnny Cooke, this shopfront restaurant is a long-time Dublin favorite. The decor is dominated by an open kitchen and art murals on the walls; there is also an outdoor seating area with antique tables and chairs. House specialties include grilled duck with pancetta, marsala balsamic sauce, and wilted endive; sautéed brill and Dover sole with capers and croutons; and baked grouper with a ragout of mussels, clams, artichokes, and tomatoes.

⊙ **Il Primo**. 16 Montague St., Dublin 2 (off Harcourt St., 50 yd. down from St. Stephen's Green). ☎ **01/478-3373.** Reservations required on weekends. Main courses £8.90–£15.90 ($13.80–$24.65); lunch menu £5.90–£9.80 ($9.15–$22.10). No service charge. AE, DC, MC, V. Mon–Sat noon–3pm and 6–11pm. MODERN ITALIAN.

Word of mouth is what brought me to Il Primo, and it's a good thing, because I doubt I would have found it myself. It's obscurely tucked away off Harcourt Street, but once inside you'll find some of the most distinguished, innovative Italian cuisine this side of Rome and Tuscany. Awaken your palate with a glass of sparkling Venetian prosecco; open with a plate of Parma ham, avocado, and balsamic vinaigrette; and then go for broke with the ravioli Il Primo, an open handkerchief of pasta over chicken, Parma ham, and mushrooms in a light tarragon cream sauce. The proprietor, Dieter Bergman, will gladly assist you in selecting appropriate wines, all of which he personally chooses and imports from Tuscany. Wines are available by the milliliter, not the bottle. Open any bottle and you pay for only what you drink. Il Primo is full of surprises.

La Mère Zou. 22 St. Stephen's Green, Dublin 2. ☎ **01/661-6669.** Reservations recommended. Lunch main courses £6–£13.50 ($9.30–$20.95), fixed-price lunch £9.50–£10.50 ($14.75–$16.30); dinner main courses £8.80–£28 ($13.65–$43.40), fixed-price 3-course early bird dinner £12.50 ($19.40) Mon–Sat 6:30–7:30pm. No service charge. AE, DC, MC, V. Mon–Thurs 12:30–2:30pm and 6–10:30pm; Fri 12:30–2:30pm and 6–11pm; Sat 6–11pm; Sun 6–9:30pm. DART to Pearse Station. Bus: 10, 11A, 11B, 13, 20B. FRENCH COUNTRY.

Chef-proprietor Eric Tydgadt has created a warm, comfortable Mediterranean ambiance in which to savor his fresh French country specialties that evoke memories of superb French cooking *en famille*. The emphasis is on perfectly cooked food accompanied by persuasive but "unarmed" sauces served in a pleasing and unpretentious manner. Mussels are a house specialty, with an array of poultry, seafood, lamb, and game offerings. The quality of ingredients and attention to enhancing the flavor of all dishes is consistent from appetizers to dessert. The excellent wine list favors the French, but also includes half-liter and 75cl. carafes of house wines for £5.90 ($9.15) and £8.75 ($13.55).

La Stampa. 35 Dawson St., Dublin 2. ☎ **01/677-8611.** Reservations recommended. Fixed-price lunch £12.95 ($20.10); dinner main courses £14.50–£18.50 ($22.50–$28.70). AE, DC, MC, V. Mon–Thurs noon–2:30pm and

6–11:30pm, Fri–Sat noon–2:30pm and 6pm–midnight, Sun 12:30–2:30pm and 6–11:30pm. DART to Pearse Station. Bus: 10, 11A, 11B, 13, 20B. FRENCH/INTERNATIONAL.

A half block from St. Stephen's Green and opposite the Lord Mayor's Mansion House, this trendy Renaissance-style restaurant is always busy and sometimes noisy, frequented by a clientele of politicians, senior government officials, models, and entertainers. It features a long and spacious dining room with a glass-domed ceiling, tall pillars, and mirrors that make it seem even larger. In spite of its Italian name, the food is international, with an emphasis on French. House specialties are lobster ravioli, fillet of cod on puree of potatoes rimmed with green beans and bacon, saddle of lamb stuffed with wild mushrooms and spinach, and grilled red mullet with a confit of fennel. For a starter, I strongly recommend the fish soup.

Trocadero. 3 St. Andrew St., Dublin 2. ☎ **01/677-5545.** Reservations recommended. Early-bird menu 6–7:30pm £10.50 ($22.50). Main courses £9.25–£29 ($14.35–$44.95). AE, DC, MC, V. Daily 6pm–midnight. DART to Tara St. Station. Bus: 16A, 19A, 22A, 55, 83. INTERNATIONAL.

Located close to the Andrews Lane and other theaters, Trocadero is a favorite gathering spot for theatergoers, performers, and press. As might be expected, the decor is theatrical, with subdued lighting, banquette seating and close-knit tables, and photos of entertainers on the walls. Steaks are the specialty, but the menu also offers rack of lamb, daily fish specials, pastas, and traditional dishes such as Irish stew and corned beef and cabbage with parsley sauce.

INEXPENSIVE

✪ **Fitzers Café.** 51 Dawson St., Dublin 2. ☎ **01/677-1155.** Reservations recommended. Lunch main courses £6.25–£9.95 ($9.70–$15.40); dinner main courses £7.95–£13.95 ($12.30–$21.60). AE, DC, MC, V. Daily 9am–11:30pm. DART to Pearse Station. Bus: 10, 11A, 11B, 13, 20B. INTERNATIONAL.

Wedged in the middle of a busy shopping street, this bright and airy Irish-style bistro has a multi-windowed facade and a modern Irish decor of light woods inside. The food, excellent and reasonably priced, is contemporary and quickly served, with choices ranging from chicken breast with hot chili cream sauce or brochette of lamb tandoori with mild curry sauce to gratin of smoked cod. Fitzers has several other Dublin locations, including one just a few blocks away at the National Gallery, Merrion Square West (☎ **01/668-6481**); another in Ballsbridge, at 24 Upper Baggot St. (☎ **01/660-0644**); and Fitzers Cafe at Temple Bar Square (☎ **01/679-0440.** Consistency is the operative word here—count on Fitzers not to disappoint.

Pasta Fresca. 3/4 Chatham St., Dublin 2. ☎ **01/679-2402.** Reservations suggested. Entrees £7–£13 ($10.85–$20.15). MC, V. Mon–Sat 11:30am–11:30pm, Sun 11:30am–6pm. Bus: 10, 11A, 11B, 13, 20B. ITALIAN.

Situated just a block from Grafton Street and St. Stephen's Green and around the corner from the Gaiety Theatre, this trattoria is popular with shoppers and for pre- and post-theater dinners. The menu features a variety of pastas, from fettuccine or tagliatelle to lasagna, spaghetti, and ravioli, as well as veal and steak dishes.

BUDGET

✪ **Bewley's Café.** 78/79 Grafton St., Dublin 2. ☎ **01/677-6761.** Reservations not required. All items £1.65–£6 ($2.55–$9.30). AE, DC, MC, V. Mon–Thurs 7:30am–1am, Thurs–Sat 7:30am–4am, Sun 8am–1am. DART to Pearse Station. Bus: 15A, 15B, 15C, 46, 55, 63, 83. IRISH.

Bewley's, a three-story landmark founded in 1840 by a Quaker named Joshua Bewley, is a quintessential part of the Dublin experience. With a traditional decor of high ceilings, stained-glass windows, and dark woods, this busy coffee shop/restaurant serves breakfast and light meals, but is best known for its dozens of freshly brewed coffees and teas, accompanied by home-baked scones, pastries, and sticky buns. There are several branches throughout Dublin, including 11/12 Westmoreland St. (☎ **01/677-6761**) and 13 S. Great George's St. (☎ **01/679-2078**).

Cafe Bell. St. Teresa's Courtyard, Clarendon St., Dublin 2. ☎ **01/677-7645.** Reservations not required. All items £1–£4 ($1.55–$6.20). No credit cards. Mon–Sat 10:30am–4pm. DART to Tara St. Station. Bus: 16, 16A, 19, 19A, 22A, 55, 83. IRISH/SELF-SERVICE.

Set in the cobbled courtyard of early 19th-century St. Teresa's Church, this serene little dining room is one of a handful of new eateries inconspicuously springing up in historic or ecclesiastical surroundings. With high ceilings and an old-world decor, it's a welcome contrast to the bustle of Grafton Street a block away and Powerscourt Townhouse Centre across the street. The menu changes daily, but usually includes homemade soups, sandwiches, salads, quiches, lasagnas, sausage rolls, hot scones, and other baked goods.

FITZWILLIAM SQUARE/MERRION SQUARE AREA
VERY EXPENSIVE

✪ **Restaurant Patrick Guilbaud.** 21 Upper Merrion St., Dublin 2. ☎ **01/ 676-4192.** Reservations required. Fixed-price lunch £22 ($34.10); main courses approx. £24 ($37.20). AE, DC, MC, V. Tues–Sat 12:30–2pm and 7:30–10:15pm. DART to Westland Row. Bus: 10, 11A, 11B, 13, 20B. FRENCH NOUVELLE.

After being tucked away for many years on James Place, this distinguished restaurant has been transferred to elegant new quarters, and taken with it the same glowing Michelin-star reputation for fine food and artful service. The menu features such dishes as casserole of black sole and prawns, steamed salmon with orange and grapefruit sauce, filet of spring lamb with parsley sauce and herb salad, roast duck with honey, and breast of guinea fowl with Madeira sauce and potato crust.

EXPENSIVE

Dobbins Wine Bistro. 15 Stephen's Lane (off Upper Mount St.), Dublin 2. ☎ **01/676-4670.** Reservations recommended. Dinner main courses £11.95–£18.50 ($18.50–$28.70). AE, DC, MC, V. Mon–Fri 12:30–3pm; Sat 7:30–11:30pm. DART to Pearse Station. Bus: 5, 7A, 8, 46, 84. IRISH/CONTINENTAL.

Almost hidden in a lane between Upper and Lower Mount Streets a block east of Merrion Square, this friendly enclave is a haven for inventive cuisine. The menu changes often, but usually includes such items as duckling with orange and port sauce; steamed paupiette of black sole with salmon, crab, and prawn filling; panfried veal kidneys in pastry; and filet of beef topped with crispy herb bread crumbs with a shallot and Madeira sauce. You'll have a choice of sitting in the bistro, with checkered tablecloths and sawdust on the floor, or on the tropical patio, with an all-weather sliding glass roof.

✪ **L'Ecrivain.** 109 Lower Baggot St., Dublin 2. ☎ **01/661-1919.** Reservations recommended. Fixed-price lunch 2-course £12.50 ($19.40), 3-course £15.50 ($24). Early bird fixed-price dinner £17.50 ($27.10) inclusive of VAT and service, Mon–Thurs 6:30–7:30pm. Fixed-price dinner 2-course £25 ($38.75), 3-course £29.50 ($45.70). Main courses £18.50 ($28.70). 10% service charge on food only. AE, DC, MC, V. Mon–Fri 12:30–2pm and 7–11pm, Sat 7–11pm. Bus: 10. FRENCH/IRISH. 5-minute walk from St. Stephen's Green. Ample street parking on nearby Merrion Sq.

This is one of Dublin's truly fine restaurants, from start to finish. The atmosphere is relaxed and welcoming, without the bother of pretense. You may choose to dine on the garden terrace, weather permitting. Each course seems to receive the same devoted attention, and most consist of traditional "best of Irish" ingredients, allowed to make their own best case without having to argue through dense sauces. The seared sea trout with sweet potato puree and the entrecôte steak with caramelized onion were perfectly prepared for me, and the presentation more than competes with anything we've seen in the Museum of Modern Art. *A final note:* the desserts here are not an afterthought, but the creations of a talented pastry chef. The crème brûlée here is the best I've tasted north of the Chunnel.

Lloyds. 20 Upper Merrion St., Dublin 2. ☎ **01/662-7240.** Reservations recommended. Fixed-price lunch 2-course £10.50 ($16.30), 3-course £13.50 ($20.95); main courses approx. £8.95–£15.95 ($13.90–$24.70). No service charge. AE, DC, MC, V. Daily 9am–midnight. DART to Westland Row. Bus: 10, 11A, 11B, 13, 20B. FRENCH NOUVELLE.

This is famed chef Conrad Gallagher's latest venture. The decor is minimalist and contemporary with hints of art deco—clear, bright, and simple. The food is another matter—bold, often intense, and nothing short of architectural in its presentation. The menu, on the page and on the plate, commands attention, though most of our dishes were a bit like a brass choir carried away with itself—the essential ingredients were taken for granted, and sometimes overlooked. That being said, a meal here is an adventure, well worth the relatively moderate price, and where else will you find a dish called "bubble and squeak" (corned beef, ground lamb, and cabbage)?

MODERATE

Grey Door. 23 Upper Pembroke St., Dublin 2. ☎ **01/676-3286.** Reservations required. 1- to 3-course fixed-price lunch £9–£14.50 ($13.95–$22.50); dinner entrees £10.25–£15.25 ($15.90–$23.65). AE, DC, MC, V. Mon–Fri 12:30–2:30pm; daily 6–11pm. Bus: 46A, 46B, 86. IRISH.

In a fine old Georgian town house with a gray front door, this place is known for chef Michael Durkin's imaginative renderings of traditional Irish cooking, beginning with fresh and familiar items such as Dublin Bay prawns, Wicklow beef, and Kildare lamb. The Grey Door also regularly provides live music, a fine mix of contemporary and traditional. One note of hesitation for some may be that even cigars are permitted in what is a relatively intimate space. Pier 32, the Grey Door's basement-level restaurant, has a more informal setting; it's much like a harborside pub, offering fresh seafood at modest prices, complete with traditional music on many nights. The Grey Door and Pier 32 are located less than a block southwest of Fitzwilliam Square near the junction of Leeson Street.

The Lane Gallery. 55 Pembroke Lane (off Pembroke St.), Dublin 2. ☎ **01/661-1829.** Reservations recommended. Fixed-price lunch £9.95 ($15.40); dinner main courses £9.95–£15 ($15.40–$23.25). MC, V. Mon 12:30–3pm, Tues–Fri 12:30–3pm and 7–11pm, Sat 7–11pm. DART to Pearse Station. Bus: 10. FRENCH.

An ever-changing display of paintings and works by local artists is a focal point at this restaurant, tucked in a lane between Baggot Street and Fitzwilliam Square, near the Focus Theatre. The decor complements the art with skylight or candlelight, whitewashed brick walls, and pastel linens. The menu is equally artistic, with choices such as rack of lamb with tomato coulis and mint jus, prawns in chive and ginger sauce, and roast brace of quail with white and black pudding and whiskey sauce. There is live piano music most evenings starting at 9pm. The lunch and dinner specials are very reasonable and offer great value.

McGrattan's in the Lane. 76 Fitzwilliam Lane, Dublin 2. ☎ **01/661-8808.** Reservations recommended. Dinner main courses £9.95–£13.95 ($15.40–$21.60). AE, MC, V. Mon–Fri noon–3pm and 6–11pm, Sat 6–11pm, Sun noon–11pm. IRISH/FRENCH.

Out of view from the general flow of traffic, this restaurant is in a lane between Baggot Street and Merrion Square. The decor ranges from a homey fireside lounge with oldies background music to a bright skylit and plant-filled dining room. The creative menu includes main dishes such as breast of chicken Fitzwilliam stuffed with cheddar cheese in pastry, roast pheasant with wild mushrooms and red wine sauce, and paupiette of salmon stuffed with scallop mousse and wrapped in a pancake of puff pastry.

INEXPENSIVE

Grays. 109D Lower Baggot St., Dublin 2. ☎ **01/676-0676.** Reservations not required. All items £2–£5.95 ($3.10–$9.20). MC, V. Mon–Fri 7:30am–4pm. DART to Pearse Station. Bus: 10. INTERNATIONAL/SELF-SERVICE.

A popular self-service eatery, this cozy old place has a decor that is eclectic, with choir benches, caned chairs, and lots of hanging plants. Seating is offered on ground and upstairs levels, including an outdoor courtyard for dining in fine weather. The menu choices concentrate on sandwiches and salads made to order, as well as pastas, quiches, curries, and casseroles.

BALLSBRIDGE/EMBASSY ROW AREA
VERY EXPENSIVE

Le Coq Hardi. 35 Pembroke Rd., Ballsbridge, Dublin 4. ☎ **01/668-9070.** Reservations required. Fixed-price lunch £21 ($32.55) for full menu, £13 ($20.15) for 1 course and coffee; dinner main courses £16–£27 ($24.80–$41.85). AE, CB, MC, V. Mon–Fri 12:30–2:30pm and 7–10:45pm, Sat 7–10:45pm. DART to Lansdowne Rd. Station. Bus: 18, 46, 63, 84. FRENCH.

Newly decorated in radiant autumn colors and offering a new cocktail bar, this plush 50-seat restaurant draws a well-heeled local and international business clientele. Chef John Howard has garnered many an award by offering such specialties as Dover sole stuffed with prawns, darne of Irish wild salmon on fresh spinach leaves, fillet of hake roasted on green cabbage and bacon with Pernod butter sauce, and filet of prime beef flamed in Irish whiskey. The 700-bin wine cellar boasts a complete collection of Château Mouton Rothschild, dating from 1945 to the present.

EXPENSIVE

Kites. 17 Ballsbridge Terrace, Ballsbridge, Dublin 4. ☎ **01/660-7415.** Reservations recommended. Lunch main courses £7–£13 ($10.85–$20.15); dinner main courses £9–£18 ($13.95–$27.90). AE, DC, MC, V. Mon–Fri 12:30–2pm and 6:30–11:30pm, Sat 6:30–11:30pm. DART to Lansdowne Rd. Station. Bus: 5, 7, 7A, 8, 46, 63, 84. CANTONESE.

Kites is renowned in Dublin for its excellent Cantonese cuisine, a reputation focused on its seafood and hot-and-spicy dishes. The menu features the usual chow mein, curries, and sweet-and-sour dishes, as well as a host of creative entrees such as king prawns with Chinese leaves in oyster sauce, stuffed crab claws, Singapore fried noodles, and bird's nests of fried potatoes.

Lobster Pot. 9 Ballsbridge Terrace, Ballsbridge, Dublin 4. ☎ **01/668-0025.** Reservations required. Dinner main courses £10–£16.25 ($15.50–$25.20). AE, DC, MC, V. Mon–Fri 12:30–2:30pm and 6:30–10:30pm, Sat 6:30–10:30pm. DART to Landsdowne Rd. Station. Bus: 5, 7, 7A, 8, 46, 63, 84. SEAFOOD.

This upstairs restaurant is known for its lobster dishes, as you might guess from its name. Other entrees on the menu range from prawns mornay, monkfish thermidor, sole on the bone, and coquilles St. Jacques, to tableside preparations of steak Diane, prawns sautéed in garlic butter, pepper steak, and steak tartare.

MODERATE

La Finezza. Over Kiely's, Donnybrook Rd. (N11), Donnybrook, Dublin 4. ☎ **01/283-7166.** Reservations recommended. Early-bird fixed-price dinner £10.95 ($17) Mon–Sat 5–7pm, Sun 4–7pm. Main courses £10.95–£12.95 ($17–$20.10). No service charge. AE, MC, V. Mon–Sat 5–11pm, Sunday 4–9:30pm. Bus: 10, 46A, 46B. ITALIAN/MEDITERRANEAN.

La Finezza is one of the Dublin restaurants causing quite a buzz these days. Already it has garnered a number of awards, including "restaurant of the year." Its candlelit mirrored-gallery decor is quite tasteful. The menu is imaginative and ambitious, perhaps overly so for a purist's palate. The pan-fried lamb cutlets and the fresh pepper and black bean mousse are simply exquisite. The presentation is delightful and the service superb. La Finezza deserves its accolades, and the early bird 3-course dinner is a real steal.

Roly's Bistro. 7 Ballsbridge Terrace, Dublin 4. ☎ **01/668-2611.** Reservations required. Fixed-price lunch £10.50 ($16.30); dinner main courses £8.50–£13.95 ($13.20–$21.60). Service charge 10%. AE, DC, MC, V. Daily noon–3pm and 6–10pm. DART to Lansdowne Rd. Station. Bus: 5, 6, 7, 8, 18, 45. IRISH/INTERNATIONAL.

Ballsbridge / Embassy Row Area Dining

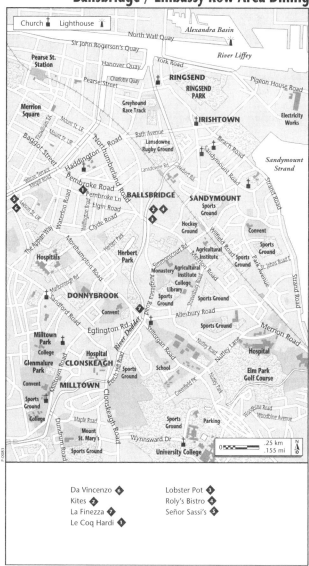

Church ✝   Lighthouse ⚲

Alexandra Basin
North Wall Quay
Sir John Rogerson's Quay
River Liffey
Pearse St. Station
Hanover Quay
York Road
Pearse Street
Charlotte Quay
RINGSEND
Pigeon House Road
Merrion Square
Mount St. LR
Mount St. UR
Fitzwilliam St.
RINGSEND PARK
Greyhound Race Track
✝IRISHTOWN
Electricity Works
Baggot Street
Haddington Road
Northumberland Road
Bath Avenue
Lansdowne Rugby Ground
Beach Road
Sandymount Road
Sandymount Strand
Pembroke Road
Lansdowne Rd.
Herbert Rd.
Wilton Terrace
Mespil Road
Pembroke Ln.
BALLSBRIDGE
SANDYMOUNT
Waterloo Road
Wellington Road
Elgin Road
Clyde Road
Strand Road
The Appian Way
Leeson St. UR
❺
❻
❷ ❹
❸
Sports Ground
Hockey Ground
Wiffield Road
Convent
Morehampton Road
Herbert Park
Herbert Park
Simmonscourt Rd.
Agricultural Institute
Merrion Road
Sports Ground
Sports Ground
Park Avenue
St. Johns Road E
Hospitals
Marlborough Rd.
Monastery
Agricultural Institute
College
Library
Anglesea Road
Sports Ground
Sports Ground
Strand Road
DONNYBROOK
Sandford Road
Convent
❼
Simmonstown Road
Aylesbury Road
Sports Ground
Merrion Road
Eglinton Rd.
River Dodder
Nutley Road
Nutley Lane
Hospital
Milltown Park
College
Nutley Park
Elm Park Golf Course
Glenmalure Park
Hospital
CLONSKEAGH
School
Greenfield Pk.
Beech Hill Road
Convent
MILLTOWN
Sports Ground
Woodbine Road
Woodbine Avenue
Sports Ground
Clonskeagh Road
Dundrum Road
Maple Road
Mount St. Mary's
Sports Ground
Wynnsward Dr.
Sports Ground
Parking
University College
0 — .25 km
.155 mi
N

Da Vincenzo ❻   Lobster Pot ❸
Kites ❷   Roly's Bistro ❹
La Finezza ❼   Señor Sassi's ❺
Le Coq Hardi ❶

85

Open since 1992, this two-story restaurant has skyrocketed to success, thanks to a magical blend of people and place—genial and astute host Roly Saul, master chef Colin O'Daly, a young and enthusiastic wait staff, a trendy location between the American Embassy and the Royal Dublin Society—and, above all, excellent and imaginatively prepared food at mostly moderate prices. The main dining rooms, with bright and airy decor and lots of windows, can be noisy when the house is full, but the nonsmoking section has a quiet enclave of booths laid out in an Orient Express style for those who prefer a quiet tête-à-tête. The bistro serves such entrees as roasted pheasant with brussels sprout puree, Dublin Bay prawns Newburg, and leek and mushroom tart. An excellent array of international wines is offered, starting at £9.95 ($15.40) a bottle.

Señor Sassi's. 146 Upper Leeson St., Dublin 4. ☎ **01/668-4544.** Reservations recommended. Dinner main courses £8.50–£12.50 ($13.20–$19.40). AE, DC, MC, V. Mon 6–11pm, Tues–Thurs noon–3pm and 6–11pm, Fri noon–3pm and 6:30–11:45pm, Sat 7–11:45pm, Sun 6:30–10pm. Bus: 10, 11A, 11B, 13, 46A, 46B. MEDITERRANEAN.

This innovative restaurant blends the simple and spicy flavors of Spain, Italy, southern France, and the Middle East in its busy location. The contemporary and casual setting includes slate floors, marble-topped tables, and walls painted a sunny shade of yellow; seating is also available in a conservatory extension overlooking a courtyard garden. The menu includes items such as Moroccan-style couscous, tagliatelle, prawns sautéed in rum with Creole sauce, charcoal steaks, tortilla Español (traditional omelet with potato and onions), vegetarian dishes, and warm salads. Be sure to try the unusual olive bread.

INEXPENSIVE

Da Vincenzo. 133 Upper Leeson St., Dublin 4. ☎ **01/660-9906.** Reservations recommended. Fixed-price lunch £6.95 ($10.80); dinner main courses £6.50–£10.10 ($10.40–$16.10). AE, DC, MC, V. Mon–Sat 12:30–11:30pm, Sun 1–10pm. Bus: 10, 11A, 11B, 46A, 46B. ITALIAN.

Located within a block of the Hotel Burlington, this informal and friendly bistro offers ground level and upstairs seating amid a casual decor of glowing brick fireplaces, pine walls, vases and wreaths of dried flowers, modern art posters, blue and white pottery, and a busy open kitchen. Pizza with a light pita-style dough, cooked in a wood-burning oven, is the specialty here. Other entrees range from pastas such as tagliatelle, lasagna, cannelloni, spaghetti, and fettuccine to veal and beef dishes, including an organically produced filet steak.

O'CONNELL STREET AREA

EXPENSIVE

Chapter One. 18 Parnell Sq. N., Dublin 1. ☎ **01/873-2266.** Reservations recommended. Fixed-price lunch £12 ($18.60); dinner main courses £9.50–£15 ($14.75–$23.25). AE, MC, V. Mon 12:30–2:30pm, Tues–Fri 12:30–2:30pm and 6–11pm, Sat 6–11pm. DART to Connolly Station. Bus: 10, 11, 11A, 11B, 12, 13, 14, 16, 16A, 19, 19A, 22, 22A, 36. IRISH.

A literary theme prevails at this restaurant, housed in the basement of the Dublin Writers Museum, just north of Parnell Square and the Garden of Remembrance. The layout is spread over three rooms and alcoves, all accentuated by stained-glass windows, paintings, sculptures, and literary memorabilia. The catering staff, affiliated with the Old Dublin Restaurant, has added a few Scandinavian influences. Main courses include fillet of salmon on a bed of avocado with smoked tomato vinaigrette; black sole with citrus fruit and dill cucumber cream sauce; and roast half-duck with apricot sauce.

MODERATE

101 Talbot. 100 Talbot St., Dublin 1. ☎ **01/874-5011.** Reservations recommended. Lunch main courses £3.25–£5.50 ($5.05–$8.50); dinner main courses £7.25–£10.50 ($11.25–$16.30). AE, DC, MC, V. Tues–Sat 10am–11pm. DART to Connolly Station. Bus: 27A, 31A, 31B, 32A, 32B, 42B, 42C, 43, 44A. INTERNATIONAL/VEGETARIAN.

Open since 1991, this second-floor restaurant features light, healthy foods, with a strong emphasis on vegetarian and vegan dishes. The setting is bright and casual, with contemporary Irish art on display, big windows, yellow rag-rolled walls, ash-topped tables, and newspapers to read. Entrees include jambalaya of lamb, smoked sausage, and black-eyed peas; vegetable satay with rice; and tandoori chicken with mango. The lunch menu changes daily, the dinner menu weekly. Espresso and cappuccino are always available for sipping, and there is a full bar. It's located at Talbot Lane near Marlborough Street, convenient to the Abbey Theatre.

INEXPENSIVE

The Winding Stair. 40 Lower Ormond Quay, Dublin 1. ☎ **01/873-3292.** Reservations not necessary. All items £1.50–£5 ($2.30–$7.75). MC, V. Mon–Sat 10am–6pm, Sun 1–6pm. Bus: 70 or 80. IRISH/SELF-SERVICE.

Retreat from the bustle of the north side's busy quays at this cafe/bookshop and indulge in a light meal while browsing through some books. There are three floors, each chock-full of used books (from novels, plays, and poetry to history, art, music, and sports), and all connected by a winding 18th-century staircase. A cage-style lift serves those who prefer not to climb the stairs. Tall and wide windows provide expansive views of the Halfpenny Bridge and River Liffey. The food is simple and healthy—sandwiches made with additive-free meats or fruits (such as banana and honey), organic salads, homemade soups, and natural juices.

DINING BETWEEN HOURS & OUTDOORS

AFTERNOON TEA   As in Britain, afternoon tea is a revered tradition in Ireland, especially in the grand hotels of Dublin. Afternoon tea in its fullest form is a sit-down event and a relaxing experience, not just a quick hot beverage taken on the run.

Properly presented, afternoon tea is almost a complete meal, including a pot of freshly brewed tea accompanied by finger sandwiches, pastries, hot scones, cream-filled cakes, and other sweets arrayed on a silver tray. To enhance the ambience, there is often live piano or harp music. Best of all, this sumptuous midafternoon pick-me-up is priced to please, averaging £7 to £9 ($10.85 to $13.95) per person, even in the lounges of the city's best hotels.

Afternoon tea hours are usually 3 to 4:30pm. Among the hotels offering this repast are the Berkeley Court, Conrad, Davenport, Gresham, Royal Dublin, Shelbourne, and Westbury (see "Accommodations" in chapter 4, for full address and phone numbers of each).

LATE NIGHT DINING   Although Dublin is keeping later and later hours, it is still nearly impossible to find anything approaching 24-hour dining. One place that comes close is the **Coffee Dock at Jurys Hotel,** Ballsbridge, Dublin 4 (☎ **01/660-5000**). It is open Monday 7am to 4:30am, Tuesday to Saturday from 6am to 4:30am, and Sunday 6am to 10:45pm. **Bewley's,** at 78/79 Grafton St., Dublin 2 (☎ **01/677-6761**), is open Sunday through Thursday until 1am; Friday and Saturday until 4am. **Juice,** at 73–83 S. Great George's St., Dublin 2 (☎ **01/475-7856**) serves a limited menu Saturdays until 4am.

PICNIC FARE   The parks of Dublin offer plenty of sylvan and relaxed settings for a picnic lunch, so feel free to park it on a bench, or pick a grassy patch and spread a blanket. In particular, try **St. Stephen's Green** at lunchtime (in the summer there are open-air band concerts), **Phoenix Park,** and **Merrion Square.** You can also take a ride on the DART to the suburbs of **Dun Laoghaire** (to the south) or **Howth** (to the north) and set up a picnic along a bay-front pier or promenade.

In recent years, some fine delicatessens and gourmet food shops ideal for picnic fare have sprung up. For the best selection of fixings, we recommend two: **Gallic Kitchen,** 49 Francis St., Dublin 8 (☎ **01/454-4912**), for gourmet prepared food to go, from salmon en croûte to pastries filled with meats or vegetables, pâtés, quiches, sausage rolls, and homemade pies, breads, and cakes; and **Magills Delicatessen,** 14 Clarendon St., Dublin 2 (☎ **01/671-3830**), for Asian and continental delicacies, meats, cheeses, spices, and salads.

6

Dublin Sights & Attractions

*D*ublin is a city of many moods and landscapes. There are medieval churches and imposing castles, graceful Georgian squares and lantern-lit lanes, broad boulevards and crowded bridges, picturesque parks and pedestrian walkways, intriguing museums and markets, gardens and galleries, and—if you have any energy left after all that—an electric nightlife. Enjoy!

SUGGESTED ITINERARIES

If You Have 1 Day

Start at the beginning, in Dublin's **medieval quarter,** the area around Christ Church and St. Patrick's Cathedrals. Tour these great churches and then walk the cobblestone streets and inspect the nearby old city walls at High Street. From Old Dublin, take a turn eastward and see **Dublin Castle** and then go down Dame Street to **Trinity College** with the famous Book of Kells. From here it's only a short distance to St. Stephen's Green, a perfect place to take a breather. Finally, if time and energy remain, cross over the River Liffey to O'Connell Street, Dublin's main thoroughfare. Walk up this wide street, passing the landmark **General Post Office** (GPO), to Parnell Square and the picturesque Garden of Remembrance. If time permits, visit the Dublin Writers Museum. Cap the day off with a show at the Abbey or the Gate Theatre, and maybe a drink or two at a nearby pub.

If You Have 2 Days

Day 1   Spend Day 1 as above.

Day 2   In the morning, take a Dublin Bus city sightseeing tour to give you an overview of the city. You'll see all of the local downtown landmarks, plus the major buildings along the River Liffey and some of the leading sites on the edge of the city, such as the **Guinness Brewery,** the Royal Hospital, the Irish Museum of Modern Art, and the Phoenix Park. In the afternoon, head for Grafton Street for some shopping. If time allows, stroll Merrion or Fitzwilliam Square to give you a sampling of the best of Dublin's Georgian architecture.

If You Have 3 Days

Days 1 and 2   Spend Days 1 and 2 as above.

Day 3   Make this a day for Dublin's artistic and cultural attractions. Visit some of the top museums and art galleries, from the mainstream—the National Museum and National Gallery, Natural History Museum, and Museum of Modern Art—to the more specialized—the Chester Beatty Library, the Museum of Childhood, or the Kilmainham Jail—to the very specialized—the Old Jameson Distillery or the Guinness Hop Store. Save time for a walk around Temple Bar, the city's Left Bank district, lined with art galleries and film studios, interesting second-hand shops, and casual eateries.

If You Have 4 Days or More

Days 1–3   Spend Days 1 through 3 as above.

Day 4   Take a ride aboard DART, Dublin's rapid transit system, to the suburbs, either southward to Dun Laoghaire, Dalkey, or Bray, or northward to Howth. The DART routes follow the rim of Dublin Bay in both directions, so you'll enjoy a scenic ride and get to spend some time in an Irish coastal village.

1 The Top Attractions

✪ **Trinity College and the Book of Kells.** College Green, Dublin 2. ☎ **01/608-1688.** Admission £3.50 ($5.40) adults, £3 ($4.65) seniors and students, free for children under 12, £7 ($10.85) family. Credit cards accepted for shop purchases only. Mon–Sat 9:30am–5pm, Sun (Oct–May) noon–4:30pm, Sun (Jun–Sept) 9:30am–4:30pm. DART to Tara St. Station. Bus: 5, 7A, 8, 15A, 15B, 15C, 46, 55, 62, 63, 83, 84.

The oldest university in Ireland, Trinity was founded in 1592 by Queen Elizabeth I. It sits in the heart of the city on a beautiful 40-acre site just south of the River Liffey, with cobbled squares, gardens, a picturesque quadrangle, and buildings dating from the 17th to the 20th centuries. The college is home to the Book of Kells, an 8th-century version of the four Gospels with elaborate scripting and illumination. One page per day is turned for public viewing. This famous treasure and other early Christian manuscripts are on permanent public view in the Colonnades, an exhibition area located on the ground floor of the Old Library. The complete Trinity College Library contains more than three million volumes. If you want a look at the place before you go, rent the 1983 Michael Caine film *Educating Rita,* in which Trinity stood in for a British university.

Trinity College

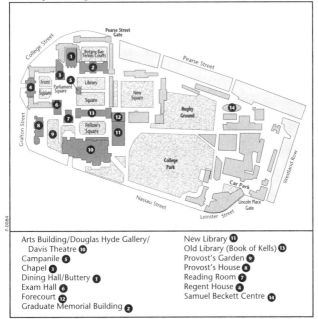

Arts Building/Douglas Hyde Gallery/
Davis Theatre ⑩
Campanile ⑤
Chapel ③
Dining Hall/Buttery ①
Exam Hall ⑥
Forecourt ⑫
Graduate Memorial Building ②

New Library ⑪
Old Library (Book of Kells) ⑬
Provost's Garden ⑨
Provost's House ⑧
Reading Room ⑦
Regent House ④
Samuel Beckett Centre ⑭

✪ **National Gallery.** Merrion Sq. West, Dublin 2. ☎ **01/661-5133.** Free admission. Mon–Sat 10am–5:30pm, Sun 2–5pm. Guided tours, Sat 3pm and Sun 2:15, 3, and 4pm. DART to Pearse Station. Bus: 5, 6, 7, 7A, 8, 10, 44, 47, 47B, 48A, 62.

Established by an act of Parliament in 1854, this gallery first opened its doors in 1864, with just over 100 paintings. Today the collection of paintings, drawings, watercolors, miniatures, prints, sculpture, and objets d'art is considered one of Europe's finest. Every major European school of painting is represented, including an extensive assemblage of Irish work. The museum features a fine gallery shop and an excellent self-service restaurant operated by "Fitzers," a name synonymous with excellent and interesting cuisine at near-budget prices. A $14 million refurbishment of the museum was completed in 1996; and a new extension is underway, scheduled to open by 2000. All public areas are wheelchair-accessible.

✪ **National Museum.** Kildare St. and Merrion St., Dublin 2. ☎ **01/ 677-7444.** Free admission. Tues–Sat 10am–5pm, Sun 2–5pm. DART to Pearse Station. Bus: 7, 7A, 8, 10, 11, 13.

Money-Saving Tips on Attractions

If you're going to spend time in Dublin and see the sights, it may make sense to invest in a **SuperSaver Card,** available at any of the Dublin Tourism Offices listed under "visitor information" as well as at any of the participating attractions: Dublin's Viking Adventure, Dublin Writers Museum, Fry Model Railway, James Joyce Museum, Malahide Castle, and Newbridge House. The price of the SuperSaverCard is: £16 ($24.80) adults, £12.50 ($19.40) seniors and students, £8.50 ($13.20) children, £37 ($57.35) family. The tickets are valid for 1 year and provide one-time discounts of up to 30% off normal admission prices.

For literary-minded visitors, the **Dublin Writers Museum,** 18 Parnell Sq., Dublin 1 (☎ **01/872-2077**), offers reduced-rate combination tickets that allow entry into the Dublin Writers Museum as well as the James Joyce Museum and/or the George Bernard Shaw Birthplace. The savings amount to approximately 15%.

A similar reduced-rate combination ticket allows entry into Trinity College's **Book of Kells Exhibition** in conjunction with admission to the **Dublin Experience,** an audiovisual presentation that tracks 1,000 years of Dublin history (see "A Sight and Sound Show," in section 2). It's available at the bookshop/visitor center at **Trinity College,** College Green, Dublin 2 (☎ **01/608-1688**).

Established in 1890, this museum is a reflection of Ireland's heritage from 2000 B.C. to the present. It is the home of many of the country's greatest historical finds, including "The Treasury" exhibit, which toured the United States and Europe in the 1970s with the Ardagh Chalice, Tara Brooch, and Cross of Cong. Other highlights range from the artifacts from the Wood Quay excavations of the Old Dublin Settlements to "Or," an extensive exhibition of Irish Bronze Age gold ornaments dating from 2200 to 700 B.C. Facilities include a shop and cafe. *Note:* the National Museum encompasses two other attractions—Collins Barracks and the Natural History Museum—each listed separately below.

Collins Barracks. Benburb St., Dublin 7. ☎ **01/677-7444.** Free admission. Tours at varying hours, depending on groups, £1 ($1.55). Tues–Sat 10am–5pm, Sun 2–5pm. Bus: 34, 70, 80.

Officially part of the National Museum, Collins Barracks is the oldest military barracks in Europe. Even if it were empty, it would be

Dublin Attractions

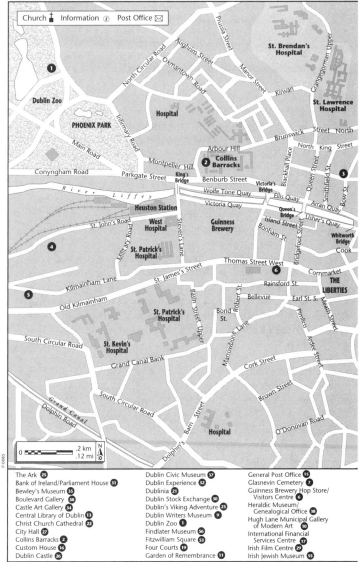

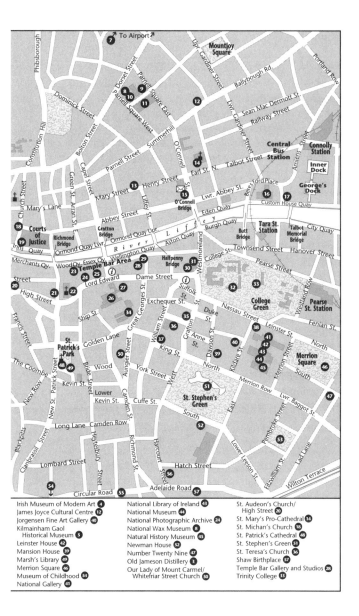

Irish Museum of Modern Art	4	National Library of Ireland	43	St. Audoen's Church/	
James Joyce Cultural Centre	12	National Museum	44	High Street	20
Jorgensen Fine Art Gallery	40	National Photographic Archive	24	St. Mary's Pro-Cathedral	14
Kilmainham Gaol		National Wax Museum	8	St. Michan's Church	18
Historical Museum	5	Natural History Museum	45	St. Patrick's Cathedral	48
Leinster House	42	Newman House	52	St. Stephen's Green	51
Mansion House	39	Number Twenty Nine	47	St. Teresa's Church	36
Marsh's Library	49	Old Jameson Distillery	3	Shaw Birthplace	57
Merrion Square	46	Our Lady of Mount Carmel/		Temple Bar Gallery and Studios	28
Museum of Childhood	54	Whitefriar Street Church	50	Trinity College	33
National Gallery	41				

well worth a visit just for the structure itself, a splendidly restored early 18th-century masterwork by Colonel Thomas Burgh, Ireland's Chief Engineer and Surveyor General under Queen Anne.

So far, the collection housed here is focused on the decorative arts. Most notable is the extraordinary display of Irish silver and furniture. Until the acquisition of this vast space, only a fraction of the National Museum's collection could be displayed; but all that is changing, as more and more treasures find their way here. This will be a prime site for touring exhibitions; so consult *The Event Guide* for details. There is also a cafe and gift shop on the premises.

Dublin Castle. Palace St. (off Dame St.), Dublin 2. ☎ **01/677-7129.** Admission £2.50 ($3.90) adults, £1.50 ($2.30) seniors and students, £1 ($1.55) children under 12. Mon–Fri 10am–5pm, Sat–Sun and holidays 2–5pm. Guided tours are conducted every 20–25 minutes. Bus: 50, 50A, 54, 56A, 77, 77A, 77B.

Built between 1208 and 1220, this complex represents some of the oldest surviving architecture in the city, and was the center of British power in Ireland for more than 7 centuries until it was taken over by the new Irish government in 1922. Highlights include the 13th-century Record Tower; the State Apartments, once the residence of English viceroys; and the Chapel Royal, a 19th-century Gothic building with particularly fine plaster decoration and carved oak gallery fronts and fittings. The newest developments are the Undercroft, an excavated site on the grounds where an early Viking fortress stood, and the Treasury, built between 1712 and 1715 and believed to be the oldest surviving office building in Ireland. At hand, as well, are a crafts shop, heritage centre, and restaurant.

Christ Church Cathedral. Christchurch Place, Dublin 8. ☎ **01/677-8099.** Admission: suggested donation £1 ($1.55) adults, 50p (80¢) children. Daily 10am–5pm. Closed Dec 26. Bus: 21A, 50, 50A, 78, 78A, 78B.

Standing on high ground in the oldest part of the city, this cathedral is one of Dublin's finest historic buildings. It dates from 1038 when Sitric, Danish king of Dublin, built the first wooden Christ Church here. In 1171, the original simple foundation was extended into a cruciform and rebuilt in stone by Strongbow. The present structure, though, dates mainly from 1871 to 1878, when a huge restoration took place. Highlights of the interior include magnificent stonework and graceful pointed arches, with delicately chiseled supporting columns. It is the mother church for the diocese of Dublin and Glendalough of the Church of Ireland.

Irish Film Centre. 6 Eustace St., Dublin 2. ☎ **01/679-5744;** cinema box office 01/679-3477. Free admission to centre; £3–£4 ($4.65–$6.20) for cinemas.

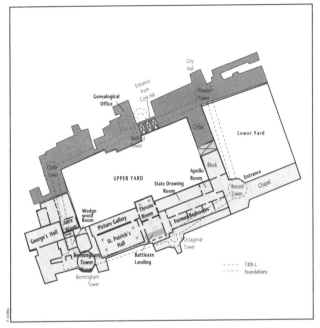

Centre Mon–Sat 10am–11pm; cinemas daily 2–11pm; cinema box office daily 1:30–9pm; *Flashback* (free of charge) Jun to mid-Sept Wed–Sun at noon. Bus: 21A, 78A, 78B.

Since it opened in 1991, this institute has fast become a focal point in Dublin's artsy Temple Bar district. The Centre houses two cinemas, the Irish Film Archive, a library, a bookshop and bar, and eight film-related organizations. The summertime Wednesday to Sunday noontime screenings of *Flashback*, a history of Irish film since 1896, followed by a lunch in the bar, make a perfect midday outing.

Dublinia. St. Michael's Hill, Christ Church, Dublin 8. ☎ **01/679-4611.** Admission £3.95 ($6.10) adults; £2.90 ($4.50) seniors, students, and children; £10 ($15.50) family. Apr–Sept daily 10am–5pm; Oct–Mar Mon–Sat 11am–4pm, Sun 10am–4:30pm. Bus: 50, 78A, 123.

What was Dublin like in medieval times? To find out, visit this historically accurate presentation of the Old City from 1170 to 1540, re-created through a series of theme exhibits, spectacles, and experiences. Highlights include an illuminated Medieval Maze complete with visual effects, background sounds, and aromas that lead

The Book of Kells

The Book of Kells is a large-format illuminated manuscript of the four Gospels in Latin, dated on comparative grounds to about A.D. 800. One cannot be more precise about its date because some leaves from the end of the book, where such information was normally recorded, are missing. It is the most majestic work of art to survive from the early centuries of Celtic Christianity, and has often been described as "the most beautiful book in the world." Produced by a team of talented scribes and artists working in a monastic scriptorium, its fascination derives from the dignified but elusive character of its main motifs and the astonishing variety and complexity of the linear ornamentation that adorns every one of its 680 pages. Its creators managed to combine new artistic influences from Eastern Christendom with the traditional interlace patterning of Celtic metalwork to produce what Gerald of Wales, a 13th-century chronicler, called "the work not of men, but of angels." The message sometimes may not be easy to read, but everyone can admire the elegant precision of the standard script, the subtlety of the color harmonies, and the exuberant vitality of the human and animal ornaments.

The Book was certainly in the possession of the Columban monastery of Kells, a town in County Meath, during most of the Middle Ages. The Annals of Ulster record its theft from the western sacristy of the stone-built monastic church in 1007, and relate that it was recovered 2 to 3 months later from "under the sod," and without the jewel-encrusted silver shrine in which such prestige books

you on a journey through time from the first arrival of the Anglo-Normans in 1170 to the closure of the monasteries in the 1530s. The next segment depicts everyday life in medieval Dublin with a diorama, as well as a prototype of a 13th-century quay along the banks of the Liffey. The finale takes you to The Great Hall for a 360-degree wrap-up portrait of medieval Dublin via a 12-minute cyclorama-style audiovisual.

St. Patrick's Cathedral. Patrick's Close, Patrick St., Dublin 8. ☎ **01/ 475-4817.** Admission £2 ($3.10) adults, £1.75 ($2.70) seniors and students, £5 ($7.75) family. Mon–Sat 9am–6pm, Sun 9am–4:30pm. Bus: 50, 50A, 54, 54A, 56A.

It is said that St. Patrick baptized converts on this site and consequently a church has stood here since A.D. 450, making it the oldest

were kept. Whether it was originally created in Kells remains an unresolved question. Some authorities think that it may have been begun, if not completed, in the great monastery founded by St. Columba himself (in about 561) on the island of Iona off the west coast of Scotland. Iona had a famous scriptorium, and remained the headquarters of the Columban monastic system until the early years of the 9th century. It then became an untenable location because of repeated Viking raids, and in 807 a remnant of the monastic community retreated to the Irish mainland to build a new headquarters at Kells. It has been suggested that the great Gospel book that we call "of Kells" may have been started in Iona, possibly to mark the bicentenary of St. Columba's death in 797, and later transferred to Kells for completion. But it is also possible to argue that the work was entirely done in Kells, and that its object was to equip the monastery with a great new book to stand on the high altar of the new foundation.

In the medieval period the Book was (wrongly) regarded as the work of St. Columba himself, and was known as the "great Gospel book of Colum Cille" (Colum of the Churches). The designation "Book of Kells" seems to have originated with the famous biblical scholar James Ussher, who made a study of its original Latin text in the 1620s. There is a large selection of illustrative materials relating to the Book of Kells in the gift shop located in the Colonnades of the Old Library in Trinity College.

—*J. V. Luce, Trinity College and the Royal Irish Academy*

Christian site in Dublin. The present cathedral dates from 1190, but because of a fire and a rebuilding in the 14th century, not much of the original foundation remains. It is mainly early English in style, with a square medieval tower that houses the largest ringing peal bells in Ireland, an 18th-century spire, and a 300-foot-long interior, making it the longest church in the country. St. Patrick's is closely associated with Jonathan Swift, who was dean here from 1713 to 1745 and whose tomb lies in the south aisle. Others who are memorialized within the cathedral include Turlough O'Carolan, a blind harpist and composer and the last of the great Irish bards; Michael William Balfe, the composer; and Douglas Hyde, the first president of Ireland. St. Patrick's is the national cathedral of the Church of Ireland.

Dublin Writers Museum. 18/19 Parnell Sq. N., Dublin 1. ☎ **01/872-2077.** Fax 01/872-2231. Admission £2.95 ($4.60) adults, £2.50 ($3.90) seniors and students, £1.30 ($2) children under 12, £8 ($12.40) families. Sept–May Mon–Sat 10am–5pm, Sun 11am–5pm; June–Aug Mon–Fri 10am–6pm, Sat 10am–5pm, Sun 11am–5pm. DART to Connolly Station. Bus: 10, 11, 11A, 11B, 12, 13, 14, 16, 16A, 19, 19A, 22, 22A, 36.

Housed in a stunning 18th-century Georgian mansion with splendid plasterwork and stained glass, the museum is itself an impressive reminder of the grandeur of the Irish literary tradition. Yeats, Joyce, Beckett, Shaw, Wilde, Swift, and Sheridan are among those whose lives and works are celebrated here. One of the museum's rooms is devoted to children's literature.

The Phoenix Park. Parkgate St., Dublin 7. ☎ **01/677-0095.** Free admission. Open daily 24 hours. Visitor Center: admission £2 ($3.10) adults, £1.50 ($2.35) seniors, £1 ($1.55) students and children, £5 ($7.75) families. Mid- to end Mar daily 9:30am–5pm, Apr–May daily 9:30am–5:30pm, Jun–Sept daily 10am–6pm, Oct daily 9:30am–5pm, Nov to mid-Mar Sat and Sun 9:30am–4:30pm. Bus: 10, 25, 26.

Two miles west of the city center, The Phoenix Park, the largest enclosed urban park in Europe, is the playground of Dublin. It's traversed by a network of roads and quiet pedestrian walkways, and its 1,760 acres are informally landscaped with ornamental gardens, nature trails, and broad expanses of grassland separated by avenues of trees, including oak, beech, pine, chestnut, and lime. The homes of the Irish president and the U.S. ambassador are on its grounds. Livestock graze peacefully on pasturelands, deer roam the forested areas, and horses romp on polo fields. The new Phoenix Park Visitor Centre, adjacent to Ashtown Castle, offers exhibitions and an audiovisual presentation on the history of the Phoenix Park, and houses its own restaurant.

2   More Attractions

ART GALLERIES

Boulevard Gallery. Merrion Sq. W., Dublin 2. Free admission. May–Sept Sat–Sun 10:30am–6pm. DART to Pearse Station. Bus: 5, 7A, 8, 46, 62.

The fence around Merrion Square doubles as a display railing on summer weekends in an outdoor display of local art similar to those you'll find in Greenwich Village or Montmartre. Permits are given to local artists only to sell their own work, so this is a chance to meet an artist as well as to browse or buy.

Hugh Lane Municipal Gallery of Modern Art. Parnell Sq. N., Dublin 1. ☎ **01/874-1903.** Free admission; donations accepted. Tues–Fri 9:30am–6pm,

Thurs (Apr–Aug only) 9:30am–8pm, Sat 9:30am–5pm, Sun 11am–5pm. DART to Connolly or Tara Stations. Bus: 3, 10, 11, 13.

Housed in a finely restored 18th-century building known as Charlemont House, this gallery is next to the Dublin Writers Museum. It is named after Hugh Lane, an Irish art connoisseur who was killed in the sinking of the *Lusitania* in 1915 and who willed his collection (including works by Courbet, Manet, Monet, and Corot) to be shared between the government of Ireland and the National Gallery of London. With the Lane collection as its nucleus, this gallery also contains paintings from the impressionist and post-impressionist traditions, sculptures by Rodin, stained glass, and works by modern Irish artists.

Irish Museum of Modern Art (IMMA). Military Rd., Kilmainham. ☎ **01/ 671-8666.** Free admission. Tues–Sat 10am–5:30pm, Sun noon–5:30pm. Bus: 78A, 79, 90.

Housed in the splendidly restored 17th-century edifice known as the Royal Hospital, IMMA is a showcase of Irish and international art from the latter half of the 20th century. The buildings and grounds also provide a venue for theatrical and musical events, overlapping the visual and performing arts. As of now, this space has not yet come close to reaching its potential. Its presentation and programs are uneven, sometimes exciting and sometimes quite disappointing. The formal gardens, an important early feature of this magnificent structure, have been recently restored (recreated) and opened to the public during the museum's hours.

Temple Bar Gallery and Studios. 5–9 Temple Bar, Dublin 2. ☎ **01/ 671-0073.** Fax 01/677-7527. www.paddynet.ie/tbgs. Free admission. Mon–Sat 10am–6pm, Sun 2–6pm. Bus: 21A, 46A, 46B, 51B, 51C, 68, 69, 86.

Founded in 1983 in the heart of Dublin's "Left Bank," this is one of the largest studio/gallery complexes in Europe. More than 30 Irish artists work here at a variety of contemporary visual arts, including sculpture, painting, printing, and photography. Only the gallery section is open to the public, but, with advance notice, you can make an appointment to view individual artists at work.

BREWERIES/DISTILLERIES

✪ **Guinness Hopstore.** Crane St. (off Thomas St.), Dublin 8. ☎ **01/ 453-6700,** ext. 5155. Admission £3 ($4.65) adults, £1.50 ($2.35) students, £1 ($1.55) seniors and children. Apr–Sept Mon–Sat 9:30am–4pm, Sun 10:30am–4:30pm; Oct–Mar Mon–Sat 9:30am–5pm, Sun noon–4pm. Bus: 21A, 78, 78A.

Founded in 1759, the Guinness Brewery is one of the world's largest breweries, producing the distinctive stout famous for its thick, creamy head. Although tours of the brewery itself are no longer allowed, visitors are welcome to explore the adjacent Guinness Hopstore, a converted 19th-century four-story building. It houses the World of Guinness Exhibition, an audiovisual presentation showing how the stout is made, plus a museum and a bar where visitors can sample a glass of the famous brew. The top two floors of the building also serve as a venue for a variety of art exhibits.

The Old Jameson Distillery. Bow St., Dublin 7. ☎ **01/872-5566.** Admission £3.50 ($5.40) adults, £3 ($4.65) seniors and students, £1.50 ($2.30) children, £9.50 ($14.70) family. Daily 9:30am–6pm, last tour at 5pm. Bus: 34, 70, 80, 90.

This museum illustrates the history of Irish whiskey, known as *uisce beatha* (the water of life) in Irish. Housed in a former distillery warehouse, it presents a short introductory audiovisual presentation, an exhibition area, and a whiskey-making demonstration. At the end of the tour, whiskey can be sampled at an in-house pub, where an array of fixed-price menus for lunch, tea, or dinner is available.

PLACES OF BUSINESS

✪ **Bank of Ireland/Parliament House.** 2 College Green, Dublin 2. ☎ **01/661-5933,** ext. 2265. Free admission. Mon–Fri 10am–4pm, Sat 2–5pm, Sun 10am–1pm. Guided 45-minute tours of the House of Lords chamber Tues and Thurs at 10:30am, 11:30am, and 1:45pm (except holidays). DART to Tara St. Station. All city center buses.

Although now a busy bank, this building was erected in 1729 to house the Irish Parliament, but it became superfluous when the British and Irish Parliaments were merged in London. In fact, the Irish Parliament voted itself out of existence, becoming the only recorded parliament in history to do so. Highlights include the windowless front portico, built to avoid distractions from the outside when Parliament was in session; and the unique House of Lords chamber, famed for its Irish oak woodwork, 18th-century tapestries, golden mace, and sparkling Irish crystal chandelier of 1,233 pieces, dating from 1765.

✪ **General Post Office (GPO).** O'Connell St., Dublin 1. ☎ **01/872-8888.** Free admission. Mon–Sat 8am–8pm, Sun 10:30am–6:30pm. DART to Connolly Station. Bus: 25, 26, 34, 37, 38A, 39A, 39B, 66A, 67A.

With a 200-foot-long, 56-foot-high facade of Ionic columns and Greco-Roman pilasters, this is more than a post office; it is the symbol of Irish freedom. Built between 1815 and 1818, it was the main stronghold of the Irish Volunteers in 1916. Set afire, the building was gutted and abandoned after the surrender and execution of many of the Irish rebel leaders. It reopened as a post office in 1929 after the formation of the Irish Free State. In memory of the building's dramatic role in Irish history, today there is an impressive bronze statue of Cuchulainn, the legendary Irish hero, on display. Look closely at the pillars outside—you can still see bullet holes from the siege.

CATHEDRALS & CHURCHES

Our Lady of Mount Carmel/Whitefriar Street Carmelite Church. 57 Aungier St., Dublin 2. ☎ **01/475-8821.** Free admission. Daily 8:30am– 6:30pm. Bus: 16, 16A, 19, 19A, 22, 22A, 83,155.

One of the city's largest churches, it was built between 1825 and 1827 on the site of a pre-Reformation Carmelite priory (1539) and an earlier Carmelite abbey (13th century). It has since been extended, with a new entrance from Aungier Street. This is a favorite place of pilgrimage on February 14th, because the body of St. Valentine is enshrined here, presented to the church by Pope Gregory XVI in 1836. The other highlight is the 15th-century black oak Madonna, Our Lady of Dublin.

St. Audeon's Church. Cornmarket (off High St.), Dublin 8. ☎ **01/ 677-8714.** Free admission. Fri–Wed 11:30am–1:30pm. Bus: 21A, 78A, 78B.

Situated next to the only remaining gate of the Old City walls (1214), this church is said to be the only surviving medieval parish in Dublin. Although it is partly in ruins, significant parts have survived, including the west doorway, which dates from 1190, and the nave from the 13th century. In addition, the 17th-century bell tower houses three bells cast in 1423, making them the oldest in Ireland. It's a Church of Ireland property, but nearby is another St. Audeon's Church, this one Catholic and dating from 1846. It was here that Father Flash Kavanagh used to say the world's fastest mass so his congregation was out in time for the football matches.

St. Mary's Pro-Cathedral. Cathedral and Marlborough sts., Dublin 1. ☎ **01/ 874-5441.** Free admission. Mon–Fri 8am–6pm, Sat 8am–9pm, Sun 8am–8pm. DART to Connolly Station. Bus: 28, 29A, 30, 31A, 31B, 32A, 32B, 44A.

Since Dublin's two main cathedrals (Christ Church and St. Patrick's) belong to the Protestant Church of Ireland, St. Mary's is the closest the Catholics get to having their own. Tucked into a corner of a rather unimpressive back street, it is situated in the heart of the city's north side and is considered the main Catholic parish church of the city center. Built between 1815 and 1825, it is of the Greek Revival Doric style, providing a distinct contrast to the

Gothic Revival look of most other churches of the period. The exterior portico is modeled on the Temple of Theseus in Athens, with six Doric columns, while the Renaissance-style interior is patterned after the Church of St. Philip de Reule of Paris. The church is noted for its Palestrina Choir, which sings every Sunday at 11am.

St. Michan's Church. Church St., Dublin 8. ☎ **01/872-4154.** Admission £1.50 ($2.35) adults, £1 ($1.55) seniors and students, 50p (80¢) children under 12. Mon–Fri 10am–12:45pm and 2–5pm, Sat 10am–12:45pm. Bus: 34, 70, 80.

Built on the site of an early Danish chapel (1095), this 17th-century edifice claims to be the only parish church on the north side of the Liffey surviving from a Viking foundation. Now under the Church of Ireland banner, it has some very fine interior woodwork and an organ (dated 1724) on which Handel is said to have played his *Messiah.* The most unique (and, let it be noted, macabre) feature of this church, however, is the underground burial vault. Because of the dry atmosphere, bodies have lain for centuries without showing signs of decomposition.

St. Teresa's Church. Clarendon St., Dublin 2. ☎ **01/671-8466.** Free admission; donations welcome. Daily 8am–8pm or longer. Bus: 16, 16A, 19, 19A, 22, 22A, 55, 83.

With its foundation stone laid in 1793, the church was opened in 1810 by the Discalced Carmelite Fathers, to be continuously enlarged until its present form was reached in 1876. This was the first post–Penal Law church to be legally and openly erected in Dublin, following the Catholic Relief Act of 1793. Among the artistic highlights are John Hogan's *Dead Christ,* a sculpture displayed beneath the altar, and Phyllis Burke's seven beautiful stained-glass windows.

WHERE THE BODIES ARE BURIED

Glasnevin Cemetery. Finglas Rd., Dublin 11. ☎ **01/830-1133.** Free admission. Daily 8am–4pm. Bus: 19, 19A, 40, 40A, 40B, 40C.

Situated north of the city center, the Irish National Cemetery was founded in 1832 and covers more than 124 acres. The majority of people buried here are ordinary citizens, but there are also many famous names to be found on the headstones, from former Irish presidents such as Eamon de Valera and Sean T. O'Kelly to other political heroes such as Michael Collins, Daniel O'Connell, Roger Casement, and Charles Stewart Parnell. Literary figures also have their place here, including poet Gerard Manley Hopkins and writers Christy Brown and Brendan Behan. Though open to all, this is primarily a Catholic burial ground, with more than the usual share of Celtic crosses. A heritage map, on sale in most bookshops, serves as a guide to who's buried where, or you can take one of the free 1-hour guided tours departing at 3pm every Wednesday and Friday from the grave of Roger Casement at the foot of the O'Connell Round Tower. You can book in advance by calling ☎ **01/ 830-1133.**

HISTORIC BUILDINGS

Custom House Visitor Centre. Custom House Quay, Dublin 1. ☎ **01/ 878-7760.** Admission £2 ($3.10) adults, £1 ($1.55) seniors and children, £5 ($7.55) family. Mon–Fri 10am–5pm, Sat and Sun 2–5pm. Bus: 27A, 27B, 53A.

The Custom House, which sits prominently on the Liffey's north bank, is one of Dublin's finest Georgian buildings. Designed by James Gandon and completed in 1791, it is beautifully propor-tioned, with a long classical facade of graceful pavilions, arcades, columns, a central dome topped by a 16-foot statue of Commerce, and 14 keystones over the doors and windows, known as the Riv-erine Heads because they represent the Atlantic Ocean and the 13 principal rivers of Ireland. Although burned to a shell in 1921, the building has been masterfully restored and its bright Portland stone recently cleaned. The new visitor centre presents the full history of the structure.

✪ **Four Courts.** Inns Quay, Dublin 8. ☎ **01/872-5555.** Free admission. Mon–Fri 11am–1pm, 2–4pm. Bus: 34, 70, 80.

Home to the Irish law courts since 1796, this fine 18th-century building overlooks the north bank of the Liffey on Dublin's west side. With a sprawling 440-foot facade, it was designed by James Gandon and is distinguished by its graceful Corinthian columns, massive dome (64 feet in diameter), and exterior statues of Justice, Mercy, Wisdom, and Moses (sculpted by Edward Smyth). The building was severely burned during the Irish Civil War of 1922, but has been artfully restored. The public is admitted only when court is in session, so it is best to phone in advance.

Leinster House. Kildare St. and Merrion Sq., Dublin 2. ☎ **01/618-3000.** Free admission. Access by guided tours only, Oct–May, Mon and Fri 10am–4:30pm; exact times vary. DART to Pearse Station. Bus: 5, 7A, 8.

Dating from 1745 and originally known as Kildare House, this building is said to have been the model for Irish-born architect James Hoban's design for the White House in Washington, D.C. It was sold in 1815 to the Royal Dublin Society, which developed it as a cultural center, with the National Museum, Library, and Gallery all surrounding it. In 1924, however, it took on a new role when it was acquired by the Irish Free State government as a parliament house. Since then, it has been the meeting place for the Dáil Eireann (Irish House of Representatives) and Seanad Eireann (Irish Senate), which together constitute the Oireachtas (National Parliament). Tickets for admission when the Dáil is in session (Oct–May Tues–Thurs) must be arranged in advance from the Public Relations Office at ☎ **01/618-3066.**

Mansion House. Dawson St., Dublin 2. ☎ **01/676-1845.** Not open to the public, but the exterior is worth a look. DART to Pearse Station. Bus: 10, 11A, 11B, 13, 20B.

Built by Joshua Dawson, this Queen Anne–style building has been the official residence of Dublin's lord mayors since 1715. It was here that the first Dáil Eireann assembled, in 1919, to adopt Ireland's Declaration of Independence and ratify the Proclamation of the Irish Republic by the insurgents of 1916.

✪ **Newman House.** 85–86 St. Stephen's Green, Dublin 2. ☎ **01/706-7422.** Fax 01/706-7211. Guided tours £2 ($3.10) adults, £1 ($1.55) seniors, students, and children under 12. June, July, and Sept Tues–Fri noon–5pm, Sat 2–5pm, Sun 11am–2pm; otherwise, by appointment only. Bus: 14, 14A, 15A, 15B.

In the heart of Dublin on the south side of St. Stephen's Green, this is the historic seat of the Catholic University of Ireland. Named for Cardinal John Henry Newman, the 19th-century writer and theologian and first rector of the university, it is comprised of two of the finest Georgian town houses in Dublin, dating from 1740 and decorated with outstanding Palladian and Rococo plasterwork, marble tiled floors, and wainscot paneling. No. 85 has been magnificently restored to its original splendor. *Note:* Every other Sunday, Newman House hosts a bi-weekly antiques and collectibles fair, where dealers from throughout Ireland sell a wide range of items, including silver, rare books, paintings and prints, coins, stamps, etc.

LIBRARIES

✪ **Chester Beatty Library and Gallery of Oriental Art.** 20 Shrewsbury Rd., Ballsbridge, Dublin 4. ☎ **01/269-2386.** E-mail: mryan@cbl.ie. Free admission. Tues–Fri 10am–5pm, Sat 2–5pm; free guided tours Wed and Sat 2:30pm. DART to Sandymount Station. Bus: 5, 6, 6A, 7A, 8, 10, 46, 46A, 46B, 64.

Bequeathed to the Irish nation in 1956 by Sir Alfred Chester Beatty, this collection contains approximately 22,000 manuscripts, rare books, miniature paintings, and objects from Western, Middle Eastern, and Far Eastern cultures.

Marsh's Library. St. Patrick's Close, Upper Kevin St., Dublin 8. ☎ **01/ 454-3511.** www.kst.dit.ie/marsh. Admission £1 ($1.55). Children free. Mon and Wed–Fri 10am–12:45pm and 2–5pm, Sat 10:30am–12:45pm. Bus: 50, 50A, 50C, 77, 77A.

This is Ireland's oldest public library, founded in 1701 by Narcissus Marsh, Archbishop of Dublin. It is a repository of more than 25,000 scholarly volumes, chiefly on theology, medicine, ancient history, maps, Hebrew, Syriac, Greek, Latin, and French literature.

National Library of Ireland. Kildare St., Dublin 2. ☎ **01/603-0200.** Fax 01/676-6690. Free admission. Mon–Wed 10am–9pm, Thurs–Fri 10am–5pm, Sat 10am–1pm. DART to Pearse Station. Bus: 10, 11A, 11B, 13, 20B.

If you're coming to Ireland to research your roots, this library should be one of your first points of reference (along with the Heraldic Museum, see below), with its thousands of volumes and records yielding ancestral information. Opened at this location in 1890, this is the principal library of Irish studies, and is particularly noted for its collection of first editions and the papers of Irish writers and political figures, such as W. B. Yeats, Daniel O'Connell, and Patrick Pearse. It also has an unrivaled collection of maps of Ireland.

National Photographic Archive. Meeting House Sq., Temple Bar, Dublin 2. ☎ **01/661-8811.** Free admission. Mon–Sat 11am–6pm. DART to Tara St. Station. Bus: 21A, 46A, 46B, 51B, 51C, 68, 69, 86.

The newest member of the Temple Bar cultural complex, the National Photographic Archive will house the extensive photo collection of the National Library and serve as its photo exhibition space. At present, it is still finding its way, but it's sure to offer exciting programs in the coming years.

MORE MUSEUMS

Dublin Civic Museum. 58 S. William St., Dublin 2. ☎ **01/679-4260.** Free admission. Tues–Sat 10am–6pm, Sun 11am–2pm. Bus: 10, 11, 13.

Located in the old City Assembly House next to the Powerscourt Townhouse Centre, this museum focuses on the history of the Dublin area from medieval to modern times. In addition to old street signs, maps, and prints, you can see Viking artifacts, wooden water mains, coal covers, and even the head from the statue of Lord Nelson, which stood in O'Connell Street until it was blown up in 1965.

Irish Jewish Museum. 3–4 Walworth Rd. (off Victoria St.), S. Circular Rd., Dublin 8. ☎ **01/453-1797.** Free admission; donations welcome. Oct–Apr Sun 10:30am–2:30pm; May–Sept Tues, Thurs, Sun 11am–3pm. Bus: 15A, 15B, 47, 47B.

Housed in a former synagogue, this is a museum of Irish/Jewish documents, photographs, and memorabilia, tracing the history of the Jews in Ireland over the last 500 years.

Natural History Museum. Merrion St., Dublin 2. ☎ **01/677-7444.** Free admission. Tues–Sat 10am–5pm, Sun 2–5pm. Bus: 7, 7A, 8.

A division of the National Museum of Ireland, the recently renovated Natural History Museum is considered one of the finest traditional museums in the world. In addition to presenting the zoological history of Ireland, it offers examples of major animal groups from around the world, including many which are rare or extinct. The Blaschka glass models of marine animals are a big attraction here.

Number Twenty Nine. 29 Lower Fitzwilliam St., Dublin 2. ☎ **01/702-6165.** Admission £2.50 ($3.90) adults, £1 ($1.55) seniors and students, children under 16 free. Tues–Sat 10am–5pm, Sun 2–5pm. Closed 2 weeks before Christmas. DART to Pearse Station. Bus: 6, 7, 8, 10, 45.

This unique museum is right in the heart of one of Dublin's fashionable Georgian streets. The restored four-story town house is designed to reflect the lifestyle of a Dublin middle-class family during the period from 1790 to 1820. The exhibition ranges from artifacts and artworks of the time to carpets, curtains, decorations, plasterwork, and bell pulls. The nursery includes dolls and toys of the era.

A SIGHT & SOUND SHOW

Dublin Experience. Trinity College, Davis Theatre, Dublin 2. ☎ **01/608-1688.** Admission £3 ($4.65) adults, £2.75 ($4.30) seniors, students, and children. Daily late May to Sept, hourly showings 10am–5pm. DART to Tara St. Station. Bus: 5, 7A, 8, 15A, 15B, 15C, 46, 55, 62, 63, 83, 84.

An ideal orientation for first-time visitors to the Irish capital, this 45-minute multimedia sight-and-sound show traces the history of Dublin from the earliest times to the present. It is presented in the Davis Theater of Trinity College, on Nassau Street.

ESPECIALLY FOR KIDS

✪ **The Ark: A Cultural Centre for Children.** Eustace St., Temple Bar, Dublin 2. ☎ **01/670-7788.** Fax 01/670-7758. Prices from 50p–£5 (80¢–$8) depending on activity or event. Daily 10am–4pm. Closed mid–Aug to mid–Sept. DART to Tara St. Station. Bus: 51, 51B, 37, 39.

The Ark is a unique new cultural center for children in the Temple Bar area where children are taught with respect and sensitivity by an experienced staff. The handsomely renovated building has three modern main floors housing a wonderful semicircular theater that can open out onto Meeting House Square, a gallery, and a workshop for hands-on learning sessions. This exciting center offers organized mini-course experiences (1 to 2 hours long) designed around particular themes in music, visual arts, and theater. In their debut year, The Ark offered numerous activities in photography, the concept of an Ark and animal-making, music and instrument-making, and the art of architecture. The workshops, performances, tours, and artist/musician-in-residence program are geared toward specific age groups and the associated activities are kept small, so check the current themes and schedule of events and book accordingly. The Ark enjoys huge popularity with children, families, and teachers.

Dublin's Viking Adventure. Temple Bar, Dublin 2 (entrance from Essex St.). ☎ **01/679-6040.** Fax 01/679-6033. Admission £4.75 ($7.40) adults, £3.95 ($6.10) seniors and students, £2.75 ($4.25) children, £13 ($20.15) family. Mar–Oct Tues–Sat 10am–1pm and 2–4:30pm. DART to Tara St. Station. Bus: 51, 51B, 37, 39.

This popular new attraction brings you on an imaginative journey through time to an era when Dublin was a bustling Norse town. A lively, authentic atmosphere is created by the "Vikings" who populate the village in their period houses and detailed costumes. The Viking townspeople engage in the activities of daily life in the Wood Quay area along the Liffey, while you watch and interact with them. The "Viking Feast" is a further opportunity to experience living history at the berserk price of £31.50 ($48.85) per adult and £20 ($31) for Viking-wannabes under 16. Feasts are held every day but Tuesday at 7:30pm. Call the number above for reservations.

✪ **Dublin Zoo.** The Phoenix Park, Dublin 8. ☎ **01/677-1425.** Admission £5.90 ($9.15) adults, £4.20 ($6.50) seniors and students, £3.20 ($5) children 3–16, £15.90 ($24.65) family. Summer Mon–Sat 9:30am–6pm, Sun 10:30am–6pm; winter Mon–Fri 9:30am–4pm, Sat 9:30am–5pm, Sun 10:30am–5pm. Bus: 10, 25, 26.

Established in 1830, this is the third-oldest zoo in the world (after London and Paris), nestled in the city's largest playground, the Phoenix Park, about 2 miles west of the city center. This 30-acre zoo provides a naturally landscaped habitat for more than 235 species of wild animals and tropical birds. Highlights for youngsters include the Children's Pets' Corner and a train ride around the zoo. New additions to the zoo, part of a $24 million redevelopment, are an Arctic exhibition called "Fringes of the Arctic," "Monkey Islands," and "City Farm." Other facilities include a restaurant, coffee shop, and gift shop.

Lambert Puppet Theatre and Museum. 5 Clifden Lane, Monkstown, County Dublin. ☎ **01/280-0974**. No box office; book by phone daily. Admission £4.50 ($7). Shows Sat–Sun 3:30pm. DART to Salthill Station. Bus: 7, 7A, 8.

Founded by master ventriloquist Eugene Lambert, this 300-seat suburban theater presents puppet shows designed to delight audiences both young and young at heart. During intermission, you can browse in the puppet museum.

Museum of Childhood. The Palms, 20 Palmerston Park, Rathmines, Dublin 6. ☎ **01/497-3223**. Admission £1.50 ($2.35) adults, £1 ($1.55) children under 12. July–Aug Wed and Sun 2–5:30pm; Sept and Nov–June Sun 2–5:30pm. Bus: 13 or 14.

Part of a large suburban house on the south side of Dublin, this museum specializes in dolls and dollhouses of all nations, made between 1730 and 1940. Among the unique items on display are dollhouses that belonged to the Empress Elizabeth of Austria and Daphne du Maurier. In addition, there are antique toys, rocking horses, and doll carriages.

National Wax Museum. Granby Row (at Upper Dorset St., off Parnell Sq.), Dublin 1. ☎ **01/872-6340**. Admission £3.50 ($5.45) adults, £2.50 ($3.90) students, £2 ($3.10) children under 12. Mon–Sat 10am–5:30pm, Sun noon–5:30pm. Bus: 11, 13, 16, 22, 22A.

For an overall life-size view of Irish history and culture, this museum presents wax figures of Irish people of historical, political, literary, theatrical, and sporting fame. In addition, there is a wide range of tableaux featuring everything from the Last Supper, Pope John Paul II, and various world leaders to music stars like U2, Michael Jackson, and Elvis Presley. For younger children, Children's World depicts characters from fairy tales such as *Jack and the Beanstalk, Sleeping Beauty,* and *Snow White.*

FOR THE GENEALOGY-MINDED

✪ **Heraldic Museum/Genealogical Office.** 2 Kildare St., Dublin 2. ☎ **01/603-0200**. Fax 01/662-1062. Free admission. Mon–Fri 10am–12:30pm, 2–4:30pm. DART to Pearse Station. Bus: 5, 7A, 8, 9, 10, 14, 15.

The only one of its kind in the world, this museum focuses on the uses of heraldry. Exhibits include shields, banners, coins, paintings, porcelain, and stamps depicting coats of arms. The office of Ireland's chief herald also offers a consultation service on the premises, for a fee of £20 ($31), so this is the ideal place to start researching your own roots.

SIGHTS FOR THE LITERARY-MINDED

James Joyce Centre. 35 N. Great George's St., Dublin 1. ☎ **01/878-8547.** Fax 01/878-8488. www.jamesjoyce.ie. Admission £2.75 ($4.25) adults, £2 ($3.10) seniors and students, 75p ($1.15) children, £6 ($9.30) family; walking tours and events charged separately. AE, MC, V. Mon–Sat 9:30am–5pm, Sun 12:30–5pm. Closed Dec 24–26. DART to Connolly Station. Bus: 1, 40A, 40B, 40C.

Located near Parnell Square and the Dublin Writers Museum, this newly restored Georgian town house, built in 1784, gives literary enthusiasts one more reason to visit Dublin's north side. Aiming to impart an increased understanding of the life and works of James Joyce, it contains various exhibits plus a Joycean archive, reference library, and workshop. In addition, there are talks and audiovisual presentations daily, and Ken Monaghan, Joyce's nephew, conducts tours of the house and, occasionally, walking tours through the neighborhood streets of "Joyce Country" in Dublin's north inner city (group tours by special arrangement only).

Shaw Birthplace. 33 Synge St., Dublin 2. ☎ **01/475-0854.** Admission £2.50 ($3.90) adults, £2 ($3.10) seniors and students, £1.30 ($2) children, £7.50 ($11.65) family. Combination ticket with the Dublin Writers Museum available at reduced rate. Apr–Oct Mon–Sat 10am–1pm and 2–5pm, Sun 2–5pm. Bus: 16, 16A, 19, 19A, 22, 22A, 155.

Situated off S. Circular Road, this simple two-story terraced house, built in 1838, was the 1856 birthplace of George Bernard Shaw, one of Dublin's three winners of the Nobel Prize for Literature. Recently restored, it has been furnished in Victorian style to re-create the atmosphere of Shaw's early days. Rooms on view are the kitchen, maid's room, nursery, drawing room, and a couple of bedrooms, including young Bernard's.

3 Organized Tours

BUS TOURS

Dublin Bus. 59 Upper O'Connell St., Dublin 1. ☎ **01/873-4222.**

This company operates several different tours. Seats can be booked in advance at the Dublin Bus office or at the Dublin Bus ticket desk, Dublin Tourism, Suffolk Street. All tours depart from the Dublin Bus office, but free pick-up from many Dublin hotels is available for morning tours. Tours include a nearly 3-hour **Grand Dublin Tour** via double-decker bus, with either an open-air or glass-enclosed upper level. It's a great vantage point for picture-taking. The cost is £9

($13.95) adults, £4.50 ($7) children under 16, and £20 ($31) for a family of 4. It operates year-round at 10:15am and 2:15pm.

For more flexible touring, there is a **Dublin City Tour,** a continuous guided bus service connecting 10 major points of interest, including museums, art galleries, churches and cathedrals, libraries, and historic sites. For the flat fare of £6 ($9.30) adults, £3 ($4.65) children under 16, £12 ($18.60) for a family of four—you can ride the bus for a full day, getting off and on as often as you wish. It operates daily from 9:30am–4:45pm.

Gray Line Tours—Ireland. Gray Line Desk, Dublin Tourism Centre, Suffolk St., Dublin 2. ☎ **01/605-7705.** Fax 01/670-8731. A branch of the world's largest sightseeing organization, this company offers a range of full-day and half-day sightseeing tours of Dublin City Mar–Nov.

The selection of tours includes a 2-hour **morning tour,** providing an overview of the city's historical sights and attractions; a 3-hour **afternoon city tour** including admission to the Book of Kells exhibit at Trinity College, the State Apartments of Dublin Castle, and St. Patrick's Cathedral; and a **full-day tour** combining the morning and afternoon tours described above to create a 7-hour exploration of Dublin's highlights. Prices range from £7–£27 ($10.85–$41.85) per person.

WALKING TOURS

Small and compact, Dublin lends itself to walking tours. You can grab a map and a pith helmet and set off on your own, of course, but if you want some guidance, some historical background, or just some company, consider one of the following tours.

SELF-GUIDED WALKING TOURS

TOURIST TRAILS   The **Dublin Tourism Office,** St. Andrew's Church, Suffolk St., Dublin 2, has pioneered in the development of self-guided walking tours around Dublin. To date, four different tourist trails have been mapped out and signposted throughout the city: Old City, Georgian Heritage, Cultural Heritage, and Rock 'n' Stroll/Music Theme. For each trail, the tourist office has produced a handy booklet that maps out the route and provides a commentary about each place along the trail.

ESCORTED GROUP WALKING TOURS

Specialty walking tours shoot up in Dublin like weeds or wildflowers, so take your pick. They're everywhere; so keep your eyes open for the latest sprout. Here's a sampling of what's available as we go to press.

Discover Dublin Tours. 20 Lower Stephen St., Dublin 2. ☎ **01/478-0193.** Fax 01/475-1324. Tickets £6 ($9.30) adults, £5 ($7.75) seniors and students.

Year-round walks with literary or musical themes are this company's specialty. Some of the tours include a 2-hour literary/historical tour during which costumed guides recite works from Dublin's literary greats while walking you through the city's famous landmarks; and a 2-hour musical pub crawl that focuses on Irish music, from traditional to rock. The tours depart from a number of venues; reservations are required.

Jameson Literary Pub Crawl. ☎ **01/670-5603.** Tickets £6 ($9.60) per person. Year-round Sun at noon plus May and Sept daily 7:30pm; June–Aug daily 3pm and 7:30pm; Oct–April Fri–Sun 7:30pm.

Walking in the footsteps of Joyce, Behan, Beckett, Shaw, Kavanagh, and other Irish literary greats, this guided tour, winner of the "Living Dublin Award," visits a number of Dublin's most famous pubs with literary connections, while actors provide appropriate performances and commentary between stops. The tour assembles at the Duke Pub on Duke Street (off Grafton Street).

Walking Tour of Revolutionary Dublin 1916–1923. Leaving from Trinity College. ☎ **01/497-4912.** Tickets £5 ($7.75) adults, £4 ($6.20) seniors and students. June–Sept Mon–Sat 10:30am and 2:30pm.

This 2^1/$_2$-hour walking tour, led by Trinity College history graduates, steps back into the turbulent years of the 1916 Easter Rising and the succeeding years of the War of Independence and the Irish Civil War, visiting sites where some of Ireland's most dramatic moments unfolded. Each tour ends up at an old Dublin pub for a round of banter and ballads. Tours assemble at Fusili; no reservations are necessary.

Historical Walking Tours of Dublin. Leaving from Trinity College. ☎ **01/845-0241.** Tickets £5 ($7.75) adults, £4 ($6.20) seniors and students. June–Sept Mon–Sat 11am, noon, 3pm; Sun 11am, noon, 2pm, 3pm. Oct–May Sat–Sun noon.

This basic 2-hour sightseeing walk takes in Dublin's historic landmarks, from medieval walls and Viking remains around Wood Quay to Christ Church, Dublin Castle, City Hall, and Trinity College. All guides are history graduates of Trinity College and participants are encouraged to ask questions. Tours assemble at the front gate of Trinity College; no reservations are needed. Walking tours of Trinity College itself are also on offer at Trinity's Front Square, just inside the front gate.

Traditional Irish Musical Pub Crawl. ☎ **01/478-0193.**

To explore and sample the Dublin traditional music scene, meet at the Oliver St. John Gogarty pub/restaurant, at the corner of Fleet Street and Anglesea Street, Temple Bar. The tour departs May to October daily at 7:30pm, November to December and January 15 to April on Friday and Saturday at 7:30pm. It costs £6 ($9.30) for adults, £5 ($7.75) for seniors and students. A song book is included in the price.

The Zosimus Experience. 28 Fitzwilliam Lane, Dublin 2. ☎ **01/661-8646.** www.clubi.ie/zozimus. £6 ($9.30) per person. Daily at 6:45pm, by appointment.

This is the latest rage on the walking tour circuit. Its creators call it a "cocktail mix" of ghosts, murderous tales, horror stories, humor, circus, history, street theater, and whatever's left, all taking place within the precincts of medieval Dublin. You've guessed by now it's indescribable, and also great fun. Meet outside the main gate of Dublin Castle, most every evening at roughly 6:45. It's essential to book in advance, at which point you'll receive all the specifics you'll need to be in the right place at the right time. Call ☎ **01/661-8646** or the Dublin Tourism Centre at 01/605-7769 to reserve a place. The experience lasts approximately 1 1/4 hours.

HORSE-DRAWN CARRIAGE TOUR

Horse-Drawn Carriage Tours. St. Stephen's Green, Dublin 2. Tickets £8–£32 ($12.40–$49.60) for 2 to 5 passengers, depending on duration of ride. Apr–Oct daily and nightly, weather permitting.

Tour Dublin in style in a handsomely outfitted horse-drawn carriage with a driver who will comment on the sights as you travel the streets and squares of the city. To arrange a ride, consult with one of the drivers stationed with carriages at the Grafton Street side of St. Stephen's Green. Rides range from a short swing around the Green to an extensive half-hour Georgian tour or an hour-long Old City tour. Rides are available on a first-come, first-served basis.

4 The Great Outdoors

BEACHES   The following beaches on the outskirts of Dublin offer safe swimming and sandy strands and can all be reached by city bus: **Dollymount,** 3.5 miles away; **Sutton,** 7 miles away; Howth, 9 miles away; and **Portmarnock** and **Malahide,** each 10 miles away. In addition, the southern suburb of **Dun Laoghaire,** 7 miles away, offers a beach (at Sandycove) and a long bay-front promenade ideal for strolling in the sea air. For more details, inquire at the Dublin Tourism Office.

BIRD WATCHING   The estuaries, salt marshes, sand flats, and islands in the vicinity of Dublin Bay provide a varied habitat for a number of bird species. **Rockabill Island,** off the coast at Skerries, is home to an important colony of roseate terns; there is no public access to the island, but the birds can be seen from shore. **Rogerstown and Malahide Estuaries,** on the north side of Dublin, are wintering grounds for large numbers of Brent geese, ducks, and waders. **The North Bull** is a spit of sand just north of Dublin Harbor, with salt marsh and extensive intertidal flats on the side facing the mainland; 198 species in all have been recorded here. **Sandymount Strand** on Dublin's south side has a vast intertidal zone; around dusk in July and August you can often see large numbers of terns here, including visiting roseate terns from Rockabill Island.

DIVING   Oceanic Adventures in Dun Laoghaire (☎ **01/280-1083**) offers a five-star PADI diving school and arranges dive vacations on the west coast.

FISHING   The greater Dublin area offers a wide range of opportunities for freshwater angling on local rivers, reservoirs, and fisheries. A day's catch might include perch, rudd, pike, salmon, sea trout, brown trout, or freshwater eel. The **Dublin Angling Initiative,** Balnagowan, Mobhi Boreen, Glasnevin, Dublin 9 (☎ **01/ 837-9209**) offers an informative and helpful guide—the *Dublin Freshwater Angling Guide,* available for £1 ($1.55)—to tell you everything you'll need to know about local fishing.

GOLF   Dublin is one of the world's great golfing capitals. A quarter of Ireland's courses—including 5 of the top 10—lie within an hour's drive of the city. Visitors are welcome, but be sure to phone ahead and make a reservation. The following four are among the leading 18-hole courses in the Dublin area.

The **Elm Park Golf Club,** Nutley Lane, Dublin 4 (☎ **01/ 269-3438**), is located on the south side of Dublin. This inland par-69 course is very popular with visitors because it is located within 3.5 miles of the city center and close to the Jurys, Berkeley Court, and Burlington hotels. Greens fees are £35 ($54.25) on weekdays and £45 ($69.75) on weekends.

The ✪ **Portmarnock Golf Club,** Portmarnock, County Dublin (☎ **01/846-2968**), is located 10 miles from the city center on Dublin's north side, on a spit of land between the Irish Sea and a tidal inlet. First opened in 1894, this par-72 championship course has been the scene of leading tournaments during the years—from the Dunlop Masters (1959, 1965), Canada Cup (1960), Alcan (1970), and St. Andrews Trophy (1968), to many an Irish Open. Many experts consider Portmarnock the benchmark of Irish golf. Greens fees are £65 ($100.75) on weekdays, £80 ($124) on weekends.

The ✪ **Royal Dublin Golf Club,** Bull Island, Dollymount, Dublin 3 (☎ **01/833-6346**), is often compared to St. Andrews in layout. This century-old par-73 championship seaside links is situated on an island in Dublin Bay, 3 miles northeast of the city center. Like Portmarnock, it has been rated among the top courses of the world and has also hosted several Irish Open tournaments. The home base of Ireland's legendary champion Christy O'Connor, Sr., the Royal Dublin is well known for its fine bunkers, close lies, and subtle trappings. Greens fees are £50 ($77.50) on weekdays, £60 ($93) on weekends.

St. Margaret's Golf Club, Skephubble, St. Margaret's, County Dublin (☎ **01/864-0400**), one of Dublin's newest championship golf venues, is a par-72 parkland course located 3 miles west of Dublin Airport. In 1995, St. Margaret's was host to the Irish Open. Greens fees are £40 ($62) every day.

HORSEBACK RIDING   For equestrian enthusiasts of any experience level, Dublin offers almost a dozen riding stables within easy reach. Prices average about £10 ($16) an hour, with or without instruction. Many stables offer guided trail-riding as well as courses in show-jumping, dressage, prehunting, eventing, and cross-country riding. Among the riding centers nearest to downtown are **Calliaghstown Riding Centre,** Calliaghstown, Rathcoole, County Dublin (☎ **01/458-9236**); **Carrickmines Equestrian Centre,** Glenamuck Road, Foxrock, Dublin 18 (☎ **01/295-5990**); and **Spruce Lodge Equestrian Centre,** Kilternan, County Dublin (☎ **01/295-2109**).

WALKING   The walk from Bray to Greystones along the rocky promontory of **Bray Head** is a great excursion, with beautiful views back toward Killiney Bay, Dalkey Island, and Bray Head. Bray, the southern terminus of the DART line, is readily accessible from Dublin. Follow the beachside promenade south through town; at the outskirts of town the promenade turns left and up, beginning the ascent of Bray Head. Shortly after the beginning of this ascent, a trail branches to the left—this is the cliffside walk, which continues another 3^1/$_2$ miles along the coast to Greystones. From the center of Greystones there is a train that will take you back to Bray. This is an easy walk, about 2 hours one-way.

Dalkey Hill and **Killiney Hill** drop steeply into the sea, and command great views of Killiney Bay, Bray Head, and Sugarloaf Mountain. To get there, go south on Dalkey Avenue from the center of Dalkey (in front of the post office), a short distance from the Dalkey DART station. About half a mile from the post office you'll pass a road ascending through fields on your left—this is the entrance to the Dalkey Hill Park. From the parking lot, climb a series of steps to the top of Dalkey Hill; from here you can see the expanse of the Bay, the Wicklow Hills in the distance, and the obelisk topping nearby Killiney Hill. If you continue on to the obelisk, there is a trail leading from there down on the seaward side to Vico Road, itself a lovely place for a seaside walk. It's about a half-mile from the parking lot to Killiney Hill.

WINDSURFING Instruction and equipment rental are available at **The Surfdock Centre,** Grand Canal Dock, Ringsend, Dublin 4 (☎ **01/668-3945;** fax 01/6681215).

5 Spectator Sports

GAELIC SPORTS If your schedule permits, try and get to a **Gaelic football** game, which vaguely resembles soccer but allows use of the hands in punching the ball, or a **hurling** match, a game in which 30 men wielding heavy sticks rush around thrashing at a hard leather ball called a sliotar. These two amateur sports are played every weekend throughout the summer at various local fields, culminating in September with the **All-Ireland Finals,** an Irish version of the Super Bowl. For schedules and admission charges, phone the **Gaelic Athletic Association,** Croke Park, Jones Road, Dublin 3 (☎ **01/836-3222**).

GREYHOUND RACING Watching these lean, swift canines is one of the leading spectator sports in the Dublin area. Races are held throughout the year at **Shelbourne Park Greyhound Stadium,** Bridge Town Road, Dublin 4 (☎ **01/668-3502**); and **Harold's Cross Stadium,** 151 Harold's Cross Rd., Dublin 6 (☎ **01/ 497-1081**). For a complete schedule and details, contact **Bord na gCon** (The Greyhound Board), Shelbourne Park, Bridge Town Road, Dublin 4 (☎ **01/668-3502**).

HORSE RACING Dublin's racing fans gather at **Leopardstown Race Course,** off the Stillorgan road (N11), Foxrock, Dublin 18 (☎ **01/289-3607**). Located 6 miles south of the city center, this is a modern facility with all-weather glass-enclosed spectator stands. Races are scheduled throughout the year, two or three times a month.

POLO   With the Dublin Mountains as a backdrop, polo is played from May to mid-September on the green fields of the Phoenix Park, on Dublin's west side. Matches take place on Wednesday evenings and on Saturday and Sunday afternoons. Any of these games can be attended free of charge. For full details, contact the **All Ireland Polo Club,** the Phoenix Park, Dublin 8 (☎ **01/677-6248**), or check the sports pages of the newspapers.

7

Shopping in Dublin

*K*nown the world over for its handmade products and fine crafts-manship, Ireland offers many unique shopping opportunities, and Dublin, as Ireland's commercial center, is a one-stop source for the country's best wares. Also, due to Ireland's wholehearted membership in the European Union, Irish shops are brimming with imported goods from the Continent.

1 VAT Tax Refunds

When shopping in the Republic of Ireland, bear in mind that the price of most goods—excluding books and children's clothing and footwear—already includes VAT (value-added tax), a government tax of 17.36%. VAT is a hidden tax—it is already included on the price tags and in prices quoted to you. Fortunately, as a visitor, you can avoid paying this tax, IF you follow a few simple procedures. (*Note:* EU residents are not entitled to a VAT refund on goods purchased.)

The easiest way to make a VAT-free purchase is to arrange for a store to ship the goods directly abroad to your home; such a shipment is not liable for VAT. However, you do have to pay for shipping, so you may not save that much in the end. If you wish to take your goods with you, then you must pay the full amount for each item, including all VAT charges. However, you can have that tax refunded to you in a number of ways. Here are the main choices:

For a store refund, obtain at the time of purchase a full receipt showing name, address, and VAT paid (cash register tally slips are not accepted by Customs). A passport and other forms of identification (e.g., driver's license) may be required. When departing Ireland, go to the Customs Office at the airport or ferryport to have your receipts stamped and goods inspected. Stamped receipts should then be sent to the store of purchase, which will then issue a VAT refund check to you by mail to your home address. Most stores will deduct a small handling fee for this service.

Europe Tax-Free Shopping is a private company offering you a cash refund on purchases made at shops displaying an ETS sticker anywhere in Ireland or throughout the EU. Refunds can be collected in the currency of your choice as you depart from Dublin or Shannon Airport. The nominal fee for this service is calculated on the amount of money you spend in each store. The ETS booths are open at Dublin Airport from 6am to 5:30pm year-round, from 7am to 6pm from the end of April to the end of October, and 9:30am to 5:30pm from the end of October to the end of April.

To obtain a refund, you must do the following:

1. Make purchases from stores displaying an ETS sticker, and be sure to obtain an ETS voucher from these participating shops each time you make a purchase.
2. Fill out each form with your name, address, passport number, and other required details.
3. When departing Ireland, have any vouchers with a value of over £200 ($320) stamped and validated by a Customs official.
4. You can then go to the ETS booth at Dublin Airport (Departures Hall) or Shannon Airport (in the Arrivals Hall), turn in your stamped ETS forms, and receive cash payments in U.S. or Canadian dollars, British pounds sterling, or Irish punts, whichever you prefer.

If you are departing from Ireland via a ferryport, or if you don't have time to get to the ETS booth before you leave, you can mail your stamped receipts to the **ETS Headquarters at Spiddal Industrial Estate,** Spiddal, County Galway (☎ **09/83258;** fax 091/83043). Your refund, issued as a check, will be mailed to your home within 21 days. You can also request to have your VAT refund applied to your credit card account.

TaxBack is a private company offering VAT refunds after you leave Ireland by charging a flat fee averaging 2% of the gross price of goods purchased. On departure from Ireland, go to the TaxBack service desk at Shannon or Dublin Airport and turn in your receipts. Any receipts over £200 ($320) in value must first be stamped by a Customs official. If time is short, you can return home, have your receipts stamped by a notary public, and then mail them to TaxBack, P.O. Box 132 CK, 125 Patrick St., Cork City, County Cork (☎ **021/277010**). If you charged your purchases on a credit card, TaxBack will arrange a credit to your account in the amount of the VAT refund; if you paid cash, then you will receive a check in U.S. dollars sent to your home with the refund.

2 The Shopping Scene

Grafton Street, though only several blocks long, is Dublin's answer to Chicago's "Miracle Mile," with a parade of fine boutiques, fashionable department stores, and specialty shops. Since it's limited to pedestrian traffic only, Grafton Street often attracts street performers and sidewalk artists, giving it a festive atmosphere. The smaller streets radiating out from Grafton—Duke, Dawson, Nassau, and Wicklow streets—are also lined with fine small book, handcraft, and souvenir shops.

Nearby is **Temple Bar,** the hub of Dublin's Left Bank artsy district and the setting for art and music shops, secondhand clothing stores, and a host of other increasingly fine and interesting boutiques.

On the north side of the Liffey, the **O'Connell Street** area is the main inner-city shopping nucleus, along with its nearby offshoots—Abbey Street for crafts, Moore Street for its open-air market, and Henry Street, a pedestrian-only strip of department stores and indoor malls. Close at hand, west of O'Connell, are both the ILAC Centre and the new Jervis Shopping Centre.

Generally, Dublin shops are open from 9 or 9:30am to 5:30 or 6pm, Monday through Saturday, with late hours on Thursday until 8pm. There are exceptions, however, particularly during tourist season (May through Sept or Oct), when many shops also have Sunday hours, usually midmorning through 4 or 5pm. Throughout the year, many bookshops are also open on Sundays.

Major department stores include **Arnotts,** 12 Henry St., Dublin 1, and 112 Grafton St., Dublin 2 (☎ **01/872-1111**); **Brown Thomas,** 15–20 Grafton St., Dublin 2 (☎ **01/679-5666**); and **Clerys,** Lower O'Connell Street, Dublin 1 (☎ **01/878-6000**).

Dublin also has several clusters of shops in **multi-story malls** or ground-level arcades, ideal for indoor shopping on rainy days. These include the **ILAC Centre,** Henry Street, Dublin 1; the **Jervis Shopping Centre,** Mary Street, Dublin 1; **Royal Hibernian Way,** 49/50 Dawson St., Dublin 2; and **St. Stephen's Green Shopping Complex,** St. Stephen's Green, Dublin 2.

3 Shopping A to Z

ART

Combridge Fine Arts. 24 Suffolk St., Dublin 2. ☎ **01/677-4652.** DART to Pearse Station. Bus: 15A, 15B, 15C, 55, 83.

In business for more than 100 years, this shop features works by modern Irish artists as well as quality reproductions of classic Irish art.

Davis Gallery. 11 Capel St., Dublin 1. ☎ **01/872-6969.** Fax 01/872-5580. Bus: 34, 70, 80.

Located 1 block north of the Liffey, this shop offers a wide selection of Irish watercolors and oil paintings, with emphasis on Dublin scenes, wildlife, and flora.

M. Kennedy and Sons Ltd. 12 Harcourt St., Dublin 2. ☎ **01/475-1749.** Bus: 62.

If you are looking for a souvenir reflecting Irish art, try this interesting shop, established more than 100 years ago. It's a treasure trove of books on Irish artists and works, and it also stocks a lovely selection of fine-arts greeting cards, postcards, and bookmarks. There are all types of artists' supplies as well, and an excellent art gallery on the upstairs level.

BOOKS

✪ **Eason and Son Ltd.** 40–42 Lower O'Connell St., Dublin 1. ☎ **01/873-3811.** Fax 01/873-3545. www.irelandathome.ie/. DART to Connolly Station. Bus: 25, 34, 37, 38A, 39A, 39B, 66A, 67A.

For more than a century, Eason's has been synonymous with books at this central location and at its many branches throughout Ireland. This branch offers a comprehensive selection of books and maps about Dublin and Ireland.

Fred Hanna Booksellers Ltd. 27–29 Nassau St., Dublin 2. ☎ **01/677-1255.** DART to Pearse Station. Bus: 5, 7A, 8, 62.

Located across from Trinity College, this is a fine, serious bookshop for academic texts as well as new, used, and antiquarian volumes on all topics.

✪ **Greene's Bookshop Ltd.** 16 Clare St., Dublin 2. ☎ **01/676-2554.** DART to Pearse Station. Bus: 5, 7A, 8, 62.

Established in 1843 and close to Trinity College, this is one of Dublin's treasures for bibliophiles. It's chock full of new and secondhand books on every topic from religion to the modern novel. Greene's catalogue of Irish interest books is issued five to six times a year.

✪ **Hodges Figgis.** 56/58 Dawson St., Dublin 2. ☎ **01/677-4754.** DART to Pearse Station. Bus: 10, 11A, 11B, 13, 20B.

This three-story landmark store has great charm and browse appeal. Although it has everything, there is a particularly good section on

Irish literature, Celtic studies, folklore, and maps of Ireland. The recently opened Hodges Figgis Cafe on the first floor seats 60 and serves wine and light meals.

Waterstone's. 7 Dawson St., Dublin 2. ☎ **01/679-1415.** DART to Pearse Station. Bus: 10, 11A, 11B, 13, 20B.

Less than a block south of Trinity College, this literary emporium has extensive sections on Irish interests, as well as crime, gay literature, health, New Age, sport, women's studies, the arts, and wine.

CERAMICS

Louis Mulcahey. 17 Kildare St., Dublin 2. ☎ **01/662-8787.** DART to Pearse Station. Bus: 10, 11A, 11B, 13, 20B.

The ceramic creations of Louis Mulcahey are internationally renowned. For years he has been exporting his work throughout Ireland and the rest of the world from his studio on the Dingle Peninsula. This modest new shop across from the Shelbourne Hotel gives him a base in Dublin. In addition to his pottery, he designs furniture, lighting, and hand-painted silk and cotton lampshades.

CHINA & CRYSTAL

The China Showrooms. 32/33 Abbey St., Dublin 1. ☎ **01/878-6211.** www.chinashowrooms.ie. DART to Connolly Station. Bus: 27B, 53A.

Established in 1939, this is now Ireland's oldest china and crystal shop in continuous operation, a one-stop source for fine china such as Belleek, Aynsley, Royal Doulton, and Rosenthal; hand-cut crystal from Waterford, Tipperary, and Tyrone; and handmade Irish pottery. World-wide shipping is available.

✪ **Dublin Crystal Glass Company.** Brookfield Terrace, Carysfort Ave., Blackrock, County Dublin. ☎ **01/288-7932.** Fax 01/283-3227. www.dublincrystal.ie. DART to Blackrock Station. Bus: 114.

This is Dublin's own distinctive hand-cut crystal business, founded in 1764 and revived in 1968. Visitors are welcome to browse in the factory shop and see the glass being made and engraved.

CRAFT COMPLEXES

✪ **DESIGNyard.** 12 E. Essex St., Temple Bar, Dublin 2. ☎ **01/677-8453.** DART to Tara St. Station. Bus: 21A, 46A, 46B, 51B, 51C, 68, 69, 86.

The first thing you'll notice about DESIGNyard is its own design: a Victorian warehouse gorgeously converted into a chic contemporary applied-arts center, whose commissioned set of four wrought-iron gates are abstracts of the city plans of Dublin, Madrid, New York, and Vienna. This is a nonprofit gallery for the finest contemporary

Irish and European jewelry, furniture, ceramics, glass, lighting, and textiles. All exhibited pieces are for sale. Whether you see it as a shop or a museum, DESIGNyard is a sight worth a visit. Open Monday through Saturday from 10:30am to 5:30pm.

Powerscourt Townhouse Centre. 59 S. William St., Dublin 2. ☎ **01/ 679-4144.** Bus: 10, 11A, 11B, 13, 16A, 19A, 20B, 22A, 55, 83.

Housed in a restored 1774 town house, this four-story complex consists of a central skylit courtyard and more than 60 boutiques, crafts shops, art galleries, snackeries, wine bars, and restaurants. The wares include all kinds of crafts, antiques, paintings, prints, ceramics, leather work, jewelry, clothing, hand-dipped chocolates, and farmhouse cheeses.

Tower Design Centre. Pearse St. (off Grand Canal Quay), Dublin 2. ☎ **01/ 677-5655.** Open Mon–Fri 9am–5:30pm. DART to Pearse Station. Bus: 2 or 3.

Located along the banks of the Grand Canal, this 1862 sugar refinery was beautifully restored in 1983 and developed into a nest of crafts workshops. Watch the artisans at work and then purchase a special souvenir, from fine-art greeting cards and hand-marbled stationery to pewter, ceramics, pottery, knitwear, hand-painted silks, copper-plate etchings, all-wool wall hangings, silver and gold Celtic jewelry, and heraldic gifts. Restaurant and limited free parking available.

FASHIONS FOR MEN

F.X. Kelly. 48 Grafton St., Dublin 2. ☎ **01/677-8211.** DART to Pearse Station. Bus: 10, 11A, 11B, 13, 20B.

A long-established men's ready-to-wear shop, this place blends old-fashioned charm with modern design. It offers a handsome selection of styles, with emphasis on conventional clothing as well as items like creased linen suits, painted ties, and designer sportswear.

✪ **Kevin & Howlin.** 31 Nassau St., Dublin 2. ☎ **01/677-0257.** DART to Pearse Station. Bus: 7, 8, 10, 11, 46A.

Located opposite Trinity College, this shop has specialized in men's tweed garments for more than 50 years. The selection includes handwoven Donegal tweed suits, overcoats, and jackets. In addition, there is a wide selection of scarves, vests, Patch caps, and Gatsby, Sherlock Holmes, and Paddy hats.

✪ **Louis Copeland and Sons.** 39–41 Capel St., Dublin 1. ☎ **01/872-1600.** Bus: 34, 70, 80.

With a distinctive old-world shopfront, this store stands out on the north side of the River Liffey. It is known for high-quality work in made-to-measure and ready-to-wear men's suits, coats, and shirts. Other branches are located at 30 Pembroke St., Dublin 2 (☎ 01/661-0110); and at 18 Wicklow St., Dublin 2 (☎ 01/677-7038).

FASHIONS FOR WOMEN

✪ **Cleo.** 18 Kildare St., Dublin 2. ☎ **01/676-1421.** www.netsolutions.ie/cleo. DART to Pearse Station. Bus: 10, 11A, 11B, 13, 20B.

For more than 50 years, the Joyce family has been creating designer ready-to-wear clothing in a rainbow of vibrant tweed colors—elegant ponchos, capes, peasant skirts, coat-sweaters, decorative crios belts, and brimmed hats.

Pat Crowley. 3 Molesworth Place, Dublin 2. ☎ **01/661-5580.** Fax 01/661-2476. DART to Pearse Station. Bus: 10, 11A, 11B, 13, 20B.

This designer emphasizes individuality, with her exclusive line of tweeds and couture evening wear.

Sybil Connolly. 71 Merrion Sq., Dublin 2. ☎ **01/676-7281.** DART to Pearse Station. Bus: 5, 7A, 8.

Irish high fashion is synonymous with this world-renowned made-to-measure designer. Evening wear and Irish linen creations are her specialty.

GIFTS & KNICKKNACKS

House of Ireland. 37–38 Nassau St., Dublin 2. ☎ **01/677-7473.** www.hoi.ie. DART to Pearse Station. Bus: 5, 7A, 15A, 15B, 46, 55, 62, 63, 83, 84.

Located opposite Trinity College, this shop is a happy blend of European and Irish products, from Waterford and Belleek to Wedgwood and Lladro, as well as tweeds, linens, knitwear, Celtic jewelry, mohair capes, shawls, kilts, blankets, and dolls. Ask about the 10% gift offer for mentioning this guide!

The Kilkenny Shop. 6–10 Nassau St., Dublin 2. ☎ **01/677-7066.** DART to Pearse Station. Bus: 5, 7A, 15A, 15B, 46, 55, 62, 63, 83, 84.

A sister operation of the Blarney Woollen Mills, this modern multilevel shop is a showplace for original Irish designs and quality products including pottery, glass, candles, woollens, pipes, knitwear, jewelry, books, and prints. There is a pleasant cafe on the premises, ideal for coffee and pastries or a light lunch.

Weir and Sons. 96 Grafton St., Dublin 2. ☎ **01/677-9678.** DART to Pearse Station. Bus: 10, 11A, 11B, 13, 20B.

Established in 1869, this is the granddaddy of Dublin's fine jewelry shops, selling new and antique jewelry as well as silver, china, and

glass items. There is a second branch at the Ilac Centre, Henry Street
(☎ **01/872-9588**).

HERALDRY

Heraldic Artists. 3 Nassau St., Dublin 2. ☎ **01/679-7020.** Fax 01/
679-4717. www.roots.ie. DART to Pearse Station. Bus: 5, 7A, 8, 15A, 15B, 46,
55, 62, 63, 83, 84.

For more than 20 years, this shop has been known for helping visitors locate their family roots. In addition to tracing surnames, it also
sells all of the usual heraldic items, from family crest parchments,
scrolls, and mahogany wall plaques to books on researching ancestry.

House of Names. 26 Nassau St., Dublin 2. ☎ **01/679-7287.** DART to Pearse
Station. Bus: 5, 7A, 8, 15A, 15B, 46, 55, 62, 63, 83, 84.

As its name implies, this company offers a wide selection of Irish,
British, and European family names affixed along with their atten-
dant crests and mottoes to plaques, shields, parchments, jewelry,
glassware, and sweaters.

KNITWEAR

Blarney Woollen Mills. 21–23 Nassau St., Dublin 2. ☎ **01/671-0068.** Fax
01/671-0156. DART to Pearse Station. Bus: 5, 7A, 8, 15A, 15B, 46, 55, 62, 63,
83, 84.

A branch of the highly successful Cork-based enterprise of the same
name, this shop is ideally located opposite the south side of Trinity College. Known for its competitive prices, it stocks a wide range
of woollen knitwear made at the home base in Blarney, as well as
crystal, china, pottery, and souvenirs.

Dublin Woollen Mills. 41–42 Lower Ormond Quay, Dublin 1. ☎ **01/
677-0301.** Bus: 70 or 80.

Situated on the north side of the River Liffey next to the Halfpenny
Bridge, since 1888 this shop has been a leading source of Aran hand-
knit sweaters, vests, hats, jackets, and scarves, as well as lambswool
sweaters, kilts, ponchos, and tweeds at competitive prices. The shop
offers a 5% discount for those with current international student
cards.

✪ **Monaghan's.** 15/17 Grafton Arcade, Grafton St., Dublin 2. ☎ **01/
677-0823.** DART to Pearse Station. Bus: 10, 11A, 11B, 13, 20B.

Established in 1960 and operated by two generations of the
Monaghan family, this store is a prime source of cashmere sweaters
for men and women, with the best selection of colors, sizes, and
styles anywhere in Ireland. Other items in stock include traditional

Aran knits, lambswool, crochet, and Shetland wool products. Also located at 4/5 Royal Hibernian Way, off Dawson Street (☎ 01/ 679-4451).

MARKETS

Blackrock Market. 19a Main St., Blackrock. ☎ **01/283-3522.**

More than 60 vendors run stalls that offer everything from gourmet cheeses to vintage clothing at great prices in an indoor/outdoor setting; open Saturday 11am to 5:30pm and Sunday noon to 5:30pm.

Moore Street Market. Moore St., Dublin 1. No phone. DART to Connolly Station. Bus: 25, 34, 37, 38A, 66A, 67A.

For a walk into the past, don't miss the Moore Street Market, full of streetside barrow vendors plus plenty of local color and chatter. It's the principal open-air fruit, flower, fish, and vegetable market of the city.

✪ **Mother Red Caps Market.** Back Lane (off High St.), Dublin 8. ☎ **01/ 453-8306.** Bus: 21A, 78A, 78B.

Located in the heart of Old Dublin, this enclosed market, calling itself the "mother of all markets," is surely one of Dublin's best. The various stalls offer a trove of "hidden treasures" (some more in hiding than others): antiques, used books and coins, silver, handcrafts, leather products, knitwear, music tapes, furniture, and even a fortune teller! It's worth a trip here just to sample the wares at the Ryefield Foods stall (farm-made cheeses, baked goods, marmalades, and jams).

SHEEPSKINS & LEATHERS

Sheepskin Shops. 20 Wicklow St., Dublin 2. ☎ **01/671-9585.** DART to Pearse Station. Bus: 5, 7A, 8, 15A, 46, 55, 62, 63, 83, 84.

As its name indicates, this is a good place to find sheepskin jackets, hats, and moccasins, as well as suede coats and lambskin wear.

UMBRELLAS & WALKING STICKS

H. Johnston. 11 Wicklow St., Dublin 2. ☎ **01/677-1249.** DART to Pearse Station. Bus: 5, 7A, 8, 15A, 46, 55, 62, 63, 83, 84.

Just in case it rains, which it will, this centrally located shop is a good source for durable umbrellas. And if you're looking for an Irish blackthorn stick, otherwise known as a shillelagh, this spot has been specializing in them for more than 110 years. Hang one on your wall and tell the grandkids you used to chase around the old country with it.

8

Dublin After Dark

*M*aybe a more appropriate title for this section would be "Dublin Almost Dark," because during high season, Dublin's nightlife takes place mostly in daylight. Situated roughly 53° north of the equator, Dublin in June gets really dark only as the pubs are closing. Night, then, is really just a state of mind.

One general fact to keep in mind concerning Dublin's nightlife is that there are very few fixed points. Apart from a handful of established institutions, venues come and go, change character, open their doors to ballet one night and cabaret the next. *In Dublin* and *The Event Guide* provide the most thorough and up-to-date listings of what's on; it can be found on almost any magazine stand.

1 The Pub Scene

The mainstay of Dublin social life, both by night and by day, is unquestionably the pub. More than 1,000 specimens are spread throughout the city; there are pubs on every street, at every turn. In *Ulysses,* James Joyce referred to the puzzle of trying to cross Dublin without passing by a pub; his characters quickly abandoned the quest as fruitless, preferring instead to sample a few in their path. Needless to say, most visitors should follow in their footsteps and drop in on a few pubs.

Typically, Dublin pubs are open from 10:30am to 11pm (sometimes a bit later during the summer) Monday through Saturday, and from 12:30 to 2pm and from 4 to 11pm on Sunday. Drink prices are more or less standardized, with hotel bars sometimes charging slightly more than the norm. A pint of draft beer or stout averages £2 ($3.20), a bottle of beer £1.90 ($3.05), a short of whiskey (a shot and then some) around £1.85 ($2.95), and a glass of wine approximately £2.50 ($4).

You will need no assistance finding a pub in Dublin, but here are a few suggestions for finding some of the city's most distinctive.

PUBS FOR CONVERSATION & ATMOSPHERE

✪ Brazen Head. 20 Lower Bridge St., Dublin 8. ☎ **01/679-5186.**

This brass-filled and lantern-lit pub claims to be the city's oldest, and it might very well be, considering that it was licensed in 1661 and occupies the site of an even earlier tavern dating from 1198. Nestled on the south bank of the River Liffey, it is at the end of a cobblestone courtyard and was once the meeting place of Irish freedom fighters such as Robert Emmet and Wolfe Tone. A full à la carte menu is now offered.

The Castle Inn. Christchurch Place, Dublin 8. ☎ **01/475-1122.**

Situated between Dublin Castle and Christ Church Cathedral, this recently rejuvenated bi-level pub exudes an "old city" atmosphere, with stone walls, flagstone steps, knightly suits of armor, big stone fireplaces, beamed ceilings, and lots of early Dublin memorabilia. It is also the setting for an Irish Ceili and Banquet (May–Sept) featuring Irish traditional musicians and set dancers.

Davy Byrnes. 21 Duke St., Dublin 2. ☎ **01/677-5217.**

Referred to as a "moral pub" by James Joyce in *Ulysses,* this imbibers' landmark has drawn poets, writers, and literature lovers ever since. Located just off Grafton Street, it dates from 1873, when Davy Byrnes first opened the doors. He presided here for more than 50 years and visitors today can still see his likeness on one of the turn-of-the-century murals hanging over the bar.

Doheny and Nesbitt. 5 Lower Baggot St., Dublin 2. ☎ **01/676-2945.**

The locals call this Victorian-style pub simply "Nesbitt's." The place houses two fine old "snugs," small rooms with trap doors where women were served drinks in days of old.

Flannery's. 47/48 Temple Bar, Dublin 2. ☎ **01/497-4766.**

Nestled in the heart of the Temple Bar district on the corner of Temple Lane, this small three-room pub was established in 1840. The decor is a homey mix of crackling fireplaces, globe ceiling lights, old pictures on the walls, and shelves filled with local memorabilia.

The Long Hall. 51 S. Great George's St., Dublin 2. ☎ **01/475-1590.**

Tucked into a busy commercial street, this is one of the city's most photographed pubs, with a beautiful Victorian decor of filigree-edged mirrors, polished dark woods, and traditional snugs. The hand-carved bar is said to be the longest counter in the city.

Neary's. 1 Chatham St., Dublin 2. ☎ **01/677-7371.**

Adjacent to the back door of the Gaiety Theatre, this celebrated enclave is a favorite with stage folk and theater-goers. Trademarks here are the pink-and-gray marble bar and the brass hands that support the globe lanterns adorning the entrance.

Palace Bar. 21 Fleet St., Dublin 2. ☎ **01/677-9290.**

This old charmer is decorated with local memorabilia, cartoons, and paintings that tell the story of Dublin through the years.

✪ **Stag's Head.** 1 Dame Court, off Dame St. (look for the stag sign inlaid into the sidewalk), Dublin 2. ☎ **01/679-3701.**

Mounted stags' heads and eight stag-theme stained glass windows dominate the decor, and there are also wrought iron chandeliers, polished Aberdeen granite, old barrels, skylights, and ceiling-high mirrors. This place is a classic.

✪ **W. Ryan.** 28 Parkgate St., Dublin 7. ☎ **01/677-6097.**

Three generations of the Ryan family have contributed to the success of this public house, located on the north side of the Liffey near the Phoenix Park. Some of Dublin's best traditional pub features are a part of the scene here, including a metal ceiling, a domed skylight, beveled mirrors, etched glass, brass lamp holders, a mahogany bar, and four old-style snugs.

PUBS WITH TRADITIONAL & FOLK MUSIC

✪ **Kitty O'Shea's.** 23–25 Upper Grand Canal St., Dublin 4. ☎ **01/ 660-9965.** No cover.

Just south of the Grand Canal, this popular pub is named after the sweetheart of 19th-century Irish statesman Charles Stewart Parnell. The decor reflects the Parnell era, with ornate oak paneling, stained-glass windows, old political posters, cozy alcoves, and brass railings. Traditional Irish music is on tap every night.

Mother Red Caps Tavern. Back Lane, Dublin 8. ☎ **01/454-4655.** No cover except for concerts, averaging £6 ($9.30).

A former shoe factory wedged in the heart of the Liberties section of the city, this large two-story pub exudes an Old Dublin atmosphere, with eclectic mahogany and stripped pine furnishings, antiques and curios on the shelves, and walls lined with old paintings and newspaper clippings dating from the 19th century. On Sundays, there is usually a midday session of traditional Irish music, with everyone invited to bring an instrument and join in. On many nights, there is also traditional music on an informal basis or in a concert setting upstairs.

O'Donoghue's. 15 Merrion Row, Dublin 2. ☎ **01/661-4303.** No cover for music.

Tucked between St. Stephen's Green and Merrion Street, this smoke-filled enclave is widely heralded as the granddaddy of traditional music pubs. A spontaneous session is likely to erupt at almost any time of the day or night.

Oliver St. John Gogarty. 57/58 Fleet St., Dublin 2. ☎ **01/671-1779.** No cover for music.

Situated in the heart of Temple Bar and named for one of Ireland's literary greats, this pub has an inviting old-world atmosphere, with shelves of empty bottles, stacks of dusty books, a horseshoe-shaped bar, and old barrels for seats. There are traditional music sessions on Saturday from 3:30 to 7pm, Sunday from 12:30 to 3pm, and every night from 9 to 11pm.

LATE-NIGHT PUBS

If you're still going strong when the pubs shut down (11pm in winter, 11:30pm in summer), you may want to crawl to a "late night pub"—a pub with a loophole allowing it to remain open after hours. Late-nighters for the 18 to 25 set include **Hogans,** 35 S. Great George's St., Dublin 2 (☎ **01/677-5904**); and **The Mean Fiddler** (see below). After-hours pubs that host the young and hip but are still congenial for those over 25 include **Whelans,** 25 Wexford St., Dublin 2 (☎ **01/478-0766**); and the second-oldest pub in Dublin, **Bleeding Horse,** 24–25 Camden St., Dublin 2 (☎ **01/475-2705**). For the over-30 late crowd, these will fill the bill and the glass: **Break for the Border,** Lower Steven's St., Dublin 2 (☎ **01/478-0300**); **Bad Bob's Backstage Bar,** East Essex Street, Dublin 2 (☎ **01/677-5482**); **Major Tom's,** South King Street, Dublin 2 (☎ **01/478-3266**); and **Sinnotts,** South King Street, Dublin 2 (☎ **01/478-4698**).

2 The Club & Music Scene

The club and music scene in Dublin is confoundingly complex and changeable. Jazz, blues, folk, country, traditional, rock, and comedy move from venue to venue, night by night. The same club may be a gay fetish scene one night and a traditional music hot spot the next, so you have to stay on your toes to find what you want. The first rule is to get the very latest listings and see what's on and where. Keeping all this in mind, a few low-risk generalizations might prove helpful to give you a sense of what to expect.

One fact unlikely to change is that the night scene in Dublin is definitively young, with a retirement age of about 25. The only exception is some hotel venues that are either outside the city center or very costly, or both. If you're over 25, your club choices are limited unless you happen to be a recognizable celebrity. In fact, even if you are or can pass for under 25, you may find yourself excluded unless you can present just the right image—a composite of outfit, hair, attitude, and natural endowment. Many of the most sizzling spots in Dublin (we'll call them *trendy* from here on) have a "strict" or "unfriendly" door policy, admitting only those who look and feel right for the scene within. The sought-after "look" might be unkindly described as "geek-chic" or, more neutrally, "retro." An advance outing to **Sé Sí** (pronounced *shay shee*), 11 Upper Fownes St., Dublin 2 (☎ **01/677-4779**), for a consultation and a costume should enhance your odds for admission.

Most trendy clubs have DJs and live music, and the genre of current choice is something called "rave," which I won't try to put into words. Another occasional ingredient of the trendy club scene in Dublin is "E" or "Ecstasy," the drug of choice among even the youngest club-goers. Clubbers on "E" don't drink anything but water, which they must consume in great quantities. Though it may seem commonplace in this milieu, Ecstasy is both illegal and potentially lethal, and definitely not a wise vacation experience.

Cover charges tend to fluctuate not only from place to place but from night to night and from person to person (some people can't buy their way in, while others glide in gratis). Average cover charges range from nominal to £8 ($12.40).

HIPPER THAN THOU

If you think you might pass muster, the most established cutting-edge clubs (with reputedly strict door policies) are the following:

The Kitchen. 6/8 Wellington Quay, Dublin 2. ☎ **01/677-6178.** Wed–Sun 11pm–2am.

Housed in the basement of the Clarence Hotel in the heart of the Temple Bar district, this is one of Dublin's hottest, hippest nightclubs, partly owned by the rock group U2.

Lillie's Bordello. 45 Nassau St., Dublin 2. ☎ **01/679-9204.** Nightly 10pm–1am or later.

A private three-story nightclub with two bars open to members and nonmembers 7 nights a week. The place has a stylish and self-consciously decadent ambience, with a mix of music 7 days a week.

POD. Harcourt St., Dublin 2. ☎ **01/478-0166.** Wed–Sun 11pm–3am or later.

POD, by the way, stands for "Place of Dance." Operated by John Reynolds (nephew of the former prime minister of Ireland, Albert Reynolds) the POD, a "European nightclub of the year," has also won a European design award for its colorful Barcelona-inspired decor and is as loud as it is dazzling to behold.

Republica. Earl of Kildare Hotel, Kildare St., Dublin 2. ☎ **01/679-4388.**

This is a new club to keep your eye on. When it opened early in 1998 it was touted as the new benchmark in hip, with a really young scene. The fire didn't catch, however, and it changed managment within a couple of months; and as of press time Republica is still finding its way. By the time you read this, it may have come into its own. Currently it hosts The Playground, a gay night, every Sunday.

Rí-Rá. 1 Exchequer St., Dublin 2. ☎ **01/677-4835.** Nightly 11:30pm–4am or later.

Though trendy, Rí-Rá has a more friendly door policy than most of its competition, so this may be the place to try first.

KINDER & GENTLER CLUBS

Another set of established clubs, while they attract young singles and couples, have friendly door policies and are places where people of most any age and ilk are likely to feel comfortable. These include:

Annabel's. Burlington Hotel, Leeson St. Upper, Dublin 4. ☎ **01/660-5222.** Tues–Sat 10pm–2am.

Located in the Burlington Hotel just south of the Lower Leeson Street nightclub strip, this club is one of the longest lasting in town. It welcomes a mix of tourists and locals of all ages to a disco party atmosphere.

Club M. Anglesea St., Dublin 2. ☎ **01/671-5622.** Tues–Sun 10pm–2am.

Housed in the basement of Blooms Hotel in the trendy Temple Bar district and close to Trinity College, this club boasts Ireland's largest laser lighting system and offers either DJ-driven dance or live music, for the over-23 age bracket.

YET MORE CLUBS

Other comparable clubs in the city center are **Buck Whaley's,** Leeson Street Lower, Dublin 2 (☎ **01/676-1755**); **Court,** Harcourt Hotel, Harcourt Street, Dublin 2 (☎ **01/478-3677**); **Rumours,** Gresham Hotel, O'Connell Street, Dublin 1 (☎ **01/872-2850**); and the **Vatican,** Harcourt Street, Dublin 2 (no phone listed—did you really expect to ring the Vatican?).

For live music, there are several top choices. On a given night, you can find most anything —jazz, blues, rock, traditional Irish, country, or folk. Rock was dominant in the '80s when Dublin spawned new bands weekly, each aspiring to be the next U2, but it is no longer in the front seat. Instead, there's a real mix, so again, check the listings. The principal ongoing live music venues include **Whelans,** 25 Wexford St., Dublin 2 (☎ **01/478-0766**); **Eamon Doran's** (mostly an under-25 crowd), 3A Crown Alley, Temple Bar, Dublin 2 (☎ **01/679-9114**); the **Mean Fiddler,** 26 Wexford St., Dublin 2 (☎ **01/475-8555**); and a real favorite, **"Midnight at the Olympia,"** 74 Dame St., Dublin 2 (☎ **01/677-7744**).

COMEDY CLUBS

The Irish comedy circuit is relatively new and quite popular. The timing, wit, and twist of mind required for comedy seems to me so native to the Irish that I find it difficult to draw a sharp line between those who practice comedy as a living and those who practice it as a way of life. You'll find both in the flourishing Dublin comedy clubs. Here are some of our favorites. Again, this is a mobile scene; so check the latest listings for details.

Comedy Improv/Comedy Cellar. International Bar, 23 Wicklow St., Dublin 2. ☎ **01/677-9250.** Comedy Improv, Mon 9–11pm; Comedy Cellar, Wed 9–11pm. Admission £3.50 ($5.60).

A very small, packed venue, full of enthusiastic exchange. This is an up-close, in-your-face improv, with nowhere to hide; so stake out your turf early.

Murphy's Corduroy Comedy Club. Norseman, 29 E. Essex St., Temple Bar, Dublin 2. ☎ **01/671-5135.** Thurs 9pm. £5 ($7.75).

Now well-established in the comedy circuit and with a new venue, Murphy's Corduroy Comedy Club hosts some of Ireland's funniest people, many of whom are on stage.

Murphy's Laughter Lounge. O'Connell Bridge, Dublin 1. ☎ **800/COMEDY.** Thurs–Sat doors open 8pm; first act 9pm. £10 ($15.50) adults, £5 ($7.75) Thurs seniors and students.

This new 400-seat comedy venue is the current prime-time king of the Irish comedy circuit, attracting the most popular stand-ups on the Irish scene—the O'Seinfelds, as it were, as well as international acts.

DINNER SHOWS & TRADITIONAL IRISH ENTERTAINMENT

Most of these shows are aimed at tourists, although they are attended and enjoyed by locals as well.

✪ **Abbey Tavern.** Abbey Rd., Howth, County Dublin. ☎ **01/839-0307.** Box office, Mon–Sat 9am–5pm; dinner/show daily Mar–Oct and Mon–Sat Nov–Feb, dinner 7pm, show 9pm. Tickets for dinner/entertainment £28–£32 ($43.40–$49.60); entertainment only £3 ($4.65).

A complete four-course meal, accompanied by Irish ballad music, with its blend of fiddles, pipes, tin whistles, and "bones," is on tap at this authentic old-world tavern.

✪ **Culturlann Na hEireann.** 32 Belgrave Sq., Monkstown, County Dublin. ☎ **01/280-0295.** Year-round ceili dances, Fri 9pm–12:30am; informal music sessions, Fri–Sat 9:30–11:30pm; June–Sept traditional music stage show, Mon–Thurs 9–10:30pm. Tickets for ceilis, £4.50 ($7); informal music sessions, £1.50 ($2.35); stage shows, £6 ($9.30).

This is the home of Comhaltas Ceoltoiri Eireann, an Irish cultural organization that has been the prime mover in encouraging a renewed appreciation of and interest in Irish traditional music. The year-round entertainment programs include old-fashioned ceili dances on Fridays and informal music sessions on Fridays and Saturdays. In the summer months, an authentic fully costumed show featuring traditional music, song, and dance is staged. No reservations are necessary for any of the events.

Jury's Irish Cabaret. Pembroke Rd., Ballsbridge, Dublin 4. ☎ **01/660-5000.** May–Oct Tues–Sun dinner 7:15pm, show 8pm. Tickets for dinner/show £36.50 ($56.60); show with 2 drinks £23 ($35.65). AE, DC, MC, V.

As Ireland's longest-running show (more than 30 years), this production offers a unique mix of traditional Irish and international music, rousing ballads and Broadway classics, toe-tapping set dancing and graceful ballet, humorous monologues and telling recitations, plus audience participation. Free parking.

3 The Gay & Lesbian Scene

New gay and lesbian bars, clubs, and venues appear monthly, it seems, and many clubs and organizations, such as the Irish Film Centre, have special gay events or evenings once a week to once a month, so it's best to check the *Gay Community News* and *In Dublin* for the latest listings. (See "For Gay & Lesbian Travelers" in Chapter 2 for details on where to pick up these publications.) Cover charges range from £2 to £8 ($3.10 to $12.40) depending on the club or venue, with discounts for students and seniors. The social scene ranges from quiet pub conversation and dancing to fetish nights and hilarious contests. Folks on the help lines through **LOT** (Lesbians Organizing Together; ☎ **01/872-7770**) and **Gay Switchboard Dublin** (☎ **01/872-1055**) are also extremely helpful in directing you to activities of particular interest. (See page 21 for their hours of operation.) All that said, here are some well established and new bars and clubs I can suggest:

The George Bar and Night Club. 89 S. Great George's St., Dublin 2. ☎ **01/ 478-2983.** Mon and Tues 12:30–11pm, Wed–Sun 12:30pm–2:30am. DART to Tara St. Station. Bus: 22A.

The George was the first gay bar established in Dublin and now houses two bars—one quiet and the other trendy with dance music—and an after-hours nightclub called The Block upstairs. It is a comfortable mixed-age venue with something for everyone.

Out on the Liffey. 27 Upper Ormond Quay, Dublin 1. ☎ **01/872-2480.** DART to Tara St. Station and walk up the Liffey; cross at Parliament Bridge. Bus: 34, 70, 80.

A 1996 addition to the gay and lesbian scene, this relaxed, friendly pub caters to a balance of men and women and serves up pub food with good conversation. In 1998, Out expanded to include a new and happening late-night venue called Oscar's, where you can dance (or drink) until you drop.

Stonewallz. The Barracks, Griffith College, S. Circular Rd., Dublin 8. ☎ **01/ 872-7770.** www.clubi.ie./stonewallz/. £3 ($4.65) cover 9–11pm, £5 ($7.75) 11pm–2am. No credit cards. Sat 9pm–2am. Bus: 19, 19A, 22.

Music from the '60s to the '90s keeps feet moving at this women-only late-night venue. Pool tables are available, plus a video screen and games for when your feet get tired. The club is wheelchair accessible.

4 The Performing Arts

THEATER

Dublin has a venerable and vital theatrical tradition, in which imagination and talent have consistently outstripped funding. Apart from some mammoth shows at the Point, production budgets and ticket prices remain modest, even minuscule, compared with those in New York or any major U.S. city. With the exception of a handful of theaters offering a more or less uninterrupted flow of productions, most theaters mount shows only as they find the funds and opportunity to do so. That said, there are a few venerable (or at least well-established) theaters offering serious drama that we can pretty much count on to be around when we need them. They include the following:

✪ **Abbey Theatre.** Lower Abbey St., Dublin 1. ☎ **01/878-7222.**
www.abbey_theatre.ie. Box office Mon–Sat 10:30am–7pm; shows Mon–Sat
8pm, Sat matinees 2:30pm. Tickets £8–£15 ($12.40–$23.25), Mon–Thurs
evening and Sat matinee reductions for students.

For more than 90 years, the Abbey has been the national theater of
Ireland. The original theater, destroyed by fire in 1951, was replaced
in 1966 by the current quite functional though uninspired 600-seat
house. The Abbey's artistic reputation within Ireland has risen and
fallen many times and is at present reasonably strong.

Andrews Lane Theatre. 12/16 Andrews Lane, Dublin 2. ☎ **01/679-5720.**
Box office Mon–Sat 10:30am–7pm; shows Mon–Sat 8pm in theater, 8:15pm in
studio. Tickets £6–£12 ($9.60–$19.20).

This relatively new venue has an ascending reputation for fine theater. It consists of a 220-seat main theater wherein is presented contemporary work from home and abroad, and a 76-seat studio geared
for experimental productions.

The Gate. 1 Cavendish Row, Dublin 1. ☎ **01/874-4045.** Fax 01/874-5373.
Box office Mon–Sat 10am–7pm; shows Mon–Sat 8pm. Tickets £12–£14
($18.60–$21.70). AE, DC, MC, V.

Situated just north of O'Connell Street off Parnell Square, this recently restored 370-seat theater was founded in 1928 by Hilton
Edwards and Michael MacLiammoir to provide a showing for a
broad range of plays. This policy prevails today, with a program that
includes a blend of modern works and the classics. Although lesser-
known by visitors, the Gate is easily as distinguished as the Abbey.

Peacock. Lower Abbey St., Dublin 1. ☎ **01/878-7222.** Box office Mon–Sat
10:30am–7pm; shows Mon–Sat 8pm. Tickets £8–£10 ($12.40–$15.50).

In the same building as the Abbey, this small, 150-seat theater features contemporary plays and experimental works, including poetry
readings and one-person shows, as well as plays in the Irish language.

OTHER THEATERS

Other theatrical venues presenting fewer though on occasion quite
impressive productions, as well as music and dance performances,
include the **City Arts Centre,** 23 Moss St. at City Quay, Dublin 2
(☎ **01/677-0643;** www.iol.ie/~cityarts); the **Focus Theatre,** 6
Pembroke Place, off Pembroke Street, Dublin 2 (☎ **01/676-3071**);
the **Gaiety Theatre,** South King Street, Dublin 2 (☎ **01/677-1717**);
the **Olympia,** 72 Dame St., Dublin 2 (☎ **01/677-7744**); the
Players, Trinity College, Dublin 2 (☎ **01/677-3370,** ext. 1239);

the **Project@The Mint,** Henry Place (off Henry Street), Dublin 1 (☎ **1850-260027**); and the **Tivoli,** 135–138 Francis St., opposite Iveagh Market, Dublin 8 (☎ **01/454-4472**).

CONCERTS

Music and dance concerts are likely to occur in a range of Dublin venues—theaters, churches, clubs, museums, sports stadiums, castles, parks, and universities—all of which can be found in the local listings. The three institutions listed below, however, stand out as venues where most world-class performances take place. Advance bookings for most large concerts may be made through **HMV,** 18 Henry St., Dublin 1 (☎ **01/873-899**) and 65 Grafton St., Dublin 2 (☎ **01/679-0080**), or at one of the many **Golden Disc** outlets such as the one at 1 Grafton Arcade, Dublin 2 (☎ **01/677-1025**).

National Concert Hall. Earlsfort Terrace, Dublin 2. ☎ **01/671-1533.** Box office Mon–Sat 11am–7pm, Sun (if concert scheduled) from 7pm. Performances at lunchtime (1:05pm) and 8pm. Tickets £3–£20 ($4.65–$31). All major credit cards accepted.

This magnificent 1,200-seat hall is home to the National Symphony Orchestra and Concert Orchestra and host to an array of international orchestras and performing artists. In addition to classical music, there are evenings of Gilbert and Sullivan, opera, jazz, and recitals. The foyer and Carolan room were recently renovated. Street parking is available.

The Point. East Link Bridge, North Wall Quay, Dublin 1. ☎ **01/836-3633.** Box office Mon–Sat 10am–6pm; matinees 2:30pm, evening shows 8pm. Most tickets £10–£60 ($15.50–$124).

With a seating capacity of 3,000, this is Ireland's newest large theater and concert venue, attracting top Broadway-caliber shows and international stars.

Royal Dublin Society (RDS). Merrion Rd., Ballsbridge, Dublin 2. ☎ **01/668-0645.** Box office hours vary according to events; shows at 8pm. Most tickets £10–£30 ($15.50–$46.50).

Although best known as the venue for the Dublin Horse Show, this huge show-jumping arena is also the setting for major music concerts, with seating/standing room for over 6,000 people.

9

Easy Excursions from Dublin

*F*anning out a little over 12 miles in each direction, Dublin's southern and northern suburbs offer a variety of interesting sights and experiences, all easy to reach via public transportation or rental car.

1 Dublin's Southern Suburbs

Stretching southward from Ballsbridge, Dublin's prime southern suburbs, Dun Laoghaire, Dalkey, and Killiney, are on the edge of Dublin Bay. They offer lovely seaside views and walks. There is also a long promenade and a bucolic park at Dun Laoghaire.

Thanks to DART service, these towns are very accessible from downtown Dublin, and there is a good selection of restaurants and fine places to stay. A hillside overlooking Dublin Bay outside the village of Killiney is the setting for the Dublin area's only authentic deluxe castle hotel, Fitzpatrick Castle (see "Accommodations," below).

If you're traveling to Ireland by ferry from Holyhead, Wales, the first glimpse of Ireland you'll see is the port of Dun Laoghaire. Many people decide to base themselves here and commute into downtown Dublin each day. As a base it is less expensive than Dalkey, but less attractive, too.

ATTRACTIONS

James Joyce Museum. Sandycove, County Dublin. ☎ **01/280-9265.** Admission £2.50 ($3.90) adults, £2 ($3.10) seniors and students, £1.30 ($2) children, £7.50 ($11.65) family. Apr–Oct Mon–Sat 10am–1pm and 2–5pm, Sun 2–6pm. DART to Sandycove Station. Bus: 8.

Sitting on the edge of Dublin Bay about 6 miles south of the city center, this 40-foot granite monument is one of a series of martello towers built in 1804 to withstand a threatened invasion by Napoleon. The tower's great claim to fame is that it was inhabited in 1904 by James Joyce, as the guest of Oliver Gogarty, who had rented the tower from the Army for an annual fee of £8 ($12.40). Joyce, in turn, made the tower the setting for the first chapter of *Ulysses,* and it has been known as Joyce's Tower ever since. Its collection of Joycean memorabilia includes letters, documents, first and rare editions, personal possessions, and photographs.

The Ferryman. Coliemore Rd. (at stone wharf, adjacent to Dalkey Island Hotel). ☎ **01/283-4298.** Island ferry round-trip £3 ($4.65) adults, £2 ($3.10) children; rowboat rental £5 ($7.75) per hour. Jun–Aug, weather permitting.

Young Aidan Fennel heads the third generation of Fennels to ferry visitors to nearby Dalkey Island, whose only current inhabitants are a small herd of wild Irish goats and the occasional seal. Aidan is a boatbuilder, and his brightly painted fleet are mostly from his hand. The island, settled about 6000 B.C., offers three modest ruins: a church over 1,000 years old, ramparts dating from the 15th century, and a martello tower constructed in 1804 to make Napoleon think twice. Now the island is little more than a lovely picnic spot. And if you want to build up an appetite and delight your children or sweetheart, row out there in one of Aidan's handmade boats.

ACCOMMODATIONS
VERY EXPENSIVE

✪ **Fitzpatrick Castle Hotel.** Killiney Hill Rd., Killiney, County Dublin. ☎ **01/284-0700.** Fax 01/285-0207. E-mail: dublin@fitzpatricks.com. 113 units. TV TEL. £99–£200+ ($153.45–$310+) double. Service charge 15%. Breakfast £8.50 ($13.20). AE, CB, DC, MC, V. DART to Dalkey Station. Bus: 59.

With a fanciful Victorian facade of turrets, towers, and battlements, this restored 1741 gem is an ideal choice for those who want to live like royalty. A 15-minute drive from the center of the city, it is situated between the villages of Dalkey and Killiney, on 9 acres of gardens and hilltop grounds with romantic vistas of Dublin Bay. Two generations of the Fitzpatrick family pamper guests with 20th-century comforts in a regal setting of medieval suits of armor, Louis XIV–style furnishings, Irish antiques, original oil paintings, and specially woven shamrock-pattern green carpets. Most of the guest rooms have four-poster or canopy beds, and many have balconies with sweeping views of Dublin and the surrounding countryside. In spite of its size and exacting standards, the castle never fails to exude a friendly, family-run atmosphere.

Dining/Diversions: Choices include a Victorian-style French/Irish restaurant known as Truffles; the Castle Grill for informal meals; the Cocktail Bar for a relaxing drink in a posh setting; and The Dungeon for a pub/nightclub atmosphere.

Amenities: 24-hour room service, concierge, laundry service, courtesy minibus service to downtown and to the airport, indoor swimming pool, gym, saunas, squash and tennis courts; hairdressing salon; guest privileges at nearby 18-hole golf course; extensive outdoor parking.

Easy Excursions from Dublin

Balbriggan

Bernagearagh Bay

ST. PATRICK'S ISLAND

Skerries

SHENICK'S ISLAND

N1

R127

R127

R128

R108

R126

LAMBAY ISLAND

Donabate

Swords

R106

Malahide

Fry Model Railway

Dublin Airport

N1

M1

R106

Portmarnock

Irish Sea

R122

R104

R107

Sutton

IRELAND'S EYE

Howth

Ben of Howth

N2

R103

NORTH BULL ISLAND

R105

N3

Clontarf

DUBLIN

Dublin Bay

N4

Liffey

Royal Canal

N7

R119

N11

R117

R112

Dun Laoghaire

Sandycove

Dalkey

DALKEY ISLAND

Dalkey Hill

Killiney Hill

R113

Killiney

To Shankill

0 4 km 2.5 mi

N

P-0087

Attractions

Ardgillan Castle 7
Casino Marino 5
Ferryman 23
Fry Model Railway 10
Howth Castle Gardens 15
James Joyce Museum 19
Malahide Castle 11
National Botanic Gardens 2
Newbridge House & Park 8

Accommodations

The Court 27
Doyle Skylon 1
Egan's House 3
Fitzpatrick's Castle 26
Forte Posthouse 6
Forte Travelodge 9
Iona House 4
Royal Marine 16
Tudor House 22

Dining

Abbey Tavern 12
Dee Gee's Wine & Steak Bar 13
De Selby's 17
Guinea Pig 24
Kellerman's 21
King Sitric 14
P.D.'s Woodhouse 20
The Queens Bar & Restaurant 25
South Bank 18

Royal Marine. Marine Rd., Dun Laoghaire, County Dublin. ☎ **800/44-UTELL** from the U.S., or 01/280-1911. Fax 01/280-1089. 104 units. TV TEL. £90–£200 ($139.50–$310) double. Includes full breakfast and service charge. AE, DC, MC, V. DART to Dun Laoghaire Station. Bus: 7, 7A, 8.

A tradition along the seafront since 1870, this four- and five-story landmark sits on a hill overlooking the harbor, 7 miles south of Dublin City. It's a good place to stay for ready access to the ferry that travels across the Irish Sea to and from Wales. Basically a Georgian building with a wing of modern bedrooms, the Royal Marine has public areas that have been beautifully restored and recently refurbished, with original molded ceilings and elaborate cornices, crystal chandeliers, marble-mantled fireplaces, and antique furnishings. The rooms, many of which offer wide-windowed views of the bay, carry on the Georgian theme, with dark woods, traditional floral fabrics, and four-poster or canopy beds. Some of the newer rooms have light woods and pastel tones. All units have up-to-date facilities, including hair dryers and garment presses.

Dining/Diversions: There is a dining room with a panoramic view of the bay, and also a lounge bar.

Amenities: 24-hour room service, concierge, laundry service, ample outdoor parking.

MODERATE

The Court Hotel. Killiney Bay Rd., Killiney, County Dublin. ☎ **800/221-2222.** Fax 01/285-2085. E-mail: book@killineycourt.ie. 86 units. TV TEL. £88.90–£129.40 ($137.80–$200.50) double. Includes full Irish breakfast and service charge. AE, DC, MC, V. DART to Killiney Station. Bus: 59.

Situated on 4 acres of gardens and lawns, this three-story Victorian hotel enjoys a splendid location overlooking Killiney Bay, with convenient access to Dublin via the nearby DART station. The hotel's multiple lounges and popular restaurants were recently refurbished and are bright and welcoming after a walk on the strand or an outing to the city. The bedrooms, many of which have views of the bay, are adequate but unremarkable. Concierge, room service, and laundry service are available, and there is ample outdoor parking. The real draw of this hotel is its lovely setting, making possible easy excursions to Dublin as well as evening strolls on one of the most beautiful beaches on Ireland's east coast. *Note:* The Court has indicated that they will give up to a 20% discount to guests carrying this guide.

Tudor House. Dalkey, County Dublin (off Castle St. between the church and Archbolds Castle). ☎ **01/285-1528.** Fax 01/284-8133. 6 units, with shower only. TV TEL. £60–£80 ($93–$124) double. Includes full breakfast and service charge. MC, V. 7-minute walk from DART; 1.75 miles from Dun Laoghaire ferry port.

This handsome Gothic Revival Victorian manor house, built in 1848, has been lovingly restored to its original elegance by Katie and Peter Haydon. Set back from the town center, nestled behind a church, Tudor House rises to give all the guest rooms a pleasing view of Dublin Bay over the roof and treetops of Dalkey. The decor throughout the house is tasteful and serene, enhanced by antiques and fresh flowers. The blue Wedgwood Room is particularly spacious and offers a firm double bed beneath a glittering chandelier, while down the hall the cozy corner room is bright and comfortable with twin beds. The nearby DART commuter rail cannot be seen but may be heard by a light sleeper. Business and touring guests alike appreciate the splendid breakfast and helpful attention of the knowledgeable hosts. The Haydons can arrange for baby-sitting, laundry, dry-cleaning, fax, and Internet services.

DINING
EXPENSIVE

Guinea Pig. 17 Railway Rd., Dalkey, County Dublin. ☎ **01/285-9055.** Reservations required. Main courses £11–£21 ($17.05–$32.55). 5-course table d'hôte £21.95 ($34). Special value menu Sun–Fri 6–9pm, Sat 6–8pm £12.95 ($20.10). AE, DC, MC, V. Sun 5–9:30pm; Mon–Sat 5:30–11:30pm. DART to Dalkey Station. Bus: 8. SEAFOOD/FRENCH.

The Guinea Pig, like its namesake, is small and easily overlooked, but to do so would be a loss—it's a fine restaurant with a well-deserved following. Emphasizing whatever is freshest and in season, the menu often includes a signature dish called symphony de la mer (a potpourri of fish and crustaceans), wild salmon with coriander sauce, fillets of lemon sole with cockle and mussel sauce, and rack of lamb. While offering a worthy wine list, the Guinea Pig goes the extra mile and offers a surprisingly adequate house white and red for a fraction of their rack-mates. The culinary domain of chef/owner Mervyn Stewart, a former mayor of Dalkey, it is decorated in a stylish Irish country motif with Victorian touches.

MODERATE

De Selby's. 17/18 Patrick St., Dun Laoghaire. ☎ **01/284-1761.** Reservations recommended. Lunch main courses £5.25–£6.95 ($8.15–$10.75); dinner main courses £6.95–£12.75 ($10.75–$19.75). AE, CB, DC, MC, V. Mon–Thurs 5–10pm, Fri–Sat 5–11pm, Sun noon–8pm. DART to Dun Laoghaire Station. Bus: 7, 7A, 8, 46A. INTERNATIONAL.

Named after a self-styled Dun Laoghaire philosopher in a Flann O'Brien book, this restaurant is in the center of the town, just off George's Street. DeSelby's now has a totally new look, with partially restored brick walls and fresh decor to accompany their new menu, which features more fresh fish entrees. There's also a new outdoor eating area. The menu includes traditional Irish stew, Dublin Bay scampi, salmon en croûte, grilled lamb cutlets, steaks, and burgers. It's a busy spot, especially on weekends, patronized by those enjoying a day's outing at the seaport.

✪ **P.D.'s Woodhouse.** 1 Coliemore Rd. (Dalkey center, several blocks from DART station). ☎ **01/284-9339.** Reservations recommended. Main courses £6.95–£14.95 ($10.75–$23.15); lunch menu £4.95–£8.95 ($7.65–$13.85). Service charge 10%. AE, MC, V. Mon–Sat 6–11pm, Sun 1–11pm. IRISH/MEDITERRANEAN.

This restaurant is brought to you by Hurricane Charlie, the worst tropical storm to hit Ireland in recent memory. The first and only oakwood barbecue bistro in Ireland, P.D.'s Woodhouse depends daily on the oaks ripped up by Charlie 7 years ago and stored now in Wicklow. Like Charlie, this bistro's wild Irish salmon in caper and herb butter is devastating, as is the white sole. But whatever you do, don't launch any meal here without trying the Halumi cheese kebabs—conversation-stopping grilled Greek goat cheese. The nut kebabs, on the other hand, one of several vegetarian entrees, are unnecessarily austere. The early bird menu—served from 6 to 7pm for £9.95 ($15.40)—is modest, limited fare: burgers, chicken, ribs, and catch of the day, grilled to satisfy discerning budget hunger.

✪ **The Queens Bar and Restaurant.** 12 Castle St., Dalkey, County Dublin. ☎ **01/285-4569.** No reservations. Dinner main courses £6.95–£12.95 ($10.75–$20.05); bar menu £1.70–£5.75 ($2.65–$8.90). Early bird menu Mon–Fri 5:30–7pm. AE, DC, MC, V. Restaurant Mon–Sat 5:30–11pm, Sun 12:30–10pm; bar food daily noon–8pm. DART to Dalkey Station. Bus: 8. INTERNATIONAL.

One of Ireland's oldest inns, the historic Queens Pub has won a pocketful of awards, including Dublin's best pub in 1992. It has great atmosphere and food to match. In the center of town, this informal trattoria has its own open kitchen—a contrast to the usual pub grub. The low end of the menu leans towards pastas and pizzas, while the high end includes spicy Jamaican jerk chicken, T-bone steak, roast half crispy duck, or the catch of the day. In addition, there are daily specials and an interesting selection of antipasti.

South Bank. 1 Martello Terrace (at Islington Ave.), Dun Laoghaire, County Dublin. ☎ **01/280-8788.** Reservations recommended. Dinner main courses £11–£16 ($17.05–$24.80). MC, V. Tues–Sat 6–10:30pm, Sun 12:30–3pm. DART to Sandycove Station. Bus: 8. IRISH/CONTINENTAL.

On the seafront across from the promenade, this cozy, candlelit restaurant is one of the few Dublin eateries that offers glimpses of the sea. A relaxing atmosphere pervades as chamber music plays in the background. The eclectic menu changes often, but usually includes such dishes as maple chicken with grapefruit and watercress; breast of turkey with bourbon and peaches; roast duck with Cointreau and kumquat sauce; and fresh salmon in a dill-and-light-lemon sauce.

INEXPENSIVE

Kellermans. 4 St. Mary's Terrace, Dalkey. ☎ **01/285-7201.** Reservations recommended Fri–Sun. Most items under £9 ($13.95). AE, MC, V. May–Aug Mon–Wed noon–10pm, Thurs noon–11pm, Sun 1–10pm; Sept–Apr Tues–Thurs 6–10pm, Fri–Sun 6–11pm. PIZZA/INTERNATIONAL.

Kellermans offers generous portions at affordable prices from its menu of pizza and daily blackboard specials such as Fresh Dalkey Fish Pie, Hot Thai Curry, and BBQ Chicken. The food is simple and fresh and is complemented by the offerings of Kellermans' wine bar. Children are made especially welcome among the wooden tables and booths lined with red cafe chairs. The young, friendly staff keeps the atmosphere casual and cozy. This is a pleasant spot for a family to have an early dinner after a day on Dalkey Island, or for a couple to enjoy a glass of wine after a walk around town.

PUBS

P. McCormack and Sons. 67 Lower Mounttown Rd. (off York Rd.), Dun Laoghaire. ☎ **01/280-5519.**

If you rent a car and head toward the city's southern seaside suburbs, this is a great pub to stop in for refreshment. Park in McCormack's lot and step into the atmosphere of your choice. The main section has an old-world feeling, with globe lamps, stained-glass windows, books and jugs on the shelves, and lots of nooks and crannies for a quiet drink. For a change of pace, there is a skylit and plant-filled conservatory area where classical music fills the air, and outdoors you'll find a festive courtyard beer garden. The pub grub here is top notch, with a varied buffet table of lunchtime salads and meats.

The Purty Kitchen. Old Dunleary Rd., Dun Laoghaire, County Dublin. ☎ **01/284-3576.** No cover charge for traditional music; £5–£6 ($7.75–$9.30) for blues and rock in The Loft.

Housed in a building that dates from 1728, this old pub has a homey atmosphere with open brick fireplaces, cozy alcoves, a large fish mural, and pub poster art on the walls. There's often free Irish traditional music in the main bar area (the schedule varies, so call ahead), and also blues and rock music upstairs in The Loft Wednesday to Saturday from 9pm and dance music with a DJ on Sundays from 9pm.

2   Dublin's Northern Suburbs

ATTRACTIONS

Dublin's northern suburbs are best known as the home of Dublin International Airport, but there's also a delightful assortment of castles, historic buildings, and gardens to draw visitors. In addition, the residential suburbs of Drumcondra and Glasnevin offer many good lodgings en route to and from the airport.

Further north, the picturesque suburb of Howth offers panoramic views of Dublin Bay, beautiful hillside gardens, and many fine seafood restaurants. Best of all, it is easily reached via DART.

Casino Marino. Malahide Rd., Marino, Dublin 3. ☎ **01/833-1618.** Admission £2 ($3.10) adults, £1.50 ($2.30) seniors/group, £1 ($1.55) students and children, £5 ($7.75) family. Feb–Apr Sun and Wed noon–4pm; May daily 10am–5pm; Jun–Sept daily 9:30am–6:30pm; Oct daily 10am–5pm; Nov Sun and Wed noon–4pm. Bus: 20A, 20B, 27, 27A, 27B, 42, 42B, 42C.

Standing on a gentle rise 3 miles north of the city center, this 18th-century building is considered one of the finest garden temples in Europe. Designed in the Franco-Roman style of neoclassicism by Scottish architect Sir William Chambers, it was constructed in the garden of Lord Charlemont's house by the English sculptor Simon Vierpyl. Work commenced in 1762 and was completed 15 years later. It is particularly noteworthy for its elaborate stone carvings and compact structure, which make it appear to be a single story from the outside, when it is actually two stories tall.

✪ **Malahide Castle.** Malahide, County Dublin. ☎ **01/845-2337.** E-mail: malahidecastle@dublintourism.ie. Admission £3 ($4.65) adults, £2.50 ($3.90) seniors and students, £1.65 ($2.55) children under 12, £8.25 ($12.80) family; gardens free. Combination tickets available with Fry Model Railway and Newbridge House. Apr–Oct Mon–Sat 10am–5pm, Sun 11am–6pm; Nov–March Mon–Fri 10am–5pm, Sat–Sun 2–5pm; gardens May–Sept daily 2–5pm. Closed for tours 12:45–2pm (restaurant remains open). Bus: 42.

About 8 miles north of Dublin, Malahide is one of Ireland's most historic castles, founded in the 12th century by Richard Talbot and occupied by his descendants until 1973. Fully restored, the interior of the building is the setting for a comprehensive collection of Irish furniture, dating from the 17th through the 19th centuries, and the walls are lined with one-of-a-kind Irish historical portraits and

tableaux on loan from the National Gallery. The furnishings and art reflect life in and near the house over the past 8 centuries.

After touring the house, you can explore the 250-acre estate, which includes 20 acres of prized gardens with more than 5,000 species of plants and flowers. The Malahide grounds also contain the Fry Model Railway Museum (see below).

✪ **Newbridge House and Park.** Donabate, County Dublin. ☎ **01/ 843-6534.** Admission £2.85 ($4.40) adults, £2.50 ($3.90) seniors and students, £1.55 ($2.40) children, £7.75 ($12) family. Apr–Sept Tues–Sat 10am–5pm, Sun 2–6pm; Oct–March Sat–Sun 2–5pm. Closed for tours 2–5pm. 12 miles north of Dublin via Suburban rail. Bus: 33B.

This country mansion 12 miles north of Dublin dates from 1740 and was once the home of Dr. Charles Cobbe, an Archbishop of Dublin. Occupied by the Cobbe family until 1984, the house is a showcase of family memorabilia such as hand-carved furniture, portraits, daybooks, and dolls, as well as a museum of objects collected on world travels. The Great Drawing Room, in its original state, is reputed to be one of the finest Georgian interiors in Ireland. The house sits on 350 acres, laid out with picnic areas and walking trails. The grounds also include a 20-acre working Victorian farm stocked with animals.

✪ **National Botanic Gardens.** Botanic Rd., Glasnevin, Dublin 9. ☎ **01/ 837-4388.** Free admission. Apr–Oct daily 9am–6pm, Nov–Mar 10am–4:30pm. Bus: 13, 19, 134.

Established by the Royal Dublin Society in 1795 on a rolling 50-acre expanse of land north of the city center, this is Dublin's horticultural showcase. The attractions include more than 20,000 different plants and cultivars, a Great Yew Walk, a bog garden, a water garden, a rose garden, and an herb garden. There are also a variety of Victorian-style glass houses filled with tropical plants and exotic species.

The Fry Model Railway. Malahide, County Dublin. ☎ **01/845-2758.** Admission £2.75 ($4.25) adults, £2.10 ($3.25) seniors and students, £1.60 ($2.50) children, £7.50 ($11.65) family. Apr–Sept Mon–Fri 10am–6pm (closed Fri Apr–May), Sat 10am–5pm, Sun 10am–6pm; Oct–Mar Sun 2–5pm. Bus: 42.

Housed on the grounds of Malahide Castle, this is an exhibit of rare handmade models of more than 300 Irish trains, from the introduction of rail to the present. The trains were built in the 1920s and 1930s by Cyril Fry, a railway engineer and draftsman. The complex includes items of Irish railway history dating from 1834, and models of stations, bridges, trams, buses, barges, boats, the River Liffey, and the Hill of Howth.

Howth Castle Rhododendron Gardens. Howth, County Dublin. ☎ **01/ 832-2624.** Free admission. Apr–Jun daily 8am–sunset. DART to Howth Station. Bus: 31

Set on a steep slope about 8 miles north of downtown, this 30-acre garden was first planted in 1875 and is best known for its 2,000 varieties of rhododendron. Peak bloom time is in May and June. *Note:* The castle and its private gardens are not open to the public.

Ardgillan Castle and Park. Balbriggan, County Dublin. ☎ **01/849-2212.** Free admission to House. Guided tour £2.75 ($4.25) adults, £1.75 ($2.70) seniors and students, £6.50 ($10.10) family. Apr–Sept Tues–Sun 11am–6pm; Oct–Dec and Feb–Mar Wed and Sun 11am–4:30pm. Closed Jan. Free parking year-round daily 10am–dusk. Bus: 33.

Located between Balbriggan and Skerries, north of Malahide, this recently restored 18th-century castellated country house sits right on the Irish coastline. The house, home of the Taylour family until 1962, was built in 1738, and has some fine period furnishings and antiques, as well as a public tea room. But the real draw here is the setting, right on the edge of the Irish Sea, with miles of walking paths and coastal views as well as a rose garden and herb garden.

ACCOMMODATIONS
MODERATE

Doyle Skylon. Upper Drumcondra Rd., Dublin 9. ☎ **800/42-DOYLE** from the U.S., or 01/837-9121. Fax 01/837-2778. 92 units. TV TEL. £117 ($181.35) double. Includes full Irish breakfast and service charge. AE, DC, MC, V. Bus: 3, 11, 16, 41, 41A, 41B.

With a modern five-story facade of glass and concrete, this hotel stands out on the city's north side, situated midway between downtown and the airport. Set on its own grounds in a residential neighborhood next to a college, it is just 10 minutes from the heart of the city via several major bus routes that stop outside the door. Guest rooms contain all the latest amenities and colorful, Irish-made furnishings.

Dining/Diversions: For full-service dining, it's The Rendezvous Room, a modern, plant-filled restaurant with an Irish/Continental menu. For drinks, try the Joycean pub.

Amenities: Concierge, room service, laundry service, gift shop, ample outdoor parking.

Egan's House. 7/9 Iona Park, Glasnevin, Dublin 9. ☎ **01/830-3611.** Fax 01/ 830-3312. 23 units. TV TEL. £84–£100 ($130.20–$155) double. Optional breakfast at extra charge. Children under 12 50% reduction when sharing room with parents. MC, V. Bus: 3, 11, 13, 13A, 19, 19A, 16, 41, 41A, 41B.

Located on the north side of the city between Botanic and Lower Drumcondra roads, this two-story red-brick Victorian guest house is in the center of a pleasant residential neighborhood, within walking distance of the Botanic Gardens. Operated by John and Betty Egan, it offers bedrooms in a variety of sizes and styles, smoking and nonsmoking, including ground-floor rooms, with such conveniences as hair dryers and tea/coffeemakers. The comfortable public rooms have an assortment of traditional dark woods, brass fixtures, and antiques. Car parking is provided for guests.

Forte Posthouse. Dublin Airport, County Dublin. ☎ **800/225-5843** from the U.S., or 01/808-0500. Fax 01/844-6002. 195 units. TV TEL. £104 ($161.20) double. Service charge 15%. AE, DC, MC, V. Bus: 41, 41C; Express Airport Coach.

This is the only hotel on the airport grounds, 7 miles north of city center. With a modern three-story brick facade, it has a sunken skylit lobby with a central courtyard surrounded by guest rooms. The bedrooms are contemporary and functional, with windows looking out into the courtyard or toward distant mountain vistas. Each unit is equipped with standard furnishings plus full-length mirror, hair dryer, tea/coffee-making facilities, and garment press. Nonsmoking and handicapped-accessible rooms may be requested. Concierge, 24-hour room service, valet laundry service, and courtesy coach between hotel and airport are available. There's a gift shop on the premises, and parking outdoors. Dining choices include the Garden Room restaurant for Irish cuisine and Sampans for Chinese food (dinner only). The Bodhrán Bar is a traditional Irish bar with live music on weekends.

INEXPENSIVE

Forte Travelodge. N1 Dublin-Belfast road, Swords, County Dublin. ☎ **800/CALL-THF** from the U.S., or 1800/709-709 in Ireland. 60 units. TV. £49.95 ($77.40) double. No service charge. AE, MC, V. Bus: 41, 43.

Located about 8 miles north of downtown and 1.5 miles north of Dublin airport on the main N1 Dublin–Belfast road, this new two-story motel offers large, no-frills accommodations at reasonable prices. The rooms, each with double bed, sofa bed, and private bath/shower, are basic and can sleep up to four people. The red-brick exterior blends nicely with the Irish countryside and the interior is clean and modern. Public areas are limited to a modest reception area, public pay phone, and adjacent budget-priced Little Chef chain restaurant and lounge.

Iona House. 5 Iona Park, Glasnevin, Dublin 9. ☎ **01/830-6217.** Fax 01/
830-6732. 11 units. TV TEL. £50–£64 ($77.50–$99.20) double. No service
charge. Rates include full breakfast. MC, V. Closed Dec–Jan. Bus: 19, 19A. 15
minutes from city center.

A sitting room with a glowing open fireplace, chiming clocks, brass
fixtures, and dark wood furnishings sets a welcoming tone for guests
to this two-story red-brick Victorian home. Built around the turn
of the century and operated as a guest house since 1963 by John and
Karen Shouldice, it is located in a residential neighborhood midway
between Lower Drumcondra and Botanic roads, within walking distance of the Botanic Gardens. The rooms offer modern hotel-style
appointments and contemporary Irish-made furnishings. Facilities
include a lounge, small patio, and outdoor parking for guests. Smoking and nonsmoking rooms available.

DINING
VERY EXPENSIVE
✪ **King Sitric.** East Pier, Howth, County Dublin. ☎ **01/832-5235.** Reserva-
tions required. Lunch main courses £7.50–£16 ($11.65–$24); dinner main
courses £16–£25 ($24–$38.75); fixed price dinner £26 ($40.30). AE, DC, MC,
V. Mon–Fri 12:30–3pm and 6:30–11pm. DART to Howth Station. Bus: 31, 31A.
SEAFOOD.

Right on the bay, 9 miles north of Dublin, this long-established restaurant is housed in a 150-year-old former harbormaster's building.
On a fine summer's evening, it is well worth a trip out here to savor the finest of local fish and crustaceans, creatively prepared and
presented. Entrees include poached ray with capers and black butter, fillet of sole with lobster mousse, roast pheasant, grilled
monkfish, sirloin steak with a red wine sauce, and Howth fish
ragout, a signature combination of the best of the day's catch.

EXPENSIVE
✪ **Abbey Tavern.** Abbey St., Howth, County Dublin. ☎ **01/839-0307.**
Reservations recommended. Main courses £11–£20 ($17.05–$31). MC, V. Mon–
Sat 7–11pm. DART to Howth Station. Bus: 31. SEAFOOD/INTERNATIONAL.

Well-known for its nightly traditional music ballad sessions, this old-
world 16th-century tavern also has a full-service restaurant upstairs.
Although the menu changes by season, entrees often include such
dishes as scallops Ty Ar Mor (with mushrooms, prawns, and cream
sauce), crepes fruit de mer, poached salmon, duck with orange and
Curaçao sauce, and veal à la crème. After a meal, you might want
to join the audience downstairs for some lively Irish music.

MODERATE

Dee Gee's Wine and Steak Bar. Harbour Rd., Howth, County Dublin.
☎ **01/839-2641.** Reservations recommended on weekends. Dinner main
courses £6.50–£13 ($10.10–$20.15). MC, V. Daily 12:30–2pm and 6–10pm.
DART to Howth Station. Bus: 31. IRISH.

If you plan a day's outing at Howth, don't miss this place. Located
opposite the local DART station and overlooking Dublin Bay across
from the harbor, this informal seaside spot is ideal for a cup of coffee, a snack, or a full meal. A self-service snackery by day and a more
formal table-service restaurant at night, it offers both indoor and
outdoor seating. The entrees at dinner range from steaks and burgers
to shrimp scampi and vegetable lasagna. At lunchtime, soups, salads,
and sandwiches are featured. Sit, relax, and watch all the activities
of Howth from a front-row seat.

10

Two Excursions Farther Out— But Not Too Far

*T*he scope of this chapter covers the two counties to the immediate south and southwest of Dublin.

These two areas, each within easy distance from Dublin city— have less rain, less bog, and more history than any other region of comparable concentration on the island. County Wicklow presents a verdant and varied panorama of gardens, lakes, mountains, and seascapes; and to the east sit the flat plains of County Kildare, Ireland's prime horse country. Pair all of this with the region's central location vis-à-vis the rest of the country and you have an area that is both a great hub from which to explore and a historical and geographic microcosm for those who don't have time to hit the four corners of the land.

1 County Wicklow: The Garden of Ireland

County Wicklow extends from Bray, 12 miles south of Dublin, to Arklow, 40 miles south of Dublin.

GETTING THERE **By Train** Irish Rail (☎ 01/836-3333) provides daily train service between Dublin and Bray and Wicklow.

By Bus Bus Eireann (☎ 01/836-6111) operates daily express bus service to Arklow, Bray, and Wicklow towns. Both Bus Eireann and **Gray Line Tours** (☎ 01/670-8822) offer seasonal sightseeing tours to Glendalough, Wicklow, and Powerscourt Gardens.

By Car Take N11 south from Dublin City and follow turn-off signs for major attractions.

VISITOR INFORMATION For information about County Wicklow, contact the **Wicklow Tourist Office,** Fitzwilliam Square, Wicklow Town, County Wicklow (☎ 0404/69117), open Monday to Friday year-round and Saturday during peak season. For additional Wicklow information, pay an online visit to www. wicklow.ie.

The East Coast

The East Coast — IRELAND

Castleblayney
Kilkeel
N2
N1
Holy Trinity Heritage Centre 1
Carlingford Lough
Greenore
CAVAN
Carrickmacross 2
Dundalk
Bailieborough
LOUTH
Dundalk Bay
Kingscourt
Ardee
Dunleer
Virginia
Clogher Head
Collon
Monasterboice 3
Clogher Head
Lough Ramor
Kells
MEATH
Baltray
Mellifont Abbey 4
Millmount Museum 5
Drogheda
Loughcrew 28
Crossakiel
Newgrange 6
Newgrange Farm 7
N2
N1
Delvin
Athboy
Hill of Tara 8
N3
Duleek
Balbriggan
Irish Sea
Trim
Summerhill
Garristown
Skerries
Rush
Swords
Malahide
Kinnegad
Enfield
Kilcock
N4
Leixlip
Lucan
Howth
DUBLIN
Prosperous
Castletown House 9
Steam Museum 10
Dublin
Liffey River
Dun Laoghaire
Dalkey
Edenderry
Newbridge
Killruddery House & Gardens 16
Bray
Monasterevan
N7
Newbridge Cutlery 14
The Curragh 13
KILDARE
Irish National Stud 11
Japanese Gardens 12
Kildare
Blessington
Enniskerry
Powerscourt Waterfall & Gardens 17
Stradbally
Ardscull
Irish Pewtermill 19
Moone High Cross 18
Newtownmountkennedy
Roundwood
WICKLOW MOUNTAINS
Glendalough 21
Laragh
Rathnew
Wicklow
N81
Rathdrum
Gleneally
Wicklow Head
Carlow
Tullow
Wicklow Mountains National Park 20
WICKLOW
Avondale 23
Avoca
Avoca Handweavers 25
Vale of Avoca 24
Brittas Bay
Aughrim
Woodenbridge
Arklow
Noritake Arklow Pottery 26
Castlecomer
N9
Shillelagh
N80
Carnew
Gorey
Huntington Castle 27
Bunclody
N11
9 mi
12 km
N
Kilkenny
WEXFORD

AREA CODES   Telephone numbers in the Co. Wicklow region use the area codes **0404, 045,** or **01.**

A FEW WORDS ABOUT WICKLOW

The borders of County Wicklow start just a dozen or so miles south of downtown Dublin, and it is within this county that you'll find some of Ireland's best rural scenery. If you're based in Dublin, you can easily spend a day or afternoon in Wicklow and still return to Dublin in time for dinner and the theater, but you'll probably want to linger overnight at one of the many fine country inns.

One quite accessible and charming gateway to County Wicklow is the small harbor town of Greystones, which I hesitate to mention because it is practically a secret. It is hands-down one of the most unspoiled and attractive harbor towns on Ireland's east coast, with no special attractions except itself, and that's enough.

Wicklow's most stunning scenery and most interesting towns and attractions are to be found inland, between Enniskerry and Glendalough. The best way to see the Wicklow Hills is on foot, following the Wicklow Way past mountain tarns and secluded glens. In this region, don't miss the picturesque villages of Roundwood, Laragh, and Aughrim.

In the southernmost corner of Wicklow the mountains become hills and share with the villages they shelter an unassuming beauty, a sleepy tranquility that can be a welcome respite from the bustle of Wicklow's main tourist attractions. In the vicinity of Shillelagh village are lovely forests, great hill-walking, and the curious edifice of Huntington Castle.

ATTRACTIONS

✪ **Glendalough.** County Wicklow. ☎ **0404/45325** or 0404/45352. Admission £2 ($3.10) adults, £1.50 ($2.35) seniors, £1 ($1.55) children/students under 16, £5 ($7.75) family. Mid-Oct to mid-Mar daily 9:30am–5pm; mid-Mar to May daily 9:30am–6pm; June–Aug daily 9am–6:30pm; Sept to mid-Oct daily 9:30am–6pm. Bus: 2 buses daily from Dublin year-round, departing from College of Surgeons, St. Stephen's Green. Located 7 miles east of Wicklow on T7 via Rathdrum.

Its name derived from the Irish phrase *Gleann Da Locha,* meaning "The Glen of the Two Lakes," this idyllically secluded setting was chosen in the 6th century by St. Kevin for a monastery. Over the centuries, it became a leading center of learning, with thousands of students from Ireland, Britain, and all over Europe. In the 12th century, St. Lawrence O'Toole was among the many abbots to follow Kevin and spread the influence of Glendalough. But, like so many early Irish religious sites, the glories of Glendalough came to an end by the 15th century at the hands of the plundering Anglo-Norman invaders.

Today, visitors can stroll from the upper lake to the lower lake and walk through the remains of the monastery complex, long since converted to a burial place. Although much of the monastic city is in ruins, the remains do include a nearly perfect round tower, 103 feet high and 52 feet around the base, as well as hundreds of time-worn Celtic crosses and a variety of churches. One of these is St. Kevin's chapel, often called St. Kevin's Kitchen, a fine specimen of an early Irish barrel-vaulted oratory with its own miniature round belfry rising from a stone roof. A striking new visitor's center at the entrance to the site provides helpful orientation with exhibits on the archaeology, history, folklore, and wildlife of the area. There is no charge to walk around Glendalough. The admission fee above is to view the center's exhibits and audiovisual presentation.

The main entrance to the monastic complex has been spoiled by a sprawling hotel and hawkers of various sorts, so you may want to cross the river at the visitor's center and walk along the banks, crossing back again at the monastic site and thus bypassing the trappings of commerce that St. Kevin himself once fled.

Killruddery House & Gardens. Off the main Dublin-Wicklow road (N11), Killruddery, Bray, County Wicklow. ☎ **01/286-2777.** House and garden tour £4 ($6.20) adults, £2.50 ($3.90) seniors and students over 12, £1 ($1.55) children; gardens only £2 ($3.10) adults, £1.50 ($2.35) seniors and students over 12, 50p (80¢) children. House open May, June, and Sept daily 1–5pm; gardens open Apr–Sept daily 1–5pm.

This estate has been the seat of the earl of Meath since 1618. The original part of its mansion, dating from 1820, features a Victorian conservatory modeled on the Crystal Palace in London. The gardens are a highlight here, with a lime avenue, a sylvan theater, foreign trees, exotic shrubs, twin canals, and a round pond with fountains that's edged with beech hedges. They are the only surviving 17th-century French-style gardens in Ireland.

✪ **Powerscourt Gardens, House Exhibition, and Waterfall.** Off the main Dublin-Wicklow road (N11), Enniskerry, County Wicklow. ☎ **01/204-6000.** Gardens and house exhibition £5 ($7.75) adults, £4.50 ($7) seniors and students, £3 ($4.65) children ages 5–16, free for children under 5; gardens only £3.50 ($5.45) adults, £3.20 ($5) seniors and students, £2 ($3.10) children ages 5–16, free for children under 5; waterfall £2 ($3.10) adults, £1.50 ($2.35) seniors and students, £1 ($1.55) children ages 5–16, free for children under 5. AE, MC, V. Gardens and House Exhibition Mar–Oct daily 9:30am–5:30pm, Nov–Feb daily 9:30am–dusk; waterfall Mar–Oct daily 9:30am–7pm, Nov–Feb daily 10:30am–dusk.

On a 1,000-acre estate less than a dozen miles south of Dublin city sits one of the finest gardens in Europe, designed and laid out by Daniel Robertson between 1745 and 1767. This property is filled with splendid Greek- and Italian-inspired statuary, decorative ironwork, a petrified-moss grotto, lovely herbaceous borders, a Japanese garden, a circular pond and fountain with statues of winged horses, and the occasional herd of deer. Stories have it that Robertson, afflicted with gout, was pushed around the grounds in a wheelbarrow to oversee the work. This service is no longer offered, but I doubt you'll mind the walk around. An 18th-century manor house designed by Richard Cassels, the architect of Russborough House (see below) and the man credited with the design of Dublin's Parliament House, stood proudly on the site until it was gutted by fire in 1974. The house has been in part structurally restored so as to house a variety of high-quality gift shops and an exhibition, complete with video presentation, on the history of Powerscourt. The additional entrance fee to "the house" is actually for entrance to this exhibition, primarily the video, which is mediocre. The Powerscourt cafeteria is pleasant and serves delicious lunches at a reasonable price and with a view not to be believed. The adjacent garden center is staffed with highly knowledgeable green-thumbs who can answer all the questions you've collected while exploring the magnificent gardens. Meanwhile, if you've brought children who by now deserve a treat of their own, there is a nearby children's park. In my opinion, the waterfall is too little too far away at too high a price. After all, if you want to see water pouring down in Ireland, most days you can just look up.

Russborough. Off N81, Blessington, County Wicklow. ☎ **045/865239.** Main rooms £3 ($4.80) adults, £2 ($3.20) seniors and students, £1 ($1.60) children under 12. Sept and May Mon–Sat 10:30am–2:30pm and Sun 10:30am–5:30pm; Oct and Apr Sun 10:30am–5:30pm; June–Aug daily 10:30am–5:30pm.

Ensconced in this 18th-century Palladian house is the world-famous Beit Art Collection, with paintings by Vernet, Guardi, Bellotto, Gainsborough, Rubens, and Reynolds. The house is furnished with European pieces and decorated with bronzes, tapestries, and some fine Francini plasterwork. If you'd like to visit the maze and rhododendron garden, be sure to call for an appointment. Facilities include a restaurant, shop, and children's playground.

✪ **Wicklow Mountains National Park.** Glendalough, County Wicklow. ☎ **0404/45425.** May–Aug daily 10am–6pm; Apr and Sept Sat–Sun 10am–6pm.

Nearly 50,000 acres of County Wicklow have been designated as a new national park. The core area of the park is centered around Glendalough, including the Glendalough Valley and Glendalough Wood Nature Reserves. You'll find an information station at the Upper Lake at Glendalough.

Mount Usher Gardens. On the main Dublin-Wicklow road (N11), Ashford, County Wicklow. ☎ **0404/40116**. Admission £3 ($4.80) adults, £2.50 ($4) seniors, students, and children ages 5–12. Guided tours may be booked in advance for £20 ($32). Mar 17 to Oct 31 Mon–Sat 10:30am–6pm, Sun 11am–6pm.

Encompassing 20 acres along the River Vartry, this sylvan site— once home to an ancient lake and more recently laid out in the informal, free-range "Robinsonian" style—offers over 5,000 tree and plant species from all parts of the world, including spindle trees from China, North American swamp cypress, and Burmese juniper trees. Fiery rhododendrons, fragrant eucalyptus trees, giant Tibetan lilies, and snowy camellias also compete for your eye. Informal and responsive to their natural setting, these gardens have an almost untended feel to them; they are a floral woodland without pretense yet with considerable charm. A spacious tea room overlooks the river and gardens. The courtyard at the entrance to the gardens contains an interesting assortment of shops, open year-round.

Avondale House & Forest Park. Rathdrum, County Wicklow. ☎ **0404/ 46111.** Admission £3 ($4.65) adults, £2 ($3.10) seniors and children under 16, £6 ($9.30) family. Daily May–Sept 10am–6pm, Oct–Apr 11am–5pm. Parking fee £2 ($3.10). Entrance to park and house signposted off R752.

In a fertile valley between Glendalough and the Vale of Avoca, this is the former home of Charles Stewart Parnell (1846–91), one of Ireland's great political leaders. Built in 1779, the house is now a museum to his memory. Set in the surrounding 523-acre estate and boasting signposted nature trails alongside the Avondale River, Avondale Forest Park is considered the cradle of modern Irish forestry. In 1998, a new exhibition area is scheduled to open which will commemorate the American side of the Parnell family, most notably Admiral Charles Stewart of the U.S.S. *Constitution.* Teas and light lunches are available in the coffee shop, featuring homemade breads and pastries.

Vale of Avoca. Rte. 755, Avoca, County Wicklow. Free admission.

Basically a peaceful riverbank, the Vale of Avoca was immortalized in the writings of 19th-century poet Thomas Moore. It's here at the "Meeting of the Waters" that the Avonmore and Avonbeg Rivers join to form the Avoca River. It's said that the poet sat under "Tom Moore's Tree," looking for inspiration and penned the lines "There is not in the wide world a valley so sweet,/as the vale in whose bosom the bright waters meet. . . ." The tree is a sorry sight now, as it's been picked almost bare by souvenir hunters, but the place is still worth a visit.

The Irish Pewtermill. Timolin-Moone, County Wicklow. ☎/fax **050/724-164.** Mon–Fri 9:30am to 4:30pm; and, in summer, Sat and Sun 10am–4pm. Signposted off N8 in Moone. Free admission.

Ensconced in an ancient mill constructed in the 11th century for the nunnery of St. Moling—after whom the village of Timolin ("House of Moling") is named—Ireland's oldest pewtermill is a real find. Traditional Irish silver-bright pewter is cast here in antique molds, some 300 years old, by six skilled craftsmen. Casting takes place just about every day, usually in the morning. A wide selection of high quality hand-cast pewter gifts, from bowls to brooches, are on display and for sale in the showroom, and prices are very reasonable. Custom-made gifts, such as tankards, engraved with family crests, may be commissioned. An additional attraction here is a set of excellent reproductions of the principal panels from Moone High Cross, with explanatory plaques, all very helpful in further understanding and appreciating this nearby treasure. If he is about, be sure to meet Sean Cleary, a veritable font of information regarding pewter casting, local history, and all things Irish, and a formidable story-teller besides.

Huntington Castle. Clonegal, County Carlow (off N80, 4 miles from Bunclody). ☎ **054/77552.** Admission £3 ($4.65) adults, £1.50 ($2.35) children. May–Aug daily 2–6pm, Sept Sun 2–6pm; other times by appointment.

Located at the confluence of the rivers Derry and Slaney, this castle was of great strategic importance from the time it was built in the early 17th century, and was at the center of conflicts in the area up to the early 20th century, when it was briefly used as an IRA headquarters. The castle is unlike many others you will visit in that it has a lived-in feel, a magnificent decrepitude evoked not least by the sometimes overwhelming assortment of debris left by previous generations, an assortment in which lurks some real treasures. The house has many stories to tell, and young Alexander Durdin-Robertson, whose ancestors built the place, seems to know them all; he gives a great tour. Don't forget to visit the garden, which hides a lovely yew walk and one of the first hydroelectric facilities in Ireland among its waist-high weeds. The castle's basement is now home to a temple of the Fellowship of Isis, a religion founded here in 1976.

SPORTS & OUTDOOR PURSUITS

ADVENTURE CENTRE   Less than an hour's drive from Dublin center and signposted on N81, the **Blessingon Adventure Centre,** Blessington, County Wicklow (☎ **045/865024**) offers a range of outdoor activity options for both adults and children. Canoeing, kayaking, sailing, and windsurfing lessons and rentals are available on the Blessington lakes; and, on land, archery, orienteering, tennis, pony-trekking and riding lessons are on offer at all levels. Some representative prices per hour for adults are £6 ($9.30) for canoeing and kayaking, £9 ($13.95) for sailing and windsurfing, and £12 ($18.60) for pony-trekking. Full-day and half-day multi-activity prices are also offered.

BIRD WATCHING & BOTANY   Courses in ornithology and wildflowers, as well as botanical sketching and painting, are offered at the **Altamont Gardens,** Tullow, County Wicklow (☎ **0503/59128**). Mrs. North, the current owner, has left a personal imprint on the gardens, reflecting her extensive knowledge of and concern for the plant and animal species of Ireland. The cost for weekend courses, including lodging in a 17th-century cottage and meals featuring organic produce from the adjacent farm and vegetable garden, averages £200 ($310) per person. The drawing and painting courses attract amateurs as well as professionals. Special scheduling and prices are negotiable for groups of six or more.

CANOEING & KAYAKING   There are weekend courses on white-water and flat-water streams at **The National Adventure Center,** Ashford, County Wicklow (☎ **0404/40169,** fax 0404/40701; www.iol.ie/~tiglin), a state-funded facility that provides training in a variety of outdoor activities. Basic equipment is provided; fees for 1 to 5-day courses range from £35 to £130 ($54.25 to $201.50). The center caters to a young clientele, and lodging is in hostels unless you arrange otherwise.

FISHING   The streams in Wicklow are not renowned fishing waters, although brown trout and river trout can be found in such rivers as the Avoca and the Aughrim. Sea angling is popular all along the Wicklow coast, but there are not any opportunities in Wicklow to hire boats or fishing equipment.

GOLF   County Wicklow's verdant hills and dales provide numerous opportunities for golfing. Among the 18-hole courses welcoming visitors are the new **Rathsallagh Golf Club,** an 18-hole, par-72 championship course at Dunlavin, County Wicklow (☎ **045/403112**), with greens fees of £25 ($38.75) on Monday, £30 ($46.50) Tuesday through Thursday, and £40 ($62) Friday through Sunday, with a weekday early-bird special (before 9:30am) of £20 ($31); the seaside **European Club,** Brittas Bay, County Wicklow (☎ **0404/ 47415**), a championship links with greens fees of £35 ($54.25) per round and £55 ($85.25) per day, any day year-round; the parkland **Glenmalure Golf Club,** Greenane, Rathdrumm, County Wicklow (☎ **0404/46679**), with greens fees from £15 ($23.25); and the **Arklow Golf Club** (☎ **0402/32492**), a seaside par-68 course with greens fees of £18 ($27.90) 7 days a week.

HORSEBACK RIDING　With its valleys and glens and its secluded paths and nature trails, County Wicklow is perfect for horseback riding. More than a dozen stables and equestrian centers offer horses for hire and instructional programs. Rates for horse hire average £10 to £20 ($15.50 to $31) per hour. Among the leading venues are: **Broomfield Riding School,** Broomfield, Tinahely, Co. Wicklow (☎ **0402/38117**); **Devil's Glen Equestrian Village,** Ashford, County Wicklow (☎ **0404/40637**); **Calliaghstown Riding Centre,** Glenmore, Blessington, County Wicklow (☎ **045/ 65538**); **Brennanstown Riding School,** Hollybrook, Kilmacanogue, County Wicklow (☎ **01/286-3778**); and the **Laragh Trekking Centre,** Laragh East, Glendalough, County Wicklow (☎ **0404/45282**). At the **Paulbeg Riding School,** Shillelagh, County Wicklow (☎ **055/29100**), experienced riders can explore the beautiful surrounding hills while beginners can partake of expert instruction from Sally Duffy, a friendly woman who gives an enthusiastic introduction to the sport.

HUNTING　The **Broomfield Riding School,** Broomfield, Tinahely, County Wicklow (☎ **0402/38117**), offers access to the hunt for those who can demonstrate adequate equestrian skills, including jumping. The riding school is open year-round for lessons and trail rides.

WALKING　**The Wicklow Way** is a signposted walking path that follows forest trails, sheep paths, and country roads from the hills south of Dublin to the trail's terminus in Clonegal. It takes about 5 to 7 days to walk the whole of the Way, with overnight stops at B&Bs and hostels along the route. Most people choose to walk sections as day trips, and for this reason I've highlighted some of my favorites below.

　Information and maps can be obtained at the Wicklow National Park center in Glendalough or in any local tourist office. Information on less strenuous walks can be found in a number of local publications. Check out the **"Wicklow Trail Sheets"** available at tourist offices. These provide a map and route description for several short walks. The Ballyknocken House B&B also publishes a list of walks beginning and ending at the house for their guests.

The most spectacular walks in Wicklow are found in the north and central parts of the county, an area traversed by the Wicklow Way and numerous short trails. One lovely walk on the Way begins at the **Deerpark parking lot** near the Dargle River, and continues to Luggala, passing Djouce Mountain; the next section, between Luggala and Laragh, traverses some wild country around Lough Dan.

You won't want to miss **the southern section of the Wicklow Way**, through Tinahely, Shillelagh, and Clonegal. Although not as rugged as the terrain in central Wicklow, the hills here are voluptuously round, with delightful woods and glens hidden in their folds. Through much of this section the path follows country roads that have been well chosen for their lack of vehicular traffic. Consider treating yourself to a night at **Park Lodge B&B,** Clonegal, Shillelagh, County Wicklow (☎ **055/29140**), located near the trail's terminus; double rooms are £68 to £76 ($105.40 to $117.80) per person. If you're on foot you can arrange with the exceedingly hospitable Osborne family to be picked up at one of several points along the trail between Shillelagh and Clonegal.

On summer weekends, and some weekdays too, the foreign tourist crowd at **Glendalough** is joined by throngs of Dubliners out for a walk in the country; and the result can be a very tight squeeze. So, once you've seen the monastic sites—which truly aren't to be missed—I strongly recommend leaving the crowds behind and taking to the high country. For more information on walks in the Glendalough area, stop by the Wicklow Mountains National Park information center (see listing above).

One walk that doesn't require much time or effort is the stroll along the shores of the Upper Lake to the Mining Village, located at the far end of the lake. There are two paths which will take you there: a small, rocky path that follows the water's edge; and a wide forest road which parallels the lakeshore about 30 feet up the hillside. Once you reach the pile of tailings and the ruins of the mine buildings, continue past to the zigzag trail which ascends alongside the Glenealo River; the cascades here can be thunderous after a good rain. At the top of the cascades are some more mine buildings, and a great view back toward the monastic buildings. From here, the intrepid can continue north to the summit of Camaderry Mountain, or south to Lugduff—ask at the National Forest Information Center for details on these walks, which require a good map and a compass.

A favorite with Dubliners out for a weekend trek in the country is **Great Sugarloaf**, that massive cone of granite prominent on the north Wicklow skyline. The most popular route begins at Calary carpark on the mountain's southern flank: this path is the most direct, but will be mobbed with people on any sunny summer weekend. If you prefer to avoid the crowds, ask in Kilmacanoge about a route which begins in the town; this path is longer and harder to find, but worth the effort if you're looking for a quiet stroll rather than a social event. To get to the carpark take N11 to Kilmacanoge, a small town 2 miles south of Bray. Drive straight through the town, and after 1.1 miles turn left at a fork in the road. After another 2.6 miles, turn left on a small side road; continue 0.4 miles on this road, and the carpark will be on your left, surrounded by a caravan settlement. The trail to the summit is well-worn, so there's no question of getting lost; give yourself 2 hours for a leisurely walk to the summit and back. The view on a clear day takes in Dublin Bay, the Wicklow and Wexford coast, and the Wicklow and Blackstairs Mountains.

SHOPPING

County Wicklow offers a wide array of wonderful crafts centers and workshops. Here is a small sampling:

✪ **Avoca Handweavers.** Avoca, County Wicklow. ☎ **0402/35105.** Weaving shed open daily May–Oct 9am–4:30pm. Shop/cafe open daily May–Oct 9am–6pm, Nov–Apr 9:30am–5:30pm.

Dating from 1723, this cluster of whitewashed stone buildings and a mill houses the oldest surviving hand-weaving company in Ireland, producing a wide range of tweed clothing, knitwear, and accessories. The dominant tones of mauve, aqua, teal, and heather reflect the local landscape. You're welcome to watch as craftspeople weave strands of yarn that has been spun from the wool of local sheep. There is a retail outlet and coffee shop on the complex. A second outlet/shop is on the main N11 road at Kilmacanogue, Bray, County Wicklow (☎ **01/286-7466**). Open daily from 9:30am to 5:30pm.

Bergin Clarke Studio. The Old Schoolhouse, Ballinaclash, Rathdrum, County Wicklow. ☎ **0404/46385.**

Stop into this little workshop and see Brian Clarke hand-fashioning silver jewelry and giftware or Yvonne Bergin knitting stylish and colorful apparel using yarns from County Wicklow. Open May through September daily from 10am to 8pm and October through April, Monday through Saturday, from 10am to 5:30pm.

Fisher's of Newtownmountkennedy. The Old Schoolhouse, Newtownmountkennedy, County Wicklow. ☎ **01/281-9404.**

This shop, located in a converted schoolhouse, stocks a wide array of men's and women's sporting clothes—quilted jackets, raincoats, footwear, blazers, and accessories. There's also a new tearoom. Open Monday through Saturday from 9:30am to 5:30pm.

Glendalough Craft Centre. Laragh, County Wicklow. ☎ **0404/45156.**

This long-established crafts shop in a converted farmhouse offers handcrafts from all over Ireland, such as Bantry Pottery and Penrose Glass from Waterford. Books, jewelry, and a large selection of hand knits from the area are also sold. Open daily from 10am to 6pm.

Noritake Arklow Pottery Ltd. South Quay, Arklow, County Wicklow. ☎ **0402/32401.** Daily 9:30am–4:45pm.

Situated in a busy seaside town, this is Ireland's largest pottery factory and the home of Noritake's Celt Craft and Misty Isle lines. The pottery produced here ranges from earthenware, porcelain, and bone china tableware to decorated teapots, casseroles, and gifts in both modern and traditional designs. Free tours are available mid-June through August with the exception of the last week of July and first 2 weeks of August, when the factory is closed for the staff's vacation.

ACCOMMODATIONS
VERY EXPENSIVE

✪ **Tinakilly House.** Off the Dublin-Wexford road, on R750, Rathnew, County Wicklow. ☎ **800/223-6510** from the U.S., or 0404/69274. Fax 0404/67806. www.tinakilly.ie. 40 units. TV TEL. £120–£170 ($186–$263.50) double, £170 ($263.50) junior suite, £220 ($341) captain's suite with sea view. Includes full breakfast. No service charge. AE, DC, MC, V. Closed Dec 23–31.

Dating from the 1870s, this was the home of Capt. Robert Charles Halpin, commander of the *Great Eastern*, who laid the first successful cable connecting Europe with America. With a sweeping central staircase said to be the twin of the one on the ship, Tinakilly is full of seafaring memorabilia, paintings, and Victorian antiques. Many of the individually furnished rooms have views of the Irish Sea. Opened as a hotel by the Power family in 1983, it is adjacent to the Broadlough Bird Sanctuary and a 7-acre garden of beech, evergreen, eucalyptus, palm, and American redwood trees.

Dining/Diversions: The Brunel Restaurant, housed in the new east wing, is well known for fresh fish and local game, and blends country cooking with nouvelle cuisine. Vegetables, fruits, and herbs come from the house gardens, and all breads are baked fresh daily on the premises.

EXPENSIVE

Glenview Hotel. Glen o' the Downs, Delgany, Dublin-Wexford road (N11), County Wicklow. ☎ **800/528-1234** or 01/287-3399. Fax 01/287-7511. 42 units. TV TEL. £116–£148 ($179–$229.40) double. Includes full Irish breakfast and service charge. AE, DC, MC, V.

With Sugar Loaf Mountain in the background, and nestled in an idyllic setting overlooking the Glen of the Downs, this hotel has been a popular stopping-off place on the main road for more than 50 years. Totally refurbished and enlarged in 1993, it has a striking new yellow facade and a bright and airy contemporary interior, yet still maintains much of its traditional charm in the guest rooms and public areas. The main dining room, the Malton Room, is noted for its wood paneling and full set of Malton prints on the walls. The Lodge Bar and Library Lounge enjoy panoramic views of the County Wicklow countryside, including the hotel's 30 acres of gardens and woodlands. A luxurious health and leisure club was recently added.

✪ **Rathsallagh House.** Dunlavin, County Wicklow. ☎ **800/223-6510** from the U.S. or 045/53112. Fax 045/53343. 17 units (8 in main house, 9 in courtyard). TV TEL. £110–£190 ($176–$294.50) double. No service charge. Includes full breakfast. AE, DC, MC, V. Closed Dec 23–31.

On the western edge of County Wicklow, this rambling, ivy-covered country house sits amid 530 acres of parks, woods, and farmland. The original house on the property was built between 1702 and 1704 and owned by a horse-breeding family named Moody. It was burned down in the 1798 Rebellion, and the Moodys moved into the Queen Anne–style stables, which were converted into a proper residence and served as a private home until the 1950s. It was purchased in 1978 by Joe and Kay O'Flynn and opened as a country house 10 years later. Each room is individually decorated and named accordingly, from the Yellow, Pink, and Blue Rooms to the Romantic, Over Arch, and Loft Rooms, and so on. Most rooms have a sitting area, huge walk-in closet, and window seats, and some have Jacuzzis. All have hair dryer, tea/coffeemaker, vanity/desk, good reading lamps over the bed, and antique furnishings. A recent recipient of the American Express Best-loved Hotels of the World Award, this much touted guest house has a particularly warm, welcoming, unpretentious feel to it, a splendid home away from home (except for children under 12, who are not catered to).

Dining/Diversions: The dining room, under the personal supervision of Kay O'Flynn, is widely noted for its excellent food, using local ingredients and vegetables and herbs from the garden.

Amenities: 18-hole championship golf course, modest-size indoor heated swimming pool, sauna, hard tennis court, archery, croquet, billiards, and lovely mature 2-acre walled garden.

MODERATE

Glendalough Hotel. Glendalough, County Wicklow. ☎ **800/365-3346** from the U.S., or 0404/45135. Fax 0404/45142. 44 units. TV TEL. £66–£88 ($102.30–$136.40) double. Includes full breakfast. AE, DC, MC, V. Closed Jan.

If location is everything, this hotel scores high. It sits in a wooded glen at the entrance to Glendalough, beside the Glendasan River. Dating from the 1800s, it was refurbished and updated a few years ago with traditional Irish furnishings and every modern comfort. Public rooms include the Glendasan Restaurant overlooking the river and the Glendalough Tavern.

INEXPENSIVE

Derrybawn House. Laragh, County Wicklow. ☎ **0404/45134.** Fax 0404/45109. 6 units. £50–£60 ($77.50–$93) double. Includes full breakfast. No service charge. No credit cards.

This elegant, comfortable fieldstone manor house in an idyllic parkland setting looks out over the surrounding hills. The rooms (all nonsmoking) are spacious, bright, tastefully furnished, and outfitted with orthopedic beds; public rooms include a sitting room, dining room, and rec room with snooker table and facilities for making tea and coffee. Located just outside Laragh village, the place is convenient to fishing streams and hiking trails (including the Wicklow Way), and a great place from which to explore Wicklow's natural wonders.

Slievemore. The Harbour, Greystones, County Wicklow. ☎ **01/287-4724.** 8 units, shower only. TV. £38 ($58.90) double. Includes full Irish breakfast. No service charge. No credit cards. Open year-round. Free parking. Signposted on N11. Bus: 84.

This mid-19th-century harbor house offers white-glove cleanliness, spacious comfort, and (if you book early and request a seafront room) a commanding view of Greystones Harbor, Bray Head, and the Irish Sea. Proprietor Pippins Parkinson says that "people stumble on Greystones, find it by accident." Whether you're accident-prone or not, stay here and reserve a table for dinner at Coopers (see "Dining," below), just paces away, and you won't forget the day you stumbled on Greystones.

SELF-CATERING

Fortgranite Estate. Baltinglass, County Wicklow. ☎/fax **0508/81396.** 3 self-catering cottages. TV TEL. £120–£350 ($186–$542.50) per week. 3 miles south-east of Baltinglass on R747.

Fortgranite is—and has been for centuries—a working farm in the rolling foothills of the Wicklow Mountains. Its meadows and stately trees create a sublime retreat. One by one Fortgranite's unique stone cottages, formerly occupied by the estate's workers, are being restored and refurbished with appreciable care and charm by M. P. Dennis. Currently, three cottages are available year-round for rental periods of a week or longer. Two are gate lodges—Doyle's Lodge and Lennon's Lodge—each with one double bedroom, sleeping two and fully equipped with all essentials. The third, Stewards's cottage, sleeps four and is furnished with lovely antiques. All have open fireplaces and each has its own grounds and garden, affording all the privacy and peace anyone deserves. Tranquility, charm, and warmth are the operative concepts at Fortgranite, so those in search of something grand and luxurious will be disappointed. Think "cottage" and "character" and you will be delighted. Also, best to plan ahead, as the word is out about Fortgranite and availability is at a premium. Golf, fishing, hill walking, horse racing and riding, and clay pigeon shooting can all be found nearby.

The Manor. Manor Kilbride, near Blessington, County Wicklow. ☎ **01/458-2105.** Fax 01/458-2607. 4 units, 3 self-catering cottages. B&B £120 ($186) double. Includes full Irish breakfast and service charge. Self-catering £350–£450 ($542.50–$697.50) per week. MC, V. 18 miles from Dublin. On N81, take Kilbride/Sally Gap turn 7km north of Blessington; then after 2km turn left again at sign for Sally Gap. Entrance gates 50 yards ahead on right. Open Apr 1 to Oct 31.

Gracefully situated amidst 40 acres of mature gardens and wooded walks in the foothills of the Wicklow Mountains, with its own small lake and stretch of the River Brittas, the Manor of Charles and Margaret Cully is a haven of charm and cordiality. The 1835 manor itself, a rambling Victorian country home, is both worn and welcoming. What it lacks in luxury, however, it surely makes up in charm and warmth. A long-time member of "Hidden Ireland," a select consortium of private homes whose doors are open to guests, the Manor offers an authentic taste of Irish country life. Elegant candlelight dinners are available to guests for an additional £21 ($32.55) and must be booked by 2pm. You can work up your appetite in the heated swimming pool. For those who wish to drop anchor and stay a week or more, there are 3 lovely stone self-catering cottages available, two in the courtyard and one set off by itself beside the River Brittas.

The two courtyard cottages sleep four, while the river lodge is better suited to a couple. These are 4-star cottages with original beams and exposed stone walls and every amenity, the kind of nookeries one could settle into quite painlessly. The Cullys are rather lavish in their welcome baskets, so there will be no need for any immediate trip to the market.

Tynte House. Dunlavin, County Wicklow. ☎ **045/401561.** Fax 045/401586. 7 B&B units. £34 ($52.70) double. 4 self-catering mews cottages (1/2/3 bedrooms). 4 self-catering apartments (1 or 2 bedrooms). TV TEL. £90–£260 ($139.50–$403) per week, depending on size and season. Stays of less than a week may be negotiated off-season, as well as special weekend rates on request. In Dunlavin center, 30 miles southwest of Dublin.

Dunlavin, despite its turbulent history, is now a drowsy three-pub town in western Wicklow, guaranteed not to keep its guests up at night. It's as convenient as it is peaceful, providing easy access to Kildare horse country, the gardens, lakes, and mountains of Wicklow, and the scenic boglands and hills of the midlands. Tynte House, a lovingly preserved 19th-century family farm complex in Dunlavin center, offers an attractive array of options for both overnight and long-term guests. With the recent addition of Tynte House apartments, these options have been enhanced even further. The driving force behind all this hospitality is Mrs. Caroline Lawler, "brought up in the business" of divining visitors' needs and surpassing their expectations. The guest rooms are warm and comfortable, while the newly created self-catering mews houses and apartments (ranging from two to four bedrooms) are brilliantly designed and furnished with one eye on casual efficiency and the other on truly good taste. Bold, bright color-schemes, light pine furniture, spacious tiled baths, bright open kitchens fully equipped with microwave, dishwasher, and washer-dryer combinations, and cable color TV begin to describe what Mrs. Lawler has waiting for you. The no. 3 mews house and the open-plan apartment are our favorites; but none will disappoint. While all of the mattresses are new, some are more firm than others; so it would be well to request a specially firm mattress if your back, like mine, looks for excuses to complain. This is a great anchorage for families, with a safe grassy play area, tennis court, and game room with Ping-Pong and pool tables.

DINING
MODERATE

✪ **Coopers.** The Harbour, Greystones, County Wicklow (above the Beach House). ☎ **01/287-3914.** Reservations recommended. Main courses £6.95–£14.95 ($12.65–$23.85); lunch £8.45–£12.95 ($13.50–$20.70). Fixed-price early-bird 2-course dinner £10 ($15.50) Mon–Fri 5:30–7:30pm. No service charge. AE, MC, V. Mon–Sat 5:30–11:30pm; Sun 5:30–10pm, Sun lunch 12:30–4pm. INTERNATIONAL/SEAFOOD.

Coopers is the perfect reward after making the cliff walk from Bray to Greystones. This is one of the most tasteful dining environments I've found in Ireland—vaulted beamed ceilings, exposed brick and stone walls, stained glass, three fireplaces, wrought-iron fixtures, and linen table settings; a warm, relaxed, and comfortable place for couples and families of any age. The menu is a rarity in that it understates its offerings, with quite ordinary descriptions like "smoked lamb" for quite extraordinary fare. The roast duckling and the steamed sea trout are two of the house specialties, enhanced by a fine wine list. There are spectacular views of the open sea on two sides, and a piano player on Friday and Saturday nights. Coopers is no secret to the locals, so book well ahead in order not to be disappointed.

✪ **Mitchell's.** Laragh, Glendalough, County Wicklow. ☎ **0404/45302.** Reservations recommended. Lunch main courses £5–£8 ($7.75–$12.40), fixed-price lunch £12.95 ($20.10); fixed-price dinner £17.95 ($27.80). AE, MC, V. Open daily 9am–9pm. Closed Good Friday, Christmas, and last 3 weeks of Jan. IRISH/INTERNATIONAL.

A 200-year-old former schoolhouse serves as the setting for this small restaurant in a garden in sight of the mountains. The unique cut-granite facade opens to a country-kitchen atmosphere, with pine furnishings and open, log-burning fireplaces. In the summer, there is seating outdoors. The menu changes daily, but often includes rack of Wicklow lamb with honey and rosemary sauce, smoked salmon on a spiced saffron-scented sauce, grilled fillet of sea trout with sorrel sauce, and filet of beef with red wine and mushroom sauce, as well as daily vegetarian entrees. All breads and scones are made on the premises, as is an assortment of ice cream.

Roundwood Inn. Main St., Roundwood, County Wicklow. ☎ **01/282-8107** or 01/282-8125. Reservations not necessary for lunch, advised for dinner. Lunch main courses £5–£12 ($7.75–$18.60); dinner main courses £10–£16 ($15.50–$24.80). MC, V. Tues–Sat 1–2:30pm and 7:30–9:30pm. IRISH/CONTINENTAL.

Dating from 1750, this old coaching inn is the focal point of an out-of-the-way spot high in the mountains called Roundwood, said to be the highest village in Ireland. The old-world atmosphere includes open log fireplaces and antique furnishings. Menu choices range from steaks and sandwiches to traditional Irish stew, fresh lobster, and smoked salmon. It's located in the middle of the village on the main road (R755).

Tara and Jenny. Dunlavin Inn, Dunlavin, County Wicklow. ☎ **045/401368.** Reservations recommended. Main courses £8.50–£15 ($13.20–$23.25); lunch menu £1.65–£5.20 ($2.55–$8.05); lunch special £3.95 ($6.10). No service charge. MC, V. Mon–Sat noon–2pm, Thurs–Sat 7:30–9:30pm. INTERNATIONAL/ IRISH.

This modest, behind-the-pub restaurant, only 2 months old at the time of this writing, is already a small legend, or at least a wild rumor. Founded by two chefs with more than their share of training and experience—Tara was trained at Ballymaloe; and Jenny, trained in Britain, has worked in France, Italy, and Greece—this humble restaurant rivals, when plate comes to plate, some of the most touted restaurants in the area, at a third of the price. The emphasis here is on the freshest local ingredients prepared well and simply to bring out the best in them. My salmon (prepared as gravalax of wild salmon with dill and mustard sauce) was caught by the chef's father, and the accompanying vegetables were organically grown. Lamb and steak too are prepared to perfection. The menu, changing daily, is consistently imaginative and diverse; and the wine list—drawing upon the vintages of five continents—is quite strong, offering stand-out wines at affordable prices. The one disappointment, not surprisingly, was the Irish cheese platter. Only curiosity would fully justify this choice, when among the alternatives are homemade Marscarpone ice cream and Pavlova with poached nectarines, both to die for. One smoke-free snug or small private room is available on request.

INEXPENSIVE

Avoca Handweavers Tea Shop. Avoca, County Wicklow. ☎ **0402/35105.** Lunch £2–£5 ($3.10–$7.75). Daily 9:30am–5pm, Mar–Oct. AE, DC, JCB, MC, V. TRADITIONAL/VEGETARIAN.

This innovative cafeteria is worth a visit for lunch, even if you're not interested in woollens. They prepare wholesome meals, surprisingly imaginative for cafeteria fare. I had a delicate pea and mint soup, prepared with vegetable stock, accompanied by a deliciously hearty spinach tart. Other dishes might include sesame glazed chicken or locally smoked Wicklow trout; the menu changes often, and the chefs give free reign to their sometimes whimsical fancy. The tea shop has a regular local clientele, in addition to the busloads of visitors attracted by the woollens.

Escape. 1 Albert Walk, Bray, County Wicklow. ☎ **01/2866755.** Lunch specials £2–£5 ($3.10–$7.75); dinner main courses £7 ($10.85). MC, V. Tues–Sat noon–10:30pm, Sun noon–8:45pm. VEGETARIAN/VEGAN.

Conveniently located on the Bray seafront, this tiny restaurant tucked away in a gift shop offers surprisingly innovative and satisfying meals at a great price. Lunch is an especially good deal, and although the options are somewhat ordinary—jacket potatoes, an assortment of quiches—they're prepared with a flair for spicing which assures that each is a delightful and unpredictable experience. Main courses at dinner might include a Sicilian crepe filled with an assortment of cheese and roasted vegetables, or perhaps a vegetable lasagna; the menu changes daily, and the evening's offerings are usually posted at 6pm. The decor is odd: it varies from spartan simplicity to outbursts of unrestrained bric-a-brac, thanks to the attached gift shop. The cross-section of customers consists of families on holiday, tough Bray teens, and kayakers or windsurfers coming in from a day on the water. The only downside here is the smoke—there isn't a genuine nonsmoking section, and ventilation within the cavelike space can be rather poor.

The Opera House. Market Sq., Wicklow Town, County Wicklow. ☎ **0404/ 66422.** Reservations recommended Fri–Sun. Main courses £6.50–£13.95 ($10.10–$21.60). No service charge. MC, V. Jun–Aug 11am–11pm, Sept–May 5–11pm. ITALIAN.

This Irish trattoria, beginning its second year at press time, is a unique find in this traditional harbor town. Inside, the faux Mediterranean decor is warm and tasteful; outside, picnic tables provide street-side dining for nonsmokers. The smoked salmon and tagliatelle flamed in a cream and vodka sauce for £5.95 ($9.50) is a delicious bargain, and the house French table wine at £8.95 ($14.30) suits both wallet and palate. The service is enthusiastic, if stretched a bit thin on weekends. For a delightful conclusion, treat yourself to the lemon brulée.

Poppies Country Cooking. Enniskerry, County Wicklow. ☎ **01/282-8869.** Reservations not necessary. All items £1.50–£4.95 ($2.40–$7.90). No credit cards. Daily 9am–7pm. IRISH/SELF-SERVICE.

This 10-table eatery opposite the main square is popular for light meals and snacks all day. The menu ranges from homemade soups and salads to homity pie, nut roast, baked salmon, vegetarian quiche, and lasagna.

Poppies Country Cooking. Trafalgar Rd., Greystones, County Wicklow. ☎ **01/287-4228.** Reservations not required. All items £1.50–£4.95 ($2.40– $7.90). No credit cards. Daily 10am–6pm, Sun 11:30am–7pm. IRISH HOMESTYLE.

Located a short walk from either bus or train, Poppies has done it again, this time in Greystones. With the warm, familiar feel of a neighbor's kitchen—the one who can really cook— this is a hangout for locals who for all sorts of reasons see no point in cooking for themselves at the moment. From fist-size whole-grain scones to vegetarian nut roast, the portions are generous and savored. Its menu outsizes its modest 10-table size, overflowing into a lovely flowered tea garden out back, if and when the sun appears. *A note of warning:* The Poppies' desserts are diet-breakers; so try not to even look unless you are prepared to fall. And for those who don't know when or how to stop, homemade jams, preserves, salad dressing, and even local artworks are on sale.

PUBS

Cartoon Inn. Main St., Rathdrum, County Wicklow. ☎ **0404/46774.**

With walls displaying the work of many famous cartoonists, this cottagelike pub claims to be Ireland's only cartoon-theme pub and is the headquarters for Ireland's Cartoon Festival, held in late May or early June each year. Pub grub is available at lunchtime.

The Coach House. Main St., Roundwood. ☎ **01/281-8157.**

Adorned with lots of colorful hanging flowerpots on the outside, this Tudor-style inn sits in the mountains in the heart of Ireland's highest village. Dating from 1790, it is full of local memorabilia, from old photos and agricultural posters to antique jugs and plates. It's well worth a visit, whether to learn about the area or to get some light refreshment.

The Meetings. Avoca, County Wicklow. ☎ **0402/35226.**

This Tudor-style country-cottage pub stands idyllically at the "Meeting of the Waters" associated with poet Thomas Moore. An 1889 edition of Moore's book of poems is on display. Good pub grub is served every day, with traditional Irish music April through October every Sunday afternoon (from 4 to 6pm), compliments of the house. Weekend music is on tap all year.

2 County Kildare: Ireland's Horse Country

15 to 30 miles west of Dublin.

GETTING THERE   Irish Rail (☎ **01/836-3333**) provides daily train service to Kildare.

Bus Eireann (☎ **01/836-6111**) operates daily express bus service to Kildare.

If you're traveling by car, take the main Dublin-Limerick road (N7) west of Dublin to Kildare or the main Dublin-Galway road (N4) to Celbridge, turning off on local road R403.

VISITOR INFORMATION　For information about County Kildare, contact the **Wicklow Tourist Office,** Wicklow Town (☎ **0404/69117**), open year-round Monday to Friday, and Saturdays during peak season. Seasonal information offices are located at Athy, County Kildare (☎ **0507/31859**) and in Kildare Town, County Kildare (☎ **045/22696**). Both are open June through mid-September.

AREA CODES　The telephone area codes used in County Kildare are **01, 045,** and **0503.**

A WORD ABOUT KILDARE

County Kildare and horse-racing go hand in hand, or should we say neck and neck? It's home of the Curragh racetrack, where the Irish Derby is held each June, and other smaller tracks at Naas and Punchestown. County Kildare is also the heartland of Ireland's flourishing bloodstock industry. In this panorama of open grasslands and limestone-enriched soil, many of Ireland's 300 stud farms are found.

Kildare is famed as the birthplace of Brigid, Ireland's second patron saint. Brigid was a bit ahead of her time as an early exponent for women's equality—she founded a co-ed monastery in Kildare in the 5th or 6th century.

ATTRACTIONS

Castletown House. R403, off main Dublin-Galway road, Celbridge, County Kildare. ☎ **01/628-8252.** Grounds open; house closed indefinitely for renovation.

Castletown—designed by Italian architect Alessandro Galilei for William Connolly (1662–1729), then Speaker of the Irish House of Commons—remains the most grand Palladian-style mansion in Ireland. In a 1722 letter to Bishop Berkeley, this architectural gem was touted as a "magnificent pile of a building . . . (destined to be) the finest Ireland ever saw." Currently, "pile" comes sadly close to the truth, as this once-and-future gem undergoes extensive renovation in the hands of the Office of Public Works, its most recent overseer. Castletown, a national treasure, will shine again, but not likely soon.

Steam Museum. Off Dublin-Limerick road (N7), Straffan, County Kildare. ☎ **01/627-3155.** Museum: £4 ($6.20) adults; £2 ($3.10) seniors, children, and students; £10 ($15.50) family. Garden £2 ($3.10). Museum April–May Sun 2:30–5:30pm, June–Aug Tues–Sun 2–6pm, Sept Sun 2:30–5:30pm. Walled garden June–July Tues–Fri and Sun 2–6pm, Aug Tues–Fri 2:30–5:30pm.

Housed in a converted church, this museum is a must for steam-engine buffs. It contains two collections: The Richard Guinness Hall has more than 20 prototypical locomotive engines dating from the 18th century, and the Power Hall has rare industrial stationary engines. The steam and garden shop stocks a variety of recent books and videos on the Irish Railway and serves as the sole outlet for National Trust Enterprises gifts, which can be excellent values. The walled garden is of 18th-century origin and features several garden rooms extending to a delightful rosery. Call ahead for information on when the engines will be in operation.

Newbridge Cutlery. Off Dublin-Limerick road (N7), Newbridge, County Kildare. ☎ **045/431301.** Free admission. Mon–Fri 9am–5pm, Sat 11am–5pm, Sun 2–5pm.

Look closely at the silverware when you sit down to eat at one of Ireland's fine hotels or restaurants—there's a good chance it'll be made by Newbridge, which for the past 60 years has been one of Ireland's leading manufacturers of fine silverware. In the visitor center, you can see a display of silver place settings, bowls, candelabras, trays, frames, and one-of-a-kind items. A video on silvermaking is also shown. Silver pieces are sold here, including "sale" items.

✪ **The Curragh.** Dublin-Limerick road (N7), Curragh, County Kildare. ☎ **045/441205.** Admission £7–£10 ($10.85–$15.50) for most races; £12–£30 ($18.60–$46.50) for Derby. AE, DC, MC, V. Hours vary; first race usually 2pm. Rail links with all major towns. Dublin-Curragh return "Racing by Rail" package for £12 ($18.60), including courtesy coach to main entrance.

Often referred to as the Churchill Downs of Ireland, this is the country's best-known racetrack, just 30 miles west of Dublin. Majestically placed at the edge of Ireland's central plain, it's home to the Irish Derby held each year in late June/early July. Horses race here at least one Saturday a month from March to October. Recently, the main stand has been extensively renovated, a new betting hall has been added, and facilities (bars, restaurants, food court, etc.) offering food and drink have been greatly expanded.

✪ **Irish National Stud & Japanese Gardens.** Off the Dublin-Limerick road (N7), Tully, Kildare, County Kildare. ☎ **045/21617.** Admission £5 ($7.75) adults; £3 ($4.65) seniors, students, and children over 12; £2 ($3.10) children under 12; £12 ($19.20) family. MC, V. Feb 12 to Nov 12 daily 9:30am–6pm. Bus: Eireann stop. Buses from Dublin each morning, returning each evening.

Some of Ireland's most famous horses have been bred on the grounds of this government-sponsored stud farm. A prototype for other horse farms throughout Ireland, it has 288 stalls to accommodate the mares, stallions, and foals. Visitors are welcome to walk around the 958-acre grounds and see the noble steeds being exercised and groomed.

A converted groom's house has exhibits on racing, steeplechasing, hunting, and show jumping, plus the skeleton of Arkle, one of Ireland's most famous horses.

The Japanese garden is considered to be among the finest Asian gardens in Europe. Laid out between 1906 and 1910, its design symbolizes the journey of the soul from oblivion to eternity. The Japanese-style visitor center has a restaurant and crafts shop.

Moone High Cross. Moone, County Kildare. Open site. Signposted off N9 on southern edge of Moone village.

This renowned high cross, recently restored on-site, stands in the ruins of Moone Abbey, the southernmost monastic settlement established by St. Columba in the 6th century. The ruins and grounds are actually enhanced by the formula of neglect and care they currently receive. The overgrown path to the site, for instance, is lined with bright annuals. The high cross, nearly 1,200 years old, is quite magnificent, a splendid example of Celtic stone carving, containing finely crafted Celtic designs as well as numerous scenes and figures from the Bible, such as the temptation of Adam and Eve, the sacrifice of Isaac, and Daniel in the lions' den. The cross also contains a number of surprises, such as a dolphin and a species of Near Eastern fish who reproduce when the male feeds the female her own eggs, which eventually hatch from her mouth. If you're nearby, you will be glad not to have passed by this exemplary co-creation of Celtic imagination and early Christian faith.

SPORTS & OUTDOOR PURSUITS

GOLF The flat plains of Kildare provide some lovely settings for parkland courses, including two new 18-hole championship courses. The par-72 **Kildare Country Club,** Straffan, County Kildare (☎ 01/ 627-3333), charges £120 ($186) per day for greens fees. The par-70 **Kilkea Castle Golf Club,** Castledermot, County Kildare (☎ 0503/45555), charges £20 ($31) weekdays and £25 ($38.75) weekends.

For a slightly less costly game, try the par-72 championship course at the **Curragh Golf Club,** Curragh, County Kildare (☎ 045/ 441238), with greens fees of £18 ($27.90) weekdays and £22 ($34.10) on weekends.

HORSEBACK RIDING Visitors who want to go horseback riding can expect to pay an average of £10 to £15 ($15.50 to

$23.25) per hour for trekking or trail riding in the Kildare countryside. To arrange a ride, contact the **Donacomper Riding School,** Celbridge, County Kildare (☎ **01/628-8221**), or the **Kill International Equestrian Centre,** Kill, County Kildare (☎ **045/ 877208**).

ACCOMMODATIONS
VERY EXPENSIVE

Kildare Hotel & Country Club. Straffan, County Kildare. ☎ **800/221-1074** from the U.S., or 01/627-3333. Fax 01/627-3312. 45 units. MINIBAR TV TEL. £280–£350 ($434–$542.50) double; £450–£550 ($697.50–$852.50) 1-bedroom suite; £700 ($1,085) 2-bedroom suite; £1,000 ($1,550) Viceroy suite. No service charge. AE, DC, MC, V.

Located 20 miles west of Dublin, this luxurious 330-acre five-star resort is a favorite among Ireland's sporting set. The focal point of the estate is Straffan House, a 19th-century mansion that serves as the core of the hotel, with an adjacent new west wing that is a replica of the original building. The bedrooms are spread out among the main hotel, courtyard suites, and a lodge. High ceilings, bow windows, wide staircases, antiques, and period pieces are all enhanced by hand-painted wall coverings and murals. The house overlooks a 1-mile stretch of the River Liffey.

Dining/Diversions: The main restaurant is the Bryerley Turk, featuring French food, while lighter fare including afternoon tea is available in the Gallery; the Legends bar overlooks the golf course.

Amenities: 24-hour room service, nightly turndown, concierge, laundry/valet service, 18-hole Arnold Palmer–designed golf course, private access to salmon and trout fishing, two indoor and two outdoor tennis courts, two squash courts, gym, indoor swimming pool, sauna, solarium.

✪ **Kilkea Castle.** Castledermot, County Kildare. ☎ **0503/45156** or 0503/ 45100. Fax 0503/45187. 36 units. TV TEL. £180–£240 ($279–$372) double. Includes full Irish breakfast and service charge. AE, DC, MC, V.

Nestled beside the River Greese and surrounded by lovely formal gardens, this tall, multi-turreted stone castle is a standout in the flat farmland of County Kildare. Considered the oldest inhabited castle in Ireland, it dates back to 1180 and was built by Hugh de Lacy, an early Irish governor, for Walter de Riddlesford, a great warrior. The castle later passed into the ownership of the legendary Geraldines and it is still supposed to be haunted by the 11th Earl of Kildare. Every 7 years, the Earl—dressed in full regalia and accompanied by his knights—is said to gallop around the castle walls.

Fully restored as a hotel in recent years, Kilkea is decorated with suits of armor and medieval banners, as well as a mix of Irish antiques and Asian tables, chests, and urns. About a third of the bedrooms are in the original castle building, with the rest in a newer courtyard addition. The furnishings include dark woods, semi-canopy beds, armoires, chandeliers, brass fixtures, gilt-framed paintings and mirrors, and floral designer fabrics; each has a modern tile-and-brass bathroom. The castle is approximately $2^1/_2$ miles from Castledermot and is well signposted from the town.

Dining/Diversions: The main dining room is de Lacy's, specializing in innovative Irish cuisine. The Geraldine Bar conveys a 12th-century atmosphere, with original stone walls, stained-glass windows, and huge fireplace crowned by a copper flue.

Amenities: Room service, concierge, baby-sitting, 18-hole golf course, indoor heated swimming pool, exercise room, saunas, spa pool, steam rooms, sunbed, toning table, fishing for brown trout on the adjacent River Greese, two floodlit hard tennis courts, clay pigeon shooting, bicycle rental, and archery range.

EXPENSIVE

✪ **Barberstown Castle.** Straffan, County Kildare. ☎ **01/628-8157.** Fax 01/627-7027. E-mail: castleir@iol.ie. USA reservations taken through Robert Reid Associates, ☎ 800/223-6510. 26 units. TV TEL. £120–£140 ($186–$217) double, £175 ($271.25) suite. Includes full Irish breakfast. Service charge 10%. MC, V. 30-minute drive from Dublin city center or airport. South on N7, take the turn for Straffan at Kill; west on N4, take the turn for Straffan at Maynooth.

This exquisite country hotel spans within its walls 750 years of Irish history. Its four segments—constructed in the 13th, 16th, 18th, and 20th centuries—somehow form a coherent and pleasing whole. Each luxurious guest room is named after one of the castle's former lords or proprietors, beginning with Nicholas Barby, who constructed the battlemented rectangular Keep in the late 13th century, and including Eric Clapton, who sold it to the present owners, Kenneth and Catherine Healy. The Barberstown story—from fortress to guest house—is a long one, with an altogether happy ending for anyone deciding to stay a while here. The rooms are warm and elegant, with sitting area, four-poster bed, antique desk, chandelier, and spacious bathroom. Two-bedroom family accommodations are available, as is a room specially designed for guests with disabilities. Smoking is limited to the lounge. The award-winning Castle Restaurant is open to nonguests by reservation. Golf can be arranged at a number of nearby courses, including the Kildare Country Club. Within an

arms-reach of Dublin, this is a perfect country getaway with more than a touch of class.

Hotel Keadeen. Off Dublin-Limerick road (N7), Newbridge, County Kildare. ☎ **045/431666.** Fax 045/434402. E-mail: keadeen@iol.ie. 55 units. TV TEL. £115–£135 ($178.25–$209.25) double; £150 ($232.50) suite. No service charge. AE, DC, MC, V.

Situated less than 2 miles east of The Curragh racetrack, this small country-style hotel is a favorite with the horse set. Just off the main road, it is well set back on its own 8 acres of grounds in a quiet garden setting. Equestrian art dominates the public rooms. The guest rooms are bright and spacious, with light woods, floral fabrics, and brass fixtures. The new "executive" rooms, each with a king-size bed and a comfortable alcove sitting area, are well worth the additional £15 ($23.25). Facilities include the Derby Room restaurant, a casual lounge with many comfortable nooks, and a beautifully designed, fully outfitted health and fitness center, complete with an 18-meter swimming pool. All of the common rooms and all but five of the guest rooms are on ground level, well-suited to visitors with disabilities.

DINING
EXPENSIVE

Moyglare Manor. Maynooth, County Kildare. ☎ **01/628-6351.** Reservations required. Fixed-price dinner £27.50 ($42.65). Service charge 12.5%. AE, DC, V. Daily 7–9:30pm. Closed Good Friday and Dec 23–26. FRENCH.

A half-hour's drive on the Dublin-Galway road (N4) will deliver you to this grand Georgian mansion/inn, whose restaurant is surprisingly intimate. Elegance is the operative word here. The roast quail, baked plaice stuffed with shrimp, panfried brill, and steaks, all with fresh vegetables from the manor's own garden, are not known to disappoint.

MODERATE/INEXPENSIVE

Silken Thomas. The Square, Kildare, County Kildare. ☎ **045/22232.** Reservations not required for lunch. Lunch main courses £5–£8 ($7.75–$12.40); dinner main courses £6–£12 ($9.30–$18.60). AE, MC, V. Daily 11am–11pm. IRISH/ INTERNATIONAL.

Formerly known as Leinster Lodge, this historic inn offers an old world–pub/restaurant with open fire and dark woods. It is named after a famous member of the Norman Fitzgerald family, whose stronghold was in Kildare. He led an unsuccessful rebellion against Henry VIII and some of the decor recalls his efforts. The menu offers a good selection of soups, sandwiches, burgers, and salads as well as steaks, roasts, mixed grills, and fresh seafood platters. It is located on the main square in Kildare town.

Index

See also separate Accommodations and Restaurant indexes, below.

Page numbers in italics refer to maps.